Praise for Alice Sebold's *Lucky*

"This carefully detailed memoir is a tour de force of memory and rage."

—*Self*

"A vivid account of Sebold's rape and its effect on her and her family . . . The rape is only the beginning of Sebold's story."

—*Los Angeles Times*

"Eloquent . . . Sebold's opening scene is as gripping and terrifying as any in a film. . . . Her voice is a powerful new plea to break the silence that still clings to this taboo, and little understood, subject. . . . This powerful memoir leaves it to readers to decide how lucky Sebold was."

—Joan Ullman, *The Cleveland Plain Dealer*

"Reading *Lucky*, which I did in a single sitting, I was struck by the awful solitude that violence brings, both at the moment and in its aftermath. In this brilliant, eloquent, funny, precise account of how she survived rape and the pursuit of justice, Alice Sebold has triumphantly broken that solitude. We, her readers, are the fortunate beneficiaries."

—Margot Livesey

"This book proves at once the astounding bravery of Alice Sebold in the face of dreadful circumstance and the extraordinary power of words to heal. Sebold has made beauty out of agony."

—Carolyn See

"A harrowing story that's still vibrating and flexible . . . Give Alice Sebold your attention for her first five pages and you're in for the whole ride."

—Sally Eckhoff, *Salon*

"A literary memoir that shines with personality. There is such openness in Sebold's brash, vibrant style that the book feels like the long version of a friend's breathless account of an ordeal."
—Carmen Scheidel, *Time Out New York*

"Gruesome and strangely enchanting . . . A controlled and meticulous account . . . The quiet achievement of Sebold's memoir is that she handles her subject with the integrity of a journalist and the care of a survivor. . . . It succeeds not just as a record of one woman's pain and healing but as fine creative nonfiction."
—Casey Greenfield, *Newsday*

"Sebold's commanding skill as a narrator (at her best, describing the awful crime itself, she brings to mind a fierce young Joan Didion) forces you to relive her terror. . . . This is a brave and modest work of demystification. . . . She tells what it's like to go through a particular kind of nightmare in order to tell what it's like—slowly, bumpily, triumphantly—to heal."
—Sarah Kerr, *Vogue*

"Sharp-eyed and unsentimental . . . It's hard to believe that a book about brutal rape and its aftermath could actually be inspirational. But despite its disturbing subject, Alice Sebold's *Lucky* is exhilarating to read. Raped in a tunnel when she was a freshman at Syracuse University, the ironic, nervy Sebold refused to let the experience diminish her . . . or her sense of humor. . . . Reading *Lucky,* you understand how Sebold succeeded in persuading a judge that what happened to her occurred precisely—word for word, detail for detail—the way she described it."
—Francine Prose, *Elle*

"*Lucky*—which reads like a John Grisham page-turner—can't help but haunt you. . . . Sebold's is a story about having the courage to speak about the unspeakable."
—Sheryl Altman, *Biography*

Books by Alice Sebold

FICTION
The Lovely Bones
The Almost Moon

MEMOIR
Lucky

LUCKY

Alice Sebold

SCRIBNER

New York London Toronto Sydney New Delhi

SCRIBNER

An Imprint of Simon & Schuster, Inc.
1230 Avenue of the Americas
New York, NY 10020

This Scribner trade paperback edition May 2017

SCRIBNER and design are registered trademarks of The Gale Group, Inc.,
used under license by Simon & Schuster, Inc., the publisher of this work.

For information about special discounts for bulk purchases,
please contact Simon & Schuster Special Sales at 1-866-506-1949
or business@simonandschuster.com.

The Simon & Schuster Speakers Bureau can bring authors to your live event.
For more information or to book an event, contact the Simon & Schuster Speakers
Bureau at 1-866-248-3049 or visit our website at www.simonspeakers.com.

Manufactured in the United States of America

3   5   7   9   10   8   6   4

Library of Congress Control Number: 99019697

ISBN 978-0-684-85782-4
ISBN 978-1-5011-7163-5 (pbk)
ISBN 978-1-4391-3085-8 (ebook)

This edition of *Lucky*
is for those who have suffered any form of sexual assault.
We are at our strongest when we move as a group.

LUCKY

AUTHOR'S NOTE

Out of respect for their privacy, I have changed the names of some of the people who appear in these pages.

In the tunnel where I was raped, a tunnel that was once an underground entry to an amphitheater, a place where actors burst forth from underneath the seats of a crowd, a girl had been murdered and dismembered. I was told this story by the police. In comparison, they said, I was lucky.

But at the time, I felt I had more in common with the dead girl than I did with the large, beefy police officers or my stunned freshman-year girlfriends. The dead girl and I had been in the same low place. We had lain among the dead leaves and broken beer bottles.

During the rape my eye caught something among the leaves and glass. A pink hair tie. When I heard about the dead girl, I could imagine her pleading as I had, and wondered when her hair had been pulled loose from her hair tie. If that was something the man who killed her had done or if, to save herself the pain in the moment—thinking, hoping, no doubt, she would have the luxury to reflect on the ramifications of "assisting the assailant" later on—she had, on his urging, undone her hair herself. I will not know this, just as I will never know whether the hair tie was hers or whether it, like the leaves, made its way there naturally. I will always think of her when I think of the pink hair tie. I will think of a girl in the last moments of her life.

ONE

This is what I remember. My lips were cut. I bit down on them when he grabbed me from behind and covered my mouth. He said these words: "I'll kill you if you scream." I remained motionless. "Do you understand? If you scream you're dead." I nodded my head. My arms were pinned to my sides by his right arm wrapped around me and my mouth was covered with his left.

He released his hand from my mouth.

I screamed. Quickly. Abruptly.

The struggle began.

He covered my mouth again. He kneed me in the back of my legs so that I would fall down. "You don't get it, bitch. I'll kill you. I've got a knife. I'll kill you." He released his grip on my mouth again and I fell, screaming, on the brick path. He straddled me and kicked me in the side. I made sounds, they were nothing, they were soft footfalls. They urged him on, they made him righteous. I scrambled on the path. I was wearing soft-soled moccasins with which I tried to land wild kicks. Everything missed or merely grazed him. I had never fought before, was chosen last in gym.

Somehow, I don't remember how, I made it back on my feet. I remember biting him, pushing him, I don't know what. Then I began to run. Like a giant who is all powerful, he reached out and grabbed the end of my long brown hair. He yanked it hard and brought me down onto my knees in front of him. That was my first missed escape, the hair, the woman's long hair.

"You asked for it now," he said, and I began to beg.

He reached around to his back pocket to draw out a knife. I

struggled still, my hair coming out painfully from my skull as I did my best to rip myself free of his grip. I lunged forward and grabbed his left leg with both arms, throwing him off balance and making him stagger. I would not know it until the police found it later in the grass, a few feet away from my broken glasses, but with that move, the knife fell from his hands and was lost.

Then it was fists.

Maybe he was angry at the loss of his weapon or at my disobedience. Whatever the reason, this marked the end of the preliminaries. I was on the ground on my stomach. He sat on my back. He pounded my skull into the brick. He cursed me. He turned me around and sat on my chest. I was babbling. I was begging. Here is where he wrapped his hands around my neck and began to squeeze. For a second, I lost consciousness. When I came to, I knew I was staring up into the eyes of the man who would kill me.

At that moment I signed myself over to him. I was convinced that I would not live. I could not fight anymore. He was going to do what he wanted to me. That was it.

Everything slowed down. He stood up and began dragging me over the grass by my hair. I twisted and half crawled, trying to keep up with him. Dimly, I had seen the dark entrance of the amphitheater tunnel from the path. As we neared it, and I realized it was our destination, a rush of fear ran through me. I knew I would die.

There was an old iron fence a few feet out from the tunnel entrance. It was three feet high and provided a narrow space through which you had to walk in order to enter the tunnel. As he dragged me, as I scrambled against the grass, I caught sight of that fence and became utterly convinced that if he brought me beyond this point, I would not survive.

For a moment, as he dragged me across the ground, I clung feebly to the bottom of that iron fence, before a rough pull yanked me clean. People think a woman stops fighting when she is physically exhausted, but I was about to begin my real fight, a fight of words and lies and the brain.

*　*　*

When people talk about climbing a mountain or riding rough water, they say they became one with it, their bodies so attuned to it that they often, when asked to articulate how they did it, cannot fully explain.

Inside the tunnel, where broken beer bottles, old leaves, and other, as yet indiscriminate, things littered the ground, I became one with this man. He held my life in his hand. Those who say they would rather fight to the death than be raped are fools. I would rather be raped a thousand times. You do what you have to.

"Stand up," he said.

I did.

I was shivering uncontrollably. It was cold out and the cold combined with the fear, with the exhaustion, made me shake from head to toe.

He dumped my purse and bag of books in the corner of the sealed-off tunnel.

"Take off your clothes."

"I have eight dollars in my back pocket," I said. "My mother has credit cards. My sister does too."

"I don't want your money," he said, and laughed.

I looked at him. Into his eyes now, as if he was a human being, as if I could speak to him.

"Please don't rape me," I said.

"Take off your clothes."

"I'm a virgin," I said.

He didn't believe me. Repeated his command. "Take off your clothes."

My hands were shaking and I couldn't control them. He pulled me forward by my belt until my body was up against his, which was up against the tunnel's back wall.

"Kiss me," he said.

And he drew my head forward and our lips met. My lips were pursed tightly together. He tugged harder on my belt, my body pressing up further against his. He grabbed my hair in his fist and balled it up. He drew my head back and looked at me. I began to cry, to plead.

"Please don't," I said. "Please."

"Shut up."

He kissed me again and this time, he inserted his tongue in my mouth. By pleading, I had left myself open to this. Again he pulled my head back roughly. "Kiss back," he said.

And I did.

When he was satisfied, he stopped and tried to work the latch on my belt. It was a belt with a strange buckle and he couldn't figure it out. To have him let go of me, for him to leave me alone, I said, "Let me, I'll do it."

He watched me.

When I was done, he unzipped the jeans I wore.

"Now take off your shirt."

I had a cardigan sweater on. I took that off. He reached over to help unbutton my shirt. He fumbled.

"I'll do it," I said again.

I unbuttoned the oxford-cloth shirt and, like the cardigan, I peeled it back from my body. It was like shedding feathers. Or wings.

"Now the bra."

I did.

He reached out and grabbed them—my breasts—in his two hands. He plied them and squeezed them, manipulating them right down to my ribs. Twisting. I hope that to say this hurt isn't necessary here.

"Please don't do this, please," I said.

"Nice white titties," he said. And the words made me give them up, lopping off each part of my body as he claimed owner-ship—the mouth, the tongue, my breasts.

"I'm cold," I said.

"Lay down."

"On the ground?" I asked, stupidly, hopelessly. I saw, among the leaves and glass, the grave. My body stretched out, disassembled, gagged, dead.

I sat first, kind of stumbled into a seated position. He took the end of my pants and tugged. As I tried to hide my nakedness—

at least I had my underpants on—he looked down at my body. I still feel that in that gaze his eyes lit up my sickly pale skin in that dark tunnel. Made it all—my flesh—suddenly horrible. *Ugly* too kind a word, but the closest one.

"You're the worst bitch I ever done this to," he said. It was said in disgust, it was said in analysis. He saw what he had bagged and didn't like his catch.

No matter, he would finish.

Here, I began to combine truth with fiction, using anything to try and get him to come over to my side. To see me as pitiful, for him to see me as worse off than him.

"I'm a foster child," I said. "I don't even know who my parents are. Please don't do this. I'm a virgin," I said.

"Lie down."

I did. Shaking, I crawled over and lay face up against the cold ground. He pulled my underpants off me roughly and bundled them into his hand. He threw them away from me and into a corner where I lost sight of them.

I watched him as he unzipped his pants and let them fall around his ankles.

He lay down on top of me and started humping. I was familiar with this. This was what Steve, a boy I liked in high school, had done against my leg, because I would not let him do what he wanted most, which was to make love to me. With Steve I was fully dressed and so was he. He went home frustrated and I felt safe. My parents were upstairs the whole time. I told myself Steve loved me.

He worked away on me, reaching down to work with his penis.

I stared right into his eyes. I was too afraid not to. If I shut my eyes, I believed, I would disappear. To make it through, I had to be present the whole time.

He called me bitch. He told me I was dry.

"I'm sorry," I said—I never stopped apologizing. "I'm a virgin," I said.

"Stop looking at me," he said. "Shut your eyes. Stop shaking."

"I can't."

"Stop it or you'll be sorry."

I did. My focus became acute. I stared harder than ever at him. He began to knead his fist against the opening of my vagina. Inserted his fingers into it, three or four at a time. Something tore. I began to bleed there. I was wet now.

It made him excited. He was intrigued. As he worked his whole fist up into my vagina and pumped it, I went into my brain. Waiting there were poems for me, poems I'd learned in class: Olga Cabral had a poem I haven't found since, "Lillian's Chair," and a poem called "Dog Hospital," by Peter Wild. I tried, as a sort of prickly numbness took over my lower half, to recite the poems in my head. I moved my lips.

"Stop staring at me," he said.

"I'm sorry," I said. "You're strong," I tried.

He liked this. He started humping me again, wildly. The base of my spine was crushed into the ground. Glass cut me on my back and behind. But something still wasn't working for him. I didn't know what he was doing.

He kneeled back. "Raise your legs," he said.

Not knowing what he meant, never having done this for a lover, or read that kind of book, I raised them straight up.

"Spread them."

I did. My legs were like a plastic Barbie's, pale, inflexible. But he wasn't satisfied. He put a hand on each calf and pressed them out farther than I could hold.

"Keep them there," he said.

He tried again. He worked his fist. He grabbed my breasts. He twisted the nipples with his fingers, lapped at them with his tongue.

Tears came out of the corners of my eyes and rolled down either cheek. I was leaving now, but then I heard sounds. Out on the path. People, a group of laughing boys and girls, passing by. I had passed a party on my way to the park, a party to celebrate the last day of school. I looked at him; he did not hear them. This was it. I made an abrupt scream and, as soon as I did, he shoved his hand in my mouth. Simultaneously I heard the laughter again. This time it was directed toward the tunnel, toward us. Yells and taunts. Good-time noises.

We lay there, his hand locked in my mouth and pressing down hard into my throat, until the group of well-wishers left. Moved on. My second chance at escape now gone.

Things weren't going the way he planned. It was taking too long. He ordered me to stand up. Told me I could put on my *panties*. Used that word. I hated it.

I thought it was over. I was trembling but I thought he'd had enough. Blood was everywhere and so I thought he'd done what he'd come for.

"Give me a blow job," he said. He was standing now. I was on the ground, trying to search among the filth for my clothes.

He kicked me and I curled into a ball.

"I want a blow job." He held his dick in his hand.

"I don't know how," I said.

"What do you mean you don't know how?"

"I've never done it before," I said. "I'm a virgin."

"Put it in your mouth."

I kneeled before him. "Can I put my bra back on?" I wanted my clothes. I saw his thighs before me, the way they belled out from the knee, the thick muscles and small black hairs, and his flaccid dick.

He grabbed my head. "Put it in your mouth and suck," he said.

"Like a straw?" I said.

"Yeah, like a straw."

I took it in my hand. It was small. Hot, clammy. It throbbed involuntarily at my touch. He shoved my head forward and I put it in. It touched my tongue. The taste like dirty rubber or burnt hair. I sucked in hard.

"Not like that," he said and brought my head away. "Don't you know how to suck dick?"

"No, I told you," I said. "I've never done this before."

"Bitch," he said. His penis still limp, he held it with two fingers and peed on me. Just a little bit. Acrid, wet, on my nose and lips. The smell of him—the fruity, heady, nauseating smell— clung to my skin.

"Get back on the ground," he said, "and do what I say."

And I did. When he told me to close my eyes I told him I had lost my glasses, couldn't even really see him. "Talk to me," he said. "I believe you, you're a virgin. I'm your first." As he worked against me, trying for more and more friction, I told him he was strong, that he was powerful, that he was a good man. He got hard enough and plunged himself inside me. He ordered me to and I wrapped my legs around his back and he drove me into the ground. I was locked on. All that remained unpossessed was my brain. It looked and watched and cataloged the details of it all. His face, his purpose, how best I could help him.

I heard more party-goers on the path, but I was far away now. He made noises and rammed it in. Rammed it and rammed it and those on the path, those so far away, living in the world where I had lived, could not be reached by me now.

"Nail her, all right!" someone yelled toward the tunnel. It was the kind of fraternity reveler's voice that had made me feel that, as a student at Syracuse University, I might never fit in.

They passed. I was staring right into his eyes. With him.

"You're so strong, you're such a man, thank you, thank you, I wanted this."

And then it was over. He came and slumped into me. I lay under him. My heart beating wildly. My brain thinking of Olga Cabral, of poetry, of my mother, of anything. Then I heard his breathing. Light and regular. He was snoring. I thought: Escape. I shifted under him and he woke.

He looked at me, did not know who I was. Then his remorse began.

"I'm so sorry," he said. "You're a good girl," he said. "I'm so sorry."

"Can I get dressed?"

He moved aside and stood up, raised his pants, zipped them.

"Of course, of course," he said. "I'll help you."

I had begun to let myself shake again.

"You're cold," he said. "Here, put these on." He held my underwear out to me, in the way a mother would for a child, by the sides of it. I was supposed to stand up and step in.

I crawled over toward my clothes. Put my bra on as I sat on the ground.

"Are you okay?" he asked. His tone was amazing to me. Concerned. But I didn't stop to think of it then. All I knew was it was better than it had been.

I stood up and took my underpants from him. I put them on, almost falling for my lack of balance. I had to sit on the ground to put my pants on. I was worried about my legs. I couldn't seem to control them.

He watched me. As I inched my pants up, his tone switched.

"You're going to have a baby, bitch," he said. "What are you going to do about it?"

I realized this could be a reason to kill me. Any evidence. I lied to him.

"Please don't tell anyone," I said. "I'll have an abortion. Please don't tell anyone. My mother would kill me if she knew about this. Please," I said, "no one can know about this. My family would hate me. Please don't talk about this."

He laughed. "All right," he said.

"Thank you," I said. I stood now and put my shirt on. It was inside out.

"Can I go now?" I asked.

"Come here," he said. "Kiss me good-bye." It was a date to him. For me it was happening all over again.

I kissed him. Did I say I had free will? Do you still believe in that?

He apologized again. This time he cried. "I'm so sorry," he said. "You're such a good girl, a good girl, like you said."

I was shocked by his tears, but by now it was just another horrible nuance I couldn't understand. So he wouldn't hurt me more. I needed to say the right thing.

"It's okay," I said. "Really."

When raped, women expected to forgive men or at least some part of what they did

"No," he said, "it's not right what I did. You're a good girl. You weren't lying to me. I'm sorry for what I did."

I've always hated it in movies and plays, the woman who is ripped open by violence and then asked to parcel out redemption for the rest of her life.

"I forgive you," I said. I said what I had to. I would die by pieces to save myself from real death.

He perked up. Looked at me. "You're a beautiful girl," he said.

"Can I take my purse?" I asked. I was afraid to move without his permission. "My books?"

He went back to business now. "You said you had eight dollars?" He took it from my jeans. It was wrapped around my license. It was a photo ID. New York State didn't have them yet but Pennsylvania did.

"What is this?" he asked. "Is this one of them meal cards I can use at McDonald's?"

"No," I said. I was petrified of him having my identification. Leaving with anything other than what he had: all of me, except my brain and my belongings. I wanted to leave the tunnel with both of them.

He looked at it a moment longer until he was convinced. He did not take my great-grandmother's sapphire ring, which had been on my hand the whole time. He was not interested in that kind of thing.

He handed me my purse and the books I'd bought that afternoon with my mother.

"Which way you going?" he asked.

I pointed. "All right," he said, "take care of yourself."

I promised that I would. I started walking. Back out over the ground, through the gate to which I'd clung a little over an hour before, and onto the brick path. Going farther into the park was the only way toward home.

A moment later.

"Hey, girl," he yelled at me.

I turned. I was, as I am in these pages, his.

"What's your name?"

I couldn't lie. I didn't have a name other than my own to say. "Alice," I said.

"Nice knowing you, Alice," he yelled. "See you around sometime."

He ran off in the opposite direction, along the chain-link fence of the pool house. I turned. I had done my job. I had convinced him. Now I walked.

I didn't see a soul until I reached the three short stone steps that led from the park to the sidewalk. On the opposite side of the street was a frat house. I kept walking. I remained on the sidewalk close to the park. There were people out on the lawns of the frat house. A kegger party just dying out. At the place where my dorm's street dead-ended into the park, I turned and started to walk downhill past another, larger dormitory.

I was aware I was being stared at. Party-goers coming home or grinds taking in the last bit of sober air before the summer. They talked. But I wasn't there. I heard them outside of me, but like a stroke victim, I was locked inside my body.

They came up to me. Some ran, but then stepped back when I didn't respond.

"Hey, did you see her?" they said to one another.

"She's really fucked up."

"Look at the blood."

I made it down the hill, past those people. I was afraid of everyone. Outside, on the raised platform that surrounded Marion Dorm's front door, were people who knew me. Knew my face if not my name. There were three floors in Marion, a floor of girls between two floors of boys. Outside now it was mostly the boys. One boy opened the outer door for me to let me pass through. Another held the inner one. I was being watched; how could I not have been?

At a small table near the door was the RSA—resident security assistant. He was a graduate student. A small, studious Arab man. After midnight they checked ID's of anyone trying to get in. He looked at me and then hurriedly stood.

"What has happened?" he asked.

"I don't have my ID," I said.

I stood before him with my face smashed in, cuts across my nose and lip, a tear along my cheek. My hair was matted with leaves. My clothes were inside out and bloodied. My eyes were glazed.

"Are you all right?"

"I want to go to my room," I said. "I don't have my ID," I repeated.

He waved me in. "Promise me," he said, "that you will take care of yourself."

Boys were in the stairwell. Some of the girls too. The whole dorm was still mostly awake. I walked by them. Silence. Eyes.

I walked down the hall and knocked on the door of my best friend Mary Alice's room. No one. I knocked on my own, hoping for my roommate. No one. Last, I knocked on the door of Linda and Diane, two of a group of six of us who had become friends that year. At first there was no answer. Then the doorknob turned.

Inside, the room was dark. Linda was kneeling on her bed and holding the door open. I had woken her up.

"What is it?" she asked.

"Linda," I said, "I was just raped and beaten in the park." She fell back and into the darkness. She had passed out. The doors were spring-hinged and so the door slammed shut. The RSA had cared. I turned around and walked back downstairs to his desk. He stood.

"I was raped in the park," I said. "Will you call the police?"

He spoke quickly in Arabic, forgetting himself, then, "Yes, oh, yes, please come."

Behind him was a room with glass walls. Though meant as an office of some sort, it was never used. He led me in there and told me to sit down. Because there was no chair, I sat on top of the desk.

Boys had gathered from outside and now stared in at me, pressing their faces near the glass.

12

I don't remember how long it took—not long because it was university property and the hospital was only six blocks south. The police arrived first, but I have no memory of what I said to them there.

Then I was on a gurney, being strapped down. Then out in the hallway. There was a large crowd now and it blocked the entrance. I saw the RSA look over at me as he was being questioned.

A policeman took control.

"Get out of the way," he said to my curious peers. "This girl's just been raped."

I surfaced long enough to hear those words coming from his lips. I was that girl. The ripple effect began in the halls. The ambulance men carried me down the stairs. The doors of the ambulance were open. Inside, as we charged, sirens screaming, to the hospital, I let myself collapse. I went somewhere deep inside myself, curled up and away from what was happening.

They rushed me through the emergency room doors. Then into an examination room. A policeman came inside as the nurse was helping me take off my clothes and change into a hospital gown. She wasn't happy to have him there, but he averted his eyes and flipped forward to a clean page in his pocket notebook.

I couldn't help but think of detective shows on television. The nurse and policeman argued over me as he began to ask questions, take my clothes for evidence as she swabbed my face and back with alcohol and promised me the doctor would be there soon.

I remember the nurse better than I do him. She used her body as a shield between us. As he gathered preliminary evidence— my basic account—she said things to me as she took items for the evidence kit.

"You must have given him a run for his money," she said.

When she took the scraping from under my nails, she said, "Good, you got a piece of him."

The doctor arrived. A female gynecologist named Dr. Husa.

She began to explain what she was going to do while the nurse shooed out the policeman. I lay on the table. She was going to inject me with Demerol in order to relax me enough for her to gather evidence. It might also make me want to pee. I was not to do that, she said, because that might disrupt the culture of my vagina and destroy the evidence the police needed.

The door opened.

"There's someone here who wants to see you," the nurse said.

Somehow, I thought it might be my mother, and I panicked.

"A Mary Alice."

"Alice?" I heard Mary Alice's voice. It was soft, afraid, even. She took my hand and I squeezed it hard.

Mary Alice was beautiful—a natural blonde with gorgeous green eyes—and on that day, particularly, she reminded me of an angel.

Dr. Husa let us talk for a moment as she prepped the area.

Mary Alice, like everyone else, had been drinking heavily at a year-end bash held at a nearby fraternity house.

"Don't say I can't sober you up," I said to her, and for the first time I cried too, letting the tears leak out as she gave me what I needed most, a small smile to acknowledge my joke. It was the first thing from my old life that I recognized on the other side. It was horribly changed and marked, my friend's smile. It was not free and open, born of the silliness our smiles had been all year, but it was a comfort to me. She cried more than I did and her face became mottled and swollen. She told me how Diane, who, like Mary Alice, was five ten, had practically lifted up the small RSA in order to get my whereabouts out of him.

"He wasn't going to tell anyone but your roommate, but Nancy was up in your room, passed out."

I smiled at the idea of Diane and Mary Alice lifting up the RSA, his feet doing a wild walk in the air like a Keystone Kop.

"We're ready," Dr. Husa said.

"Will you stay with me?" I asked Mary Alice.

She did.

Dr. Husa and the nurse worked together. Every so often they needed to massage my thighs. I asked them to explain everything they did. I wanted to know everything.

"This is different from a regular exam," Dr. Husa explained. "I need to take samples in order to make up a rape kit."

"That's evidence so you can get this creep," the nurse said.

They took pubic clippings and pubic combings and samples of blood and semen and vaginal discharge. When I would wince, Mary Alice squeezed my hand harder. The nurse tried to make conversation, asked Mary Alice what she majored in up at the school, told me I was lucky to have such a good friend, said that being beaten up like I had would make the cops listen to me more attentively.

"There is so much blood," I heard Husa say worriedly to the nurse.

As they did the combings, Dr. Husa said, "Ah, now, there is a hair from him!" The nurse held the evidence bag open and Dr. Husa shook the combings into it.

"Good," the nurse said.

"Alice," Dr. Husa said, "we are going to let you urinate now but then I will have to take stitches inside."

The nurse helped me sit up and then scooted a bedpan under me. I urinated for such a long time that the nurse and Mary Alice made a point of it, and laughed each time they thought I'd stopped. When I was done, what I saw was a bedpan full of blood, not urine. The nurse covered it quickly with paper from the examining table.

"You don't need to be looking at that."

Mary Alice helped me lie back down.

Dr. Husa had me scoot down so she could take the stitches.

"You'll be sore down here for a few days, maybe a week," Dr. Husa said. "You shouldn't do much, if you can avoid it."

But I couldn't think in terms of days or weeks. I could only focus on the next minute and believe that with each minute it would get better, that slowly all of this might go away.

I told the police not to call my mother. Unaware of my appearance, I believed I could hide the rape from her and from my family. My mother had panic attacks in heavy traffic; I was certain my rape would destroy her.

* * *

After the vaginal exam was completed, I was wheeled into a bright white room. This room was used to store large, incredible machines with lifesaving abilities, all shining with stainless steel and spotless fiberglass. Mary Alice had gone back out to the waiting room. I noticed the machines and their details, how clean and new they seemed, because it was the first time I had been alone since the wheels of my rescue were set in motion. I lay on the gurney, naked under the hospital gown, and I was cold. I was not sure why I was there, stored alongside these machines. It was a long time before anyone came.

It was a nurse. I asked her if I could take a shower in the shower stall in the corner. She looked at a chart on the end of the gurney, which I hadn't known was there. I wondered what it said about me, and pictured the word *RAPE*, in bold red letters, written diagonally across the page.

I lay still and took shallow breaths. The Demerol worked hard to relax me but, still dirty, I fought back. Every inch of my skin prickled and burned. I wanted him off of me. I wanted to shower and scrub my skin raw.

The nurse told me I was waiting for the psychiatrist on call. Then she left the room. It was only fifteen minutes—but with the buggy crawl of contamination spreading over me, it felt very long—when a harried psychiatrist entered the room.

I thought, even then, that this doctor needed the Valium he prescribed for me more than I did. He was exhausted. I remember telling him I knew about Valium and so he didn't need to explain.

"It will make you calm," he said.

My mother had been addicted to it when I was little. She had lectured me and my sister on drugs and as I grew older I understood her fear—that I would get drunk or high and lose my virginity to some fumbling boy. But in these lectures what I always pictured was my vibrant mother diminished somehow, lessened—as if a gauze had been thrown over her sharp edges.

I couldn't see Valium as the benign drug the doctor made it

out to be. I told him this but he pooh-poohed it. When he left the room I did what I knew I would do almost immediately, and crumpled up the prescription to throw it into the waste bin. It felt good to do it. A sort of "fuck you" to the idea that anyone could sweep this thing I'd suffered under the carpet. Even then I thought I knew what could happen if I let people take care of me. I would disappear from view. I wouldn't be Alice anymore, whatever that was.

A nurse came in and told me she could send in another one of my friends to help me. With the painkillers I would need a nurse or someone else to help me keep my balance in the shower. I wanted Mary Alice, but I didn't want to be mean, so I asked for Tree, Mary Alice's roommate and one of our group of six.

I waited and as I did, I tried to think of what I could tell my mother—some kind of story that would explain why I was so sleepy. I could not know, despite the doctor's warnings, how sore I would be in the morning, or that an elegant latticework of bruises would appear along my thighs and chest, on the undersides of my upper arms and around my neck, where, days later, at home in my bedroom, I would begin to make out the individual pressure points of his fingertips on my throat—a butterfly of the rapist's two thumbs interlocking in the center and his fingers fluttering out and around my neck. "I'm gonna kill you, bitch. Shut up. Shut up. Shut up." Each repetition punctuated by the smash of my skull against brick, each repetition cutting off, tighter and tighter, the airflow to my brain.

Tree's face, and her gasp, should have told me that I couldn't hide the truth. But she recovered herself quickly and helped me navigate over to the shower stall. She was uncomfortable around me; I was no longer like her but was other than.

I think the way I survived in the early hours after the rape was by spiraling the obsession of how not to tell my mother over and over again in my brain. Convinced it would destroy her, I ceased thinking of what had happened to me and worried about her instead. My worry for her became my life raft. I clung to it, coming in and out of consciousness on my way to the hospital, during the internal stitches of the pelvic exam, and while the psychiatrist gave me the prescription for the very pills that had once made my mother numb.

The shower was in the corner of the room. I walked like a wobbly old lady and Tree steadied me. I was concentrating on my balance and so did not see the mirror to my right until I looked up and I was almost right in front of it.

"Alice, don't," Tree said.

But I was fascinated, the way I had been as a child when, in a special room with low light, I saw an exhibit at the University of Pennsylvania's Museum of Archaeology. It was nicknamed Blue Baby and it was a mummy, with the disintegrated face and body of a child who had died centuries ago. I recognized something alike in it—I was a child as this Blue Baby had been a child.

I saw my face in the mirror. I reached my hand up to touch the marks and cuts. That was me. It was also an undeniable truth: No shower would wipe the traces of the rape away. I had no choice but to tell my mother. She was too savvy to believe any story I could now fashion. She worked for a newspaper, and she took pride in the fact that it was impossible to pull the wool over her eyes.

The shower was small and made of white tile. I asked Tree to turn on the water. "As hot as you can," I said.

I took off the hospital gown and handed it to her.

I had to grip the tap and a handle on the side of the shower to stay upright. This left me unable to scrub myself. I remember telling Tree I wished I had a wire brush but that even that wouldn't be enough.

She drew the curtain and I stood there, letting the water beat over me.

"Can you help me?" I asked.

Tree pulled the curtain back a few inches.

"What do you want me to do?"

"I'm afraid I'll fall down. Can you take the soap and help wash me?"

She reached through the water and got the large square brick of soap. She drew it down my back, nothing but the bar of soap touching me. I felt the rapist's words, "worst bitch," as I would feel them almost constantly for years when I undressed in front of other people.

"Forget it," I said, unable to look at her. "I'll do it myself. Just put the soap back."

She did, then pulled the curtain closed, before leaving.

I sat down in the shower. I took a washcloth and lathered it up. I scrubbed hard with the rough towel, under a tap so hot my skin had already turned beet red. The last thing I did was put the towel over my face and with both hands rubbed it back and forth over and over again until the cuts and their blood turned the small white towel pink.

After the hot shower, I dressed in clothes that Tree and Diane had hurriedly selected from the few clean clothes I had. They had forgotten any underwear so I had no bra or underpants. What I did have was a pair of old jeans that I had embroidered flowers on while still in high school and then, when the knees ripped open, had sewn intricate handmade patches on—long strips of pleated paisley and deep-green velvet. My grandmother had labeled them my "rebel" pants. On top, I wore a thin white-and-red-striped blouse. I left the shirttails out, hoping to hide as much as possible of the jeans.

The heat of the shower and the Demerol worked together to make me groggy during the drive to the police station. I remember seeing the resident advisor, a sophomore named Cindy, outside the security door on the third floor of the police station, called the Public Safety Building. I wasn't prepared to see anyone with such a bright face, such an all-American-coed presence.

Mary Alice stayed outside with Cindy as police officers led me through a security door. I met a plainclothes detective inside. He was short, with longish black hair. He reminded me of Starsky from *Starsky and Hutch*, and seemed different from the other policemen. He was nice to me but his shift was ending. He assigned me to Sergeant Lorenz, who had not yet arrived at the station.

In hindsight I can only imagine how I appeared to them. My

face was swollen, my hair wet, my clothes—the "rebel" pants especially and the lack of a bra—and on top of this, the Demerol.

I made a composite from microfilm features. I worked with an officer and was frustrated because none of my rapist's features seemed to be among the fifty or so noses, eyes, and lips. I gave exact descriptions but when nothing was acceptable to me among the tiny black-and-white features I could select, the policeman decided on what was best. The composite that went out that night looked little like him.

The police then took a series of pictures of me, never knowing another series had been taken earlier that night. Ken Childs, a boy I liked, had shot almost a whole roll of film, snapping candids of me in various poses throughout his apartment.

Ken had a crush on me, and I knew that he was taking the pictures to show to people at home over the summer. I knew the photos would be judged. Was I pretty? Did I look smart? Would his friends be reduced to "She seems nice"? Or, worse still, "That's a nice sweater she's swearing"?

I had gained weight, but the jeans I wore were still too big for me, and I'd borrowed my mother's white oxford-cloth shirt and a tan cable cardigan sweater. The word that comes to mind here is *frumpy*.

So, in the "before" photos taken by Ken Childs, I am at first posing, then giggling, then laughing openly. For all my self-consciousness, I also got lost in the giggling silliness of our crush. I balance a box of raisins on my head, I stare at the writing on the back as if it were a gripping text, I prop my feet up on the edge of his dining table. I smile, smile, smile.

In the "after" photos the police took, I stand shocked. The word *shock*, in this context, is meant to mean I was no longer there. If you have seen police photos of crime victims, you will know that they appear either bleached or unusually dark. Mine were of the overexposed variety. There were four types of poses. Face. Face and neck. Neck. Standing with identity number. No one tells you at the time how important these photos will be. The cosmetics of rape are central to proving any case. So far, in appearance, I was two for two: I wore loose, unenticing clothes; I had clearly been beaten. Add this to my virginity, and you will begin to understand much of what matters inside the courtroom.

Finally, I was allowed to leave the Public Safety Building with Cindy, Mary Alice, and Tree. I told the officers in the station that I would return in a few hours and could be counted on to give an affidavit and look through mug shots. I wanted them to see I was serious, I wouldn't let them down. But they were working the night shift. Even when I did come back—and in their minds, it was far from certain that I would—they wouldn't be there to see I'd kept my word.

The police drove us back to Marion Dorm. It was early in the morning. Light had begun to creep up over Thorden Park at the top of the hill. I had to tell my mother.

The dorm was deathly quiet. Cindy went into her room at the top of the hall and Mary Alice and I agreed we would meet her there momentarily. Neither of us had a private phone.

We went to my room, where I found a bra and underwear to put on under my clothes.

Back out in the hallway, we ran into Diane and her boyfriend, Victor. They had been up all night, waiting for me to come home.

My relationship to Victor, before that morning, consisted primarily of not understanding what he had in common with Diane, whom I found loud. He was handsome and athletic and very, very quiet around all of us. He had entered school already having chosen his major. It was something like electrical engineering. Very different from poetry. Victor was black.

"Alice," Diane said.

Other people came out of Cindy's open doorway. Girls I knew vaguely or those I didn't know.

"Victor wants to hug you," Diane said.

I looked at Victor. This was too much. He was not my rapist, I knew that. That was not the issue. But he was blocking my way to the last thing on earth I wanted to do and the thing I knew I had to do. Make that call to my mother.

"I don't think I can," I said to Victor.

"He was black, wasn't he?" Victor asked. He was trying to get me to look at him, look right at him.

"Yes."

"I'm sorry," he said. He was crying. The tears ran slowly down the outside of his cheeks. "I'm so sorry."

I don't know whether I hugged him because I could not stand to see him crying (so odd in the Victor I knew, the quiet Victor who studied diligently or smiled shyly at Diane), or because I was prompted further by those around us. He held me until I had to pull away and then he let me go. He was miserable, and I cannot even now imagine what was going on inside his head. Perhaps he already knew that both relatives and strangers would say things to me like "I bet he was black," and so he wanted to give me something to counter this, some experience in the same twenty-four hours that would make me resist placing people in categories and aiming at them my full-on hate. It was my first hug from a man after the rape—black or white—and all I knew was that I couldn't give anything back. The arms around me, the vague threat of physical power, were all too much.

By the end, Victor and I had an audience. It was something I would have to get used to. Standing close to him, but separated from the embrace, I was aware of Mary Alice and of Diane. They belonged. The others were foggy and off to the side. They were watching my life as if it were a movie. In their version of the story, where did they fit? I would find out over the years that in a few versions, I was their best friend. Knowing a victim is like knowing a celebrity. Particularly when the crime is clouded in taboo. When I was doing research for this book, back in Syracuse, I met a woman like this. Without recognizing me at first, only knowing I was writing a book on Alice Sebold's rape case, she hurried in from another room and told me and those assisting me that "the victim in that case was my best friend." I had no idea who she was. When someone referred to me by name, she blinked and then came forward, embracing me to save face.

*　*　*

In Cindy's room, I sat down on the bed closest to the door. Cindy, Mary Alice, and Tree were there, perhaps Diane. Cindy had shooed the others out and shut her door.

It was time. I sat with the phone in my lap. My mother was only a few miles away, having driven up the day before to take me home from Syracuse. She would be up and puttering around her hotel room at the Holiday Inn. At that time she traveled with her own coffeemaker because she made decaf in her room. She was coming down from as much as ten cups of coffee a day, and restaurants weren't yet in the custom of serving decaf.

Before she had dropped me off at Ken Childs's house the evening before, we had agreed she would come to the dorm around 8:30 A.M.—a late start for her but a concession to the fact that I would have been up late saying good-bye to friends. I looked around at my girlfriends, hoping they would say, "You don't look so bad," or provide me with the single and perfect story to explain the cuts and bruises on my face—the story that I hadn't been able to come up with during the night.

Tree dialed the phone.

When my mother picked up, Tree said, "Mrs. Sebold, this is a friend of Alice's, Tree Roebeck."

Maybe my mother said hello.

"I'm going to put Alice on the phone now. She needs to speak with you."

Tree handed me the phone.

"Mom," I started.

She must not have heard what I thought was the obvious quaver in my voice. She was irritated.

"What is it, Alice? You know I'm due over soon; can't it wait?"

"Mom, I need to tell you something."

She heard it now. "What, what is it?"

I said it as if I were reading a line from a script.

"Last night I was beaten and raped in the park."

My mother said, "Oh, my God," and then, after a quick inhalation of breath, a startled gasp, she reeled herself in. "Are you all right?"

"Can you come get me, Mommy?" I asked.

She said it would be twenty minutes or so, she had to pack up and check out, but she would be there.

I hung up the phone.

Mary Alice suggested that we wait in her room until my mother arrived. Someone had bought bagels or doughnuts.

In the time since our arrival back at the dorm, students had woken up. There was hurry all around me. Many students, including my friends, were meeting parents for breakfast or rushing to bus stations and airports. People would attend to me and then switch off to finish packing. I sat with my back against the cinder-block dorm wall. As people came in and out and the door opened, I could hear bits of conversation.

"Where is she?" "Raped . . ." " . . . see her face?" " . . . she know him?" " . . . always weird . . ."

I had not eaten anything since the night before—since the raisins at Ken Childs's house—and I could not look at the bagels or doughnuts without feeling what—the rapist's penis—had last been in my mouth. I tried to stay awake. I had been up for more than twenty-four hours—far longer, what with the all-nighters that I'd pulled during finals week—but I was afraid to fall asleep before my mother got there. My girlfriends and the resident advisor, who, after all, was only nineteen, tried to take care of me, but I had begun to notice that I was now on the other side of something they could not understand. I didn't understand it myself.

TWO

While I waited for my mother, people began to leave. I ate a cracker, offered by Tree or Mary Alice. Friends were saying good-bye. Mary Alice wasn't leaving until later in the day. She had done instinctively what few people do in the face of a crisis: She had signed on for the whole ride.

I felt I needed to dress up for my mother and for the ride home. Mary Alice had already been shocked when, at Christmas and spring break, I had insisted on putting on a skirt and suit jacket to take the bus home to Pennsylvania. Both times, Mary Alice waited on the curb outside the dorm in sweatpants and a lumpy down jacket, trash bags of laundry lined up and ready to be loaded by her parents into their car. But my parents liked to see me look nice, debated my choice of clothing many mornings during high school. I had begun dieting at eleven and my weight, and how it marred my beauty, was a major topic of conversation. My father was the king of the backhanded compliment. "You look just like a Russian ballerina," he said once, "only too fat." My mother repeatedly said, "If you weren't so beautiful in the first place, it wouldn't matter." The implication being, I guess, that I was supposed to know they thought I was beautiful. The result, of course, was that I only thought I was ugly.

There was probably no better way to confirm this for me than to be raped. In high school, two boys had, in the Senior Class Will, left me toothpicks and pigment. The toothpicks were for my Asian-looking eyes, the pigment for my white skin. I was pale, always pale, and unmuscled. My lips were big and my eyes small. The morning of the rape my lips were cut, my eyes were swollen.

I put on a green-and-red kilt and made sure to use the kilt pin

25

that my mother had searched stores for after we purchased the skirt. The indecency of any wrap skirt was something she underlined to me often, particularly when we saw a woman or girl who was unaware that the flap had blown open and we, her audience in parking lot or shopping mall, could see more leg than, as my mother said, "anyone would want to."

My mother believed in buying clothes big, so, as I grew up, I listened to my older sister, Mary, complain about how all the clothes Mom bought us were huge. In the dressing rooms of department stores, my mother would test the size of all pants or skirts by putting her hand in the waistband. If she couldn't easily slide her hand between our underwear and whatever outfit we were trying on, then it was too tight. If my sister complained, my mother would say, "Mary, I don't know why you insist on wanting pants that are so tight they leave nothing, and I mean nothing, to the imagination."

We sat with our legs crossed. Our hair was neat and pulled back over the ears. We were not allowed to wear jeans more than once a week until we reached high school. We had to wear a dress to school at least once a week. No heels except pumps from Pappagallo, which were primarily for church and, even then, the heels did not exceed 1.5 inches. I was told whores and waitresses chewed gum and only tiny women could wear turtlenecks and ankle straps.

I knew, now that I had been raped, I should try to look good for my parents. Having gained the regulation freshman fifteen meant that my skirt that day fit. I was trying to prove to them and to myself that I was still who I had always been. I was beautiful, if fat. I was smart, if loud. I was good, if ruined.

While I dressed, Tricia, a representative from the Rape Crisis Center, arrived. She passed out pamphlets to my friends and left stacks of them in the front hall of the dorm. If anyone had wondered what all the commotion the night before had been about, now they knew for sure. Tricia was tall and thin with light brown hair that fell about her head in thin and wispy waves. Her approach, a sort of comforting "I'm here for you" stance, was

[handwritten margin note: clothing restrictions set by her mom.]

not one I trusted. I had Mary Alice. My mother was coming. I did not appreciate the soft touch of this stranger and I did not want to belong to her club.

I got a two-minute warning that my mother was coming up the stairs. I wanted Tricia to shut up—didn't see how what she was saying could help me with this encounter—and I paced the room, wondering if I should go out and greet my mother in the hall.

"Open the door," I said to Mary Alice. I breathed deeply and stood in the middle of the room. I wanted my mother to know I was all right. Nothing could get to me. I'd been raped but I was fine.

Within seconds, I saw that my mother, who I had expected would collapse, had the kind of fresh energy that was needed to get me through the rest of that day.

"I'm here now," she said. Both of our chins wobbled when we were on the verge of tears, a trait we shared and hated.

I told her about the police, that we had to go back. They needed a formal affidavit and there were mug books to look at. My mother spoke to Tricia and to Cindy, thanked Tree and Diane, and especially Mary Alice, whom she had met previously. I watched as she took over. I let her do it, willingly, for now not questioning its toll on her.

The girls helped my mother pack and bring my things out to the car. Victor helped too. I stayed in the room. The hallway had become a difficult place for me. Doorways there led into rooms where people knew about me.

Before my mother and I took our leave, and as a final way to show her love, Mary Alice worked among the tangles in my hair to make a French braid. It was something she knew how to do that I didn't. Something she had tons of practice with, from having groomed horses whose manes she braided for competition. It hurt while she did it, my scalp was very sore from the rapist yanking and pulling me by my hair, but with each hank of hair she braided in, I tried to gather what energy I had left. I knew before Mary Alice and my mother walked me downstairs and to the car, where Mary Alice hugged me and said good-bye, that I was going to pretend, as best as I could, that I was fine.

We drove downtown to the Public Safety Building. There was this one chore before we could go home.

I looked at mug shots, but I didn't see the man who raped me. At 9:00 A.M. Sergeant Lorenz arrived and the first order of business was to take my affidavit. My body was shutting down now and I was having trouble staying awake. Lorenz led me to the interrogation room, the walls of which were covered with thick carpet. While I told my story, he sat at a desk behind an upright typewriter, typing slowly in a hunt-and-peck style. I was drifting, trying hard to remain alert, but I told him everything. It was Lorenz's job to pare it down to one page for the file and to this effect he would at times bark angrily, "That's inconsequential, just the facts." I took each reprimand for what it was: an awareness that the specificity of my rape did not matter, but only how and if it conformed to an established charge. Rape 1, Sodomy 1, etc. How he twisted my breasts or shoved his fist up inside me, my virginity: inconsequential.

Through my struggle to remain conscious, I took the temperature of this man. He was tired, fatigued, did not like the paperwork side of being a member of the Syracuse PD, and taking an affidavit in a rape case was a crappy way to start his day.

He was also uncomfortable around me. First because I was a rape victim and had facts that would make anyone uncomfortable to hear, but also because I was having trouble staying awake. He squinted hard at me, sizing me up from behind his typewriter.

When I said I did not know a man had to be erect in order to enter me, Lorenz looked over at me.

"Come on, Alice," he said and smiled. "You and I both know that isn't possible."

"I'm sorry," I said, chastened. "I don't know that, I've never had sex with a man before."

He was quiet and then looked down. "I'm not used to virgins in my line of work," he said.

I decided to like Sergeant Lorenz and to think of him as fatherly. He was the first person to whom I had uttered the details of what had happened. I could not fathom that he might not believe me.

On 8 May 81 I left my friend's home on 321 Westcott St. at approx 12:00 AM. I proceeded to walk towards my dorm at 305 Waverly Ave by walking through Thorden Park. At approx 12:05 AM while walking on the path past the bathhouse and near the amphitheater I heard someone walking behind me. I started to walk faster and was suddenly overtaken from behind and grabbed around the mouth. This man said "be quiet I'm not going to hurt you, if you do what I say." He loosened up his grip on my mouth and I screamed. He then threw me on the ground and yanks my hair and said "don't ask any questions, I could kill you right now." We were both on the ground and he threatened me with a knife I never saw. He then began to struggle with me and told me to walk over to the area of the amphitheater. While walking I fell down and he became angry, grabbed my hair and pulled me into the amphitheater. He proceeded to undress me until I was left with my bra and panties. I took off my bra and panties, he told me to lie down which I did. He took off his pants and proceeded to have intercourse with me. After he was done he got up and asked me to give him a "blow job." I said that I didn't know what it meant and he said "just suck on it." He then took my head and forced my mouth on his penis. After he was done he told me to lie down on the ground and again had intercourse with me. He fell asleep on me for a short time. He got up and helped me dress and took $9.00 from my back pocket. I was then allowed to leave and went back to Marion Dorm where I notified the University police.

I wish to state that the man I encountered in the park is a Negro approx 16–18 years of age, small and muscular build of 150 lbs, wearing dark blue sweatshirt and dark jeans, with short afro-style hair cut. I desire prosecution in the event this individual is caught.

Lorenz handed me the voluntary affidavit to sign.

"It was eight dollars, not nine," I said. "And what about what he did to my breasts and his fist?" I asked. "We fought more than that." All I saw were what I thought of as the errors he had made, the things he had left out or the word she had substituted for what had actually been said.

"All that doesn't matter," he said. "We just need the gist of it. As soon as you sign it, you can go home."

I did. I left for Pennsylvania with my mother.

Early that morning, once my mother had arrived at the dorm, I'd asked her if she had to tell Dad. By that time she already had. He was the first person she called. They debated in that phone call whether to tell my sister just then. She had one more final to take at Penn. But my father needed to tell my sister as much as my mother needed to tell him. He called her in her dorm room in Philadelphia that morning as my mother and I made our way home. Mary would take her last exam knowing I had been raped.

And so, soon after, I began to come up with my theory of primary versus secondary. It was okay for primary people, my mother and father, my sister and Mary Alice, to share the story. They needed to, it was only natural. But the people they told, the secondary people, should not tell others. In this way, I thought I could contain the news of what had happened to me. I conveniently forgot all the faces in the dorm of those who had no vested interest in keeping faith with me.

I was returning home.

My life was over; my life had just begun.

THREE

Paoli, Pennsylvania, is an actual town. It has a center and a train line named after it, the Paoli Local. It was where I told people I was from. I wasn't. I was from Malvern. Or at least that was my mailing address. But actually I was from Frazer. I grew up in an amorphous valley of converted farmland that had been divided into treeless lots and sold off to developers. Our development, Spring Mill Farms, was one of the first to have been built in the area. For many years it was as if the fifteen or so original houses had landed in the midst of an ancient site of a meteor crash. There was nothing, save the equally new and treeless high school, for miles around. New families like mine moved into the two-story houses and bought sod or small, whirring seed spreaders that the fathers walked back and forth across the dirt lots as if they were the most disciplined of pets. Heartsick at her inability to grow anything resembling the lawns in magazines, my mother opened her arms wide to the advent of crabgrass. "To hell with it," she said. "At least it's green!"

The houses came in two options: garage sticking out in front, garage tucked to the side. There were two or three color options for the shingles and shutters. It was, to my teenage mind, a wasteland that involved endless trimming, mowing, planting, weeding, and keeping up with the neighbors on either side. We even had a white picket fence. I knew every picket, as it was my sister's and my job to crawl around on our hands and knees and use manual clippers on the grass that the mower couldn't reach.

Eventually other developments cropped up around us. Only the original residents of Spring Mill Farms could distinguish where our development ended and the others began. It was back

31

to this collapsing Chinese fan of suburbia that I went after I was raped.

The old mill, for which my neighborhood was named, had not yet been restored when I was a teenager and the mill owner's house across the street was one of the few old homes in the area. Someone had torched it and the big white house now had black holes for windows and a green wooden railing that was charred and falling-in in places.

Driving by with my mother, as I did every time we went out of the development, I was fascinated by it—its age, the overgrown weeds and grass, and the marks of the fire—how the flames had licked out of the windows and left black ash scars above their rims like crowns.

Fires are something that seemed part of my childhood, and they beckoned to me that there was another side to life I hadn't seen. Fires were horrible, no doubt, but what I became obsessed with was how they seemed, inevitably, to mark a change. A girl I had known down the block, whose house was struck by lightning, moved. I never saw her again. And there was an aura of evil and mystery around the burning of the mill house that gave flight to my imagination every time I passed.

When I was five, I walked into a house near the old Zook graveyard out on Flat Road. I was with my father and grandmother. The house had been ravaged by fire and was set far off from the road. I was frightened but my father was intrigued. He thought that we might scavenge things inside that would add to the boxlike home he and my mother had just moved into. My grandmother agreed.

In the front yard some distance from the house was a half-charred Raggedy Andy doll. I went to pick it up and my father said, "No! We only want salvageable things, not some child's toy." I think that was when it struck me, that we were walking into a place where people like me—children—had lived, but didn't anymore. Couldn't.

Once inside, my grandmother and father got down to business. Most of the house was ruined; what was any good was so blackened by smoke as to be unsalvageable. There was furniture, still, and rugs and things on the wall, but they were black and abandoned.

So they decided to take the banisters from the stairs. "Good old wood," my grandmother said.

"What about upstairs?" my father asked.

My grandmother attempted to dissuade him. "It's black as night up there; besides, I wouldn't trust those stairs."

I'm a good stair tester. I always watch for this in movies where there is a fire and heroes rush in. Do they test the stairs first? If not, the critic in me cries, "Fake!"

My father decided that since I was little I could risk it best. He sent me up the stairs as he and my grandmother worked to dislodge the railings. "Call out what you see!" he said. "Any furniture or such."

What I remember is a child's room strewn with toys, most specifically Matchboxes, which I collected. They lay on their sides and backs on a braided rug, the die-cast metal bright in yellows and blues and greens in the dark, burned house. There were children's clothes in the open closet, singed along all their hems; an unmade bed. It had happened at night, I remember thinking when I was older. They were sleeping.

In the center of this bed was a small, dark, charred cavity that went through to the floor. I stared at it. A child had died in there.

When we got home, my mother called my father an idiot. She was livid. He arrived with what he thought might be a prize. "These banisters will make great table legs," he announced. I chose to remember the Matchboxes and the Raggedy Andy, but what child leaves behind these toys, even if slightly blackened? Where were the parents, I wondered all that night and in the nightmares that followed. Had they survived?

Out of fire grew narrative. I created for this family a new life. I made it a family like I had wanted: Mom and Dad and a boy and girl. Perfect. The fire was a new beginning. Change. What was left behind was done so on purpose; the little boy had grown out of his Matchboxes, I imagined. But the toys haunted me. The face of the Raggedy Andy on the path outside, his black and shiny eyes.

The first judgment of my family came from a six-year-old playmate of mine. She was small and blond, that kind of towheaded blondness that dissolves with age, and she lived down the road at the end of the block. There were only three girls my age in the whole neighborhood, including me, and she and I played at being friends until we got lost in the wider world of grade school and junior high.

We were sitting on my front lawn near the mailbox pulling up grass. We had just that week begun to ride on the bus together. As we pulled grass up in fistfuls and made a little pile by our knees, she said, "My mom says you're weird."

Shocked into a sort of mock adulthood, I said, "What?"

"You won't be mad, will you?" she pleaded. I guaranteed her I wouldn't.

"Mom and Dad and Jill's mom and dad said your family is weird."

I began to cry.

"I don't think you're weird," she said. "I think you're fun."

Even then I knew envy. I wanted her blond, strawlike hair, which she wore down, not my stupid brunet braids with the bangs my mother cut by strapping plastic tape across them and cutting along its edge. I wanted her father, who spent time outside and, on the few occasions I ever visited her, said things like "What's shakin', bacon?" and "See you later, alligator." I heard my parents in one ear: Mr. Halls was low-class, had a beer gut, wore workman's clothes; and my playmate in the other: My parents were weird.

My father worked behind closed doors inside the house, had a huge ancient Latin dictionary on a wrought-iron stand, spoke Spanish on the phone, and drank sherry and ate raw meat, in the form of chorizo, at five o'clock. Until the day in the yard with my playmate I thought this was what fathers did. Then I began to catalog and notice. They mowed lawns. They drank beer. They played in the yard with their kids, walked around the block with their wives, piled into campers, and, when they went out, wore joke ties or polo shirts, not Phi Beta Kappa keys and tailored vests.

The mothers were a different matter and I loved mine so fiercely that I never wanted to admit to envy there. I did note that my mother seemed more anxious and less concerned with makeup, clothes, and cooking than the other mothers did. I wished my mother were normal, like other moms, smiling and caring, seemingly, only for her family.

I saw a movie with my father one night on television, *The Stepford Wives*. My father loved it; it scared the hell out of me. I, of course, thought my mother was Katharine Ross, the only real woman in a town where every wife was replaced with a perfect, automated robot of a wife. I had nightmares for months afterward. I may have wanted my mother to change but not to die and never, never to be replaced.

When I was little, I worried about losing my mother. She was often hidden behind the locked door of her bedroom. My sister or I would want her attention in the mornings. We would see our father leave her room and, as we approached, he would explain.

"Your mother has a headache this morning," he might say, or, "Your mother doesn't feel well. She'll be out in a while."

I learned that if I knocked anyway, after my father went downstairs and shut himself up in his study, where we were not allowed to disturb him, that my mother sometimes let me in. I would crawl into bed with her and make up stories or ask her questions.

She threw up in those days and I saw this once when my father hadn't thought to lock the door. When I went inside her bedroom, which had its own bathroom, I could see my father standing in the bathroom doorway with his back to me. I could hear my mother making horrible noises. I rounded the corner in time to see bright red vomit spewing from her mouth into the sink. She saw me staring at her, my eyes hip-level with my father and reflected back to her from the mirror in front of the sink. In her gagging, she pointed me out to my father, who shooed me out of the bedroom and locked the door. They fought later. "For Christ's sakes, Bud," my mother said, "you know well enough to lock the door."

My mother's pillows when I was little smelled like cherries. It was a sickeningly sweet smell. It was the same way my rapist smelled on the night of the rape. I would not admit to myself until years later that this was the smell of alcohol.

I like the story of how my parents met. My father was working at the Pentagon, a better paper-pusher than a soldier. (When, in basic training, he and an army buddy were ordered to scale a wall, he broke his partner's nose by stepping on it, instead of inside the stirrup of this man's hands.) My mother lived with her parents in Bethesda, Maryland, and worked first for *National Geographic Magazine*, and then *The American Scholar*.

The two of them were set up on a blind date. They hated each other. My mother thought my father was a "pompous ass," and after a double date with the two people who had set them up, they put the experience behind them.

But they met again a year later. They didn't hit it off exactly, but this time they didn't hate each other, and my father asked my mother out a second time. "Your father was the only one who would take the bus out from the capital and then walk the five miles from the last station to our house," my mother always pointed out. This endeared him to my grandmother, apparently, and eventually my parents wed.

By then my father had a Ph.D. in Spanish Literature from Princeton, and my parents moved to Durham, North Carolina, where he held down his first academic job at Duke University. It was there, alone all day and unable to make friends in this new place, that my mother's drinking took a turn: She began drinking secretly.

My mother had always been nervous; she never acclimated to her prescribed role as housewife. She would repeatedly tell my sister and me how lucky we were to be in our generation. We believed her. The fifties seemed horrible to us. Her father and mine had convinced her to leave her full-time job by emphasizing that a married woman didn't work.

She drank for less than a decade—but long enough for my sister and me to come into the world and have our childhoods. Long enough for my father to move up the academic ranks by taking promotions that took the two of them, and then the four of us, to Madison, Wisconsin; Rockville, Maryland; and, finally, Paoli, Pennsylvania.

By 1977, my mother had been sober for ten years. During this period, she began having things we called "flaps." Flaps were our name for when Mommy went crazy. If my father was an absence—sometimes literally gone to Spain for months—my mother was too much a presence. Her anxiety and panic was infectious, making every moment twice as long and twice as hard when she was under their sway. Unlike normal families, we could not trust that, having left to get food at the local supermarket, we would actually achieve our goal. Two steps into the store, she might begin to have a flap.

"Grab a cantaloupe or something," she would say as I got older, and thrust a bill into my hand. "I'll meet you in the car." She would hunch over during a flap and rapidly rub her breastbone to soothe what she described as her exploding heart. I would rush into the store to buy that cantaloupe and maybe something on sale near the front, wondering all the time, Will she make it to the car? Will she be all right?

In movies and in life, the burly men in white suits who stand on either side of a mental patient are nondescript and indistinguishable. So, in many ways, were my sister and I. Mary is absent from many of my memories because my mother and her illness are so dominant. When I remember, Oh, yeah, Mary was along on that ride, that's exactly how I see her: the other support for our always potentially collapsing mother.

Sometimes, Mary and I functioned as a caretaking unit. Mary would husband her to the car and I would grab the cantaloupe.

But I watched my sister develop from a child who thought the world would fall apart to a young adult who resented how the flaps made us different, exciting stares and comments in public. "Stop rubbing your tits," she would hiss at my mother.

As Mary grew less and less sympathetic, I compensated and became the emotional overlord—soothing my mother and condemning my sister. When Mary helped, I was glad to have her there. When she whined and entered her own incipient version of my mother's panic, I shut her out.

The only memory I have of my father expressing physical affection for my mother was a brief kiss as we were dropping him off to catch a suburban limo to the airport, where he would embark on his annual academic trip to Spain. The reason for this isolated incident could come under the heading of "Let's Not Have a Scene." Simply, it was my prompting, then begging, then whining that brought on the kiss.

By then, I had begun to notice that unlike my parents, other couples touched each other, held hands, and kissed on cheeks. They did this in supermarkets, walking around the block, at school occasions to which parents were invited, and in front of me, in their homes.

But it was the kiss my father gave that day upon my urging that let me know my parents' relationship, if solid, was certainly not passionate. He was, after all, leaving us for a number of months, as he did yearly, and I felt that, with an absence of that length, an expression of love was owed my mother.

My mother had gotten out of the car to help my father with his bags and to say good-bye. Mary and I were in the backseat. This was my first time seeing him off on his yearly trip. He was flustered as he always was. My mother, always nervous, was flustered too. Sitting in the backseat, I remember I got it into my head that something was not right with the picture in front of me. I started whining, "Kiss Mom good-bye."

My father said something akin to "Now, Alice, that's not necessary."

Surely the result was not what he hoped for.

"Kiss Mom good-bye!" I yelled louder and popped my head out the back window. "Kiss Mom good-bye!"

"Just do it, Dad," my sister said bitterly beside me. She was three years older and maybe, as I imagined later, she knew the score.

But if what I'd wanted was to gain confirmation that my parents really were like the rest of the couples in Spring Mill Farms, and perhaps like that famous TV couple of the time, Mr. and Mrs. Brady, the forced kiss didn't do the job. It opened the door for me. It made me know that in the Sebold house, love was duty. He kissed her on the forehead, the kind of kiss that would fulfill the demand of his child but nothing else.

Many years later, I would find black-and-white photos of my father with daisies in his hair and submerged in water with flowers surrounding him. He was smiling, showing the teeth he hated because they came in helter-skelter and his family hadn't had the money to fix them. But he had been happy enough in these photos not to care. Who took them? Not my mother, this much I know. The box of photos had arrived at our house after my grandmother Sebold died. I searched among the photos for clues. Against my mother's stern warning not to take any of the photos in this box, I tucked one inside the waistband of my skirt.

Even then I felt the absence of something I couldn't then name and it hurt me for my mother, who I instinctively knew needed it, and would, I imagined, flourish under it. I never begged or made a scene over his lack of affection again because I didn't want to encounter that emptiness in their marriage.

I soon discovered that only the unconscious touch slipped by inside my house. As a little girl I would sometimes plan my attack, the goal: to be touched. My mother would be sitting at her end of the couch, doing needlepoint or reading a book. For my purposes it was best if she was reading a book and watching television at the same time. The more distraction, the less chance she would notice my approach.

I would take my seat on the far end of the couch and slowly

inch my way down to her end, where I would contrive to put my head in her lap. If I made it, she might rest her stitching hand if she was doing needlepoint, and casually finger the locks of my hair. I remember the cool feeling of the thimble as it touched my forehead and how, with a thief's awareness, I could tell when she became conscious of her actions. I might encourage her then by saying I had a headache. But even if this bought me a few extra strokes, I knew the jig was up. I debated, until I became too old to play such games, whether it was better to remove myself from her or to be pulled, reluctantly, off her, and told to sit up or go read a book.

The soft things in my life were our dogs: two sloppy, loving bassetts named Feijoo and Belle. One name was that of a Spanish author my father admired and one, condescendingly for him, a word that the "uneducated" might recognize. "French for 'beautiful,'" my father would point out. My father commonly called my sister and me by the dogs' names and this was a clue as much to who was closest to all of our hearts as it was to how preoccupied with work my father was. Dogs and children were the same to him when he was working. Small things that begged attention and needed to be put out.

What the dogs knew was that there were four distinct environments in our house and they rarely came together. There was my father's study, my mother's bedroom, my sister's bedroom, and wherever, throughout the house, I might be holed up. So Feijoo and Belle, and later Rose, had four places to try for attention. Four places where a hand would, distractedly, reach out to fondle their ears or reach down for a good hot spot scratch. They were like comfort caravans, carting their lumbering, drooling selves from room to room. They were our comedians and our glue, for otherwise my father, mother, and sister lived in books.

I struggled to be quiet in the house. While the three of them read or worked, I kept myself busy. I experimented with making food in odd ways. I squirreled away Jell-O and made it under my tall four-poster bed. I tried to make rice on the dehydrator in the basement. I mixed my mother's and father's perfumes in little bottles to create new scents. I drew. I climbed boxes up to the crawl space in the basement and sat for hours in the dark cement hole with my knees drawn up. I played histrionic games with Ken and Barbie where Barbie, by sixteen, had married, given birth, and gotten divorced from Ken. At the mock trial, where the courthouse was made out of poster board I'd cut up, Barbie gave her reason for divorce: Ken didn't touch.

But I would get bored. Hours and hours of "finding ways to occupy myself" gave way to hatching plots. The bassetts were often my unwitting assistants. Like all dogs, they nosed through the trash and under beds. They carried away trophies: smelly clothes, used socks, unattended food containers, and whatnot. The more they loved it, the harder they fought to keep it, and the thing they loved the most, with an animal passion that makes sense of the phrase, was my mother's discarded maxi-pads. Basset hounds and maxipads are a love marriage complete. No one could tell Feijoo and Belle that that particular item was not meant for them. They were wedded to it.

And, oh, the scene, the lovely scene. It wasn't a one-person or two-person job, it was the whole thundering house. The "horror" of it made my father hysterical and my mother adamant that he get involved in the chase. The sheer thought of it was obscene! Maxipads! The bassetts and I were happy because it meant everyone came out of their rooms to run and jump and scream.

The downstairs of our house was laid out in a kind of circle and the bassetts had figured this out. We chased them round and round from front hall to back through family room, kitchen, dining room, and living room. The bassett assisting—the one sans maxi-pad—would bark and bark and cut us off at the pass when we attempted to make a lunge at the lucky one. We got smarter in our tactics, tried to block them with doors or corral them in the corner of a room. But they were wily and they had a clandestine assistant.

I let them get by. I false-lunged. I gave my parents and sister misdirection. "Back hall, back hall!" I would yell, and three hysterical people would run that way. Meanwhile the bassetts were happily hiding with their snare underneath the table in the dining room.

Eventually, I took matters in my own hands and, when my mother stepped downstairs to the kitchen or was reading outside on the porch, I would lead the most available bassett into her bedroom and turn my back.

Within minutes:

"Bud! Feijoo has a Kotex!"

"For Christ's sakes!"

"Mom," I'd say helpfully, "he's tearing it up!"

Doors burst open, footsteps on stairs and rug. Screaming, barking, raucous, joyous scene.

Always, though, as these scenes resolved themselves—disgruntled bassetts going away to lick their paws—my mother, father, and Mary would return to their rooms. I would be in the house at large again. Lonely.

In high school I began as a geek. A geek because I played the alto saxophone and, as was required of almost every musician save the lucky violinists, if you played, you marched. I was in jazz band, where, as second alto, I jammed on such tunes as the "Funky Chicken" and "Raindrops Keep Falling on My Head." But getting down with my bad self was not enough recompense to be labeled a band geek. So, after marching in a Philadelphia Eagles half-time show where our band formed the shape of the Liberty Bell on the field (as an indication of my marching skills, I was asked to be part of the crack), I quit band. Later, without me, the band won a state championship for marching. The feelings of joy over my absence were mutual.

I went from music to art. Ours was a crafts-oriented art department and I loved the raw materials. There was silver, hunks of it. And, if you were good enough, gold. I made jewelry and cut silk screens and fired enamel. Once, with Mrs. Sutton, half of the husband-and-wife team who ran the department, I spent a whole afternoon pouring molten pewter into coffee cans of cold water. Wow! The shapes! I loved the Suttons. They approved all my projects, no matter how impossible to complete. I made a long-haired-Medusa silk screen, and an enamel choker of two hands holding a bouquet of flowers. I worked swiftly to finish a set of bells for a present for my mother. They featured the head of a lady with two arms forming a frame. Inside the frame were two bells with blue-heart nipples as the clappers. The bells made a fine sound.

I followed in the wake, academically, of my perfect sister. She was quiet, neat, and got straight *A*'s. I was loud, weird, and obsolete. I dressed like Janis Joplin ten years after her death and I defied anyone to make me study or care. I still got by. Teachers, individuals, touched me. The Suttons and a few English teachers combined to make me care just enough—if you didn't point it out to me—not to become a druggie or a pothead or spend the free periods outside in the smoking lounge hiding doobies in my boots.

But I could never be a druggie because I had a secret. More than anything, I finally decided, I wanted to be an actress. And not just any actress but a Broadway one. A loud Broadway one. Ethel Merman, to be exact.

I loved her. I think I loved her even more because my mother said she couldn't sing and couldn't act but that her force of personality was so strong that she took the attention away from everyone else on stage. I wore an old feather boa and a sequined jacket that Father Breuninger held back for me from a church clothes drive. What I sang, as loudly and as charismatically, I hoped, as my idol, was her signature song. Traipsing up and down our spiral stairs with the bassetts as my audience, I belted out "There's No Business Like Show Business." It made my mother and sister laugh and my father loved it more than anyone. I couldn't sing either, but I would cultivate what Merman had, or try: force of personality. Bassetts at my feet. A little extra weight. Seven years of braces and rubber bands. There seemed no better time to break into song.

My obsession with Broadway and bad singing led me to friendships with gay boys in school. We sat outside Friendly's ice cream shop on Route 30 and sang the soundtrack from Bette Midler's *The Rose*. Gary Freed and Sally Shaw, voted the cutest couple in our school, walked by on their way to Gary's '65 Mustang after a Saturday-night sundae. They laughed at us in our black clothes and the silver jewelry we made for cheap in art class.

Sid, Randy, and Mike were gay. We were infatuated with people like Merman, Truman Capote, Odetta, Bette Midler, and the producer Alan Carr, who appeared on *Merv* in large, brightly colored muumuus, and who made Merv laugh in a way that other guests didn't. We wanted to be stars because as stars, you could get out.

We hung outside Friendly's because there was nowhere to go. We all rushed home to watch *Merv* if we knew Capote or Carr would be on. We studied Liberace. Once he flew in on a guy wire over his piano and candelabra with his cape spread out. My father loved him but my friend Sid didn't. "He's making an idiot out of himself and he's really talented," he said, as we smoked cigarettes outside Friendly's near the Dumpsters. Sid was going to drop out of school and move to Atlantic City. He knew a hairdresser there who, over the summer, had promised to help him out. Randy was sent to military school by his parents after "an incident in a park." We weren't allowed to talk to him anymore. Mike fell in love with a football player and got beat up.

"I'm going to live in New York when I grow up," I began to say. My mother loved the idea. She told me about the Algonquin Round Table and the people who sat there, how special they were. She had an outsider's mythology of New York and New Yorkers. She thrilled at the idea of me ending up there.

The year I turned fifteen my mother decided my birthday present would be a trip to New York. I think she worked herself up to go by pretending my excitement about it would keep her from collapse.

On the Amtrak train up from Philadelphia, she began to have a version of her panic. The dreaded flap. It grew worse as we sped toward New York. I was so excited to be going but as she rocked back and forth in her seat and her hands trembled—one on her right temple and one rubbing the space between her breasts—I decided we should go home.

"We'll come another time, Mom," I said. "It's okay."

She argued. "But we're on our way. You want this so much." Then, "Let me try."

She pushed herself. She fought to function normally. We should have turned back when we reached Penn Station. Both of us probably knew this. She was a mess. She couldn't walk upright. She had wanted to walk up from Penn Station to the Metropolitan Museum of Art on Eighty-second and Fifth so we could see the shops and Central Park along the way. She had spent the weeks before planning it. Told me that on Forty-fourth was the Algonquin, and that I would get to see the Ritz and the Plaza, where she was sure my idol, Merman, often stayed. Maybe we would take a ride in a hansom cab around Central Park and see the famous apartment building, the Dakota. Bergdorf's and Lexington. The theater district, where Merman's musicals were playing. My mother wanted to stand in front of Sherman's statue and, as a daughter of the South, say a silent prayer. The duck pond, the carousel, the old men with their model sailboats. It was my mother's gift.

But she couldn't walk. We stood in the cab line out on Seventh Avenue and got in one. She could not sit up straight. She kept her head between her knees so she would not throw up. She said, "I'm taking my daughter to the Met."

"You all right, lady?" the cab driver asked.

"Yes," she said. She implored me to look out the window. "This is New York," she said as she stared at the dirty floor of the cab.

I don't remember the drive up save for crying. Trying to do what she said. The buildings and people were a blur to me. "I'm not going to make it," she began saying. "I want to, Alice, but I'm not going to make it."

The cab driver was relieved to reach the Met. At first my mother stayed in the backseat.

"Mom, let's just turn around and go back," I pleaded.

"In or out?" the cab driver said. "What's the story?"

We got out. We crossed the street. In front of us were the monumental steps up to the entrance of the Met. I was trying to look around and take it in. I wanted to run up those steps thronged with people smiling and taking pictures. Slowly, with me leading my bent-over mother, we made it up some twenty stairs.

"I have to sit down," she said. "I can't go in."

We were so close.

"Mom," I said, "we made it, we have to go in."

"You go in," she said.

My fragile suburban mother sat in her good dress on the hot cement, rubbing her chest and trying not to throw up.

"I can't go in without you," I said.

She opened her purse and took a twenty from her wallet. She shoved it in my hand. "Run into the gift shop and buy yourself something," she said. "I want you to have a souvenir of the trip."

I left her there. I did not look back at her smallness on the steps. In the gift shop I was overwhelmed and twenty dollars didn't buy much. I saw a book called *Dada and the Art of Surrealism* for $8.95. I rushed back out after paying for it. People had surrounded my mother and were trying to help. There was no pretending now.

"Can we help you in some way?" a West German man and his concerned wife asked in perfect English.

My mother ignored them. The Sebolds did everything themselves.

"Alice," she said, "you need to flag a cab, I can't do it."

"Mom, I don't know how," I said.

"Go to the edge of the sidewalk and stick your hand out," she said. "One will stop."

I left her and did as I was told. An old bald man in a yellow Checker cab pulled up. I explained that my mother was the one on the steps. I pointed to her. "Could you help?"

"What's wrong with her? She sick? I don't want sick people in my cab," he said with a heavy Yiddish accent.

LUCKY

"She's just nervous," I said. "She won't throw up. I can't move her by myself."

He helped me. After living in New York as an adult I know how rare this was. But something about my desperation and, to be honest, my mother, he felt sorry for. We made it to the cab and while I sat in the backseat my mother lay down at my feet on the old Checker's big back floor.

The cabbie kept up the kind of patter you pray for. "You just stretch out there, missus," he said. "I wouldn't drive one of those new cabs. Checkers are the only kind of cab for me. Roomy. Makes people feel comfortable. How old are you, young lady? You look a lot like your mother, you know that?"

On the train ride home my mother's panic gave way to utter exhaustion. My father picked us up at the station and once we got home, she went immediately to her room. I was glad we were on vacation at school. I would have time to make up a good story.

FOUR

On the day of the rape, I lay across the backseat of the car and tried to sleep while my mother drove. I did so fitfully. The interior of the car was blue, and I pretended I was on the ocean, floating out to sea. But the closer we got to home, the more I thought about my father.

I had learned early that if I interrupted him in his study I had better have something that would dissipate his anger at being disturbed. I often played myself off my more serious sister. I tried to be a bawdy boy for the benefit of a man who lived in a house where he often complained he was "outnumbered by females." (My father took great joy in their new dog—a poodle mix—openly declaring how good it was to finally have another male in the house.) I wanted to be the child I had always been for my father.

My mother and I pulled into the driveway and walked into the house through the garage.

My father is a tall man and I knew him best as a man obsessed with his work—with editing, writing, and speaking Spanish on the phone with colleagues and friends. But that day he was shaking when I saw him at the end of the long hall in the back entranceway of our house.

"Hey, Dad," I said.

Mom followed down the long hall. I saw him look quickly up at her and then focus, or try to focus, on me as I advanced.

We hugged each other. We were awkward, ill-fitting.

I don't remember him saying anything to me. If he did say, "Oh, honey, it's good to have you home," or, "Alice, I love you," it would have been so uncharacteristic that I think I would have remembered it, but perhaps I don't remember it for that very reason. I did not want new experience. I wanted what I knew, the house I had left that fall for the first time in my life, and the father I recognized.

"How you doing, Dad?" I asked. I had thought of this simple question all the way home.

With flushed relief, he said, "After your mother called, I had five shots of whiskey and I've never been more sober in my life."

I lay down on the couch in the family room. My father, in an effort to stay busy that morning, had prepared some lunch fixings in the kitchen.

"Would you like something to eat?" he asked me.

In my response, I wished to slam-dunk the fact that no one needed to worry about this tough customer.

"That would be nice," I said, "considering the only thing I've had in my mouth in the last twenty-four hours is a cracker and a cock."

To the outsider this might sound awful; to my father, standing in the doorway of the kitchen, and to my mother, who was fussing with our bags, it both shocked them and meant only one thing: The kid they knew was still there.

"Jesus, Alice," my father responded. He was waiting there on the precipice for my directions.

"I'm still me, Dad," I said.

My parents went into the kitchen together. I don't know how long they spent in there, putting together sandwiches that were, probably, already made. What did they do? Did they hug? I can't imagine this, but they might have. Did my mother whisper details about the police and my physical condition, or did she promise she would tell him what she knew after I slept?

My sister had made it through finals. The day following my homecoming, when my parents went to pick her up in Philadelphia and pack her things for the summer, I went too.

My face was still bruised. My father drove one car and my mother drove the other. The plan was that I would stay in the car while the three of them loaded my sister's things. I was only there for my sister to see, so she would know immediately that I was okay. I also went because I didn't want them alone together and talking about me.

I rode up front with my mother. She preferred to take a local route into the city. It took longer, but we all agreed it was more scenic. Of course the real reason was that the Schuylkill Expressway, known unofficially as the Surekill by those along the Main Line of Philadelphia, was guaranteed to bring on a flap. So we took Route 30, then snaked along various secondary roads toward our ultimate goal of U-Penn.

Over time, the abandoned tracks of the Philadelphia El came to mark the official entrance into the city for me. It was here that pedestrian traffic began, where a man sold papers to drivers from the middle of the road, and a Baptist church played host, year-round, to weddings and funerals whose attendees spread out into the streets in formal clothes.

I had taken this trip many times with my mother. We would meet my father at his office or use the faculty-insurance services through the University of Pennsylvania Hospital. A regular aspect of these trips was my mother's increasing anxiety as we drew closer and closer to the city. Down Chestnut Street, once past the El, my mother always drove in the middle lane of three lanes on the one-way road. My job was to sit in the passenger seat and anticipate an attack.

The day we went to pick up my sister, the dynamic shifted. Once past the blocks of row houses, alternating block by block in terms of how well maintained they were, the street widened. Abandoned buildings, seedy gas stations, and government brick buildings lined the street. Occasionally, one or two still-standing row houses clung together in the midst of a block.

In the past, on these drives, I had focused on the buildings; I liked the stair notches in the sides of the remaining row houses, seeing them as the fossils of former lives. Now, my focus shifted. So did my mother's. In the car behind us, I would realize soon, so had my father's. It shifted to the people on the streets. Not the women, not the children.

It was hot. Hot in the humid, dank way of Northeastern cities during summer. The smell of trash and exhaust fumes seeped through the open windows of our un-air-conditioned car. Our ears perked up at random shouts. We listened for menace in the greetings of friend to friend, and my mother questioned why so many men were clustered at street corners and slouched in front of buildings. This part of Philadelphia, excepting a diminishing Italian population, was black.

We passed a corner where three men stood. Behind them, two older men sat in rickety folding chairs, brought out onto the sidewalk to escape the heat inside their homes. I could sense my mother's body tense beside me. The bruises and cuts on my face stung. I felt that every man on that street could see me, that every man knew.

"I feel sick," I said to my mother.

"We're almost there."

"It's weird, Mom," I said, as I tried to stay calm. I knew the old men hadn't raped me. I knew the tall black man in a green suit, sitting on a bus-station bench, hadn't raped me. I was still afraid.

"What's weird, Alice?" She began to knead her knuckles into her chest.

"How I feel like I've lain underneath all these men."

"That's ridiculous, Alice."

We had stopped at a light. When it turned green, we accelerated. But we were going slowly enough so that my eyes lingered on the upcoming corner.

He was there, back from the street and squatting on the cement, leaning against the clean brick of a newish building. I met his eyes. He met mine. "I've lain with you," I said inside my head.

It was an early nuance of a realization that would take years to face. I share my life not with the girls and boys I grew up with, or the students I went to Syracuse with, or even the friends and people I've known since. I share my life with my rapist. He is the husband to my fate.

We passed out of that neighborhood and into the world of the University of Pennsylvania, where my sister lived. Doors were open in the houses that rented to students, and U-Hauls and Ryder trucks were double-parked along the curb. Someone had come up with the idea to throw a move-out-day keg party. Tall white boys in muscle tees, or no shirts at all, sat on couches on the sidewalk and drank beer from plastic cups.

My mother and I made our way to my sister's dorm and parked.

My father arrived a moment later and parked his car nearby. I stayed in the car. My mother, trying to hide a flap from me, had gotten out and was pacing nearby.

This was what I heard my father say before my mother shot him a warning look.

"Did you see those goddamn animals hanging off of every post and—"

My mother looked quickly at me and then back at my father. "Hush, Bud," she said.

He came over to me and bent down into the window.

"Are you okay, Alice?"

"I'm fine, Dad," I said.

He was sweaty and red-faced. Helpless. Afraid. I had never heard him refer to blacks like this, or to any other minority by condemning them as a group.

My father went in to tell my sister we had arrived. I sat in the car with my mother. We didn't talk. I watched the activities of moveout day. Students used large canvas bins, like those to shuttle mail in the back rooms of post offices, to heap their possessions in. They rolled them across the parking lot to their parents' cars. Families greeted one another. On a scrubby patch of lawn two boys played Frisbee. Radios blared from the windows of my sister's dorm. There was freedom and release in the air; summer like an infection, spreading across the campus.

There she was. I saw my sister emerge from the building. I got to watch her walk all the way from the door, which was maybe a hundred feet away, the same distance I was from my rapist when he said, "Hey, girl, tell me your name."

I remember her leaning down into the car.

"Your face," she said. "Are you okay?"

"It sure took me long enough," I joked to her, "but I finally figured out how to wreck your straight *A*'s."

"Now, Alice," my father said, "your sister asked you how you are."

"I'm getting out of the car," I said to my mother. "I feel like an idiot."

My family was uncomfortable with this, but I got out and stood there. I said I wanted to see Mary's room, see where she lived, help.

I was not hurt badly enough to notice immediately. If you weren't looking my way, you wouldn't have known I was different. But as my family and I walked back toward my sister's dorm, faces at first took in a family like anyone else's—mother, father, and two girls—but then their eyes lingered, just for a moment, and caught something. My swollen eye, the cuts along my nose and cheek, my bloated lips, the delicate purples of bruises blossoming. As we walked, the stares gathered in number, and I felt them but pretended I didn't. Beautiful Ivy League boys and girls, brains and nerds, surrounded me. I believed I was doing all this for my family, because they couldn't deal. But I was doing it for myself as well. We took the elevator up and in it I saw vivid graffiti.

A girl had been gang-raped at a fraternity that year. She had filed a complaint and charges. She was trying to prosecute. But the fraternity members and their friends had made it impossible for her to stay in school. By the time I visited Penn's campus she had withdrawn. In the elevator of my sister's dormitory was a crude ballpoint drawing of her with her legs spread open. A group of male figures were waiting in line beside her. The caption read, "Marcie pulls a train."

I was crammed in the elevator with my family and Penn students going back up for another load. I stood with my face to the wall, staring at the drawing of Marcie. I wondered where she was and what would become of her.

My memories of my family that day are splotchy. I was busy performing, thinking that it was for this that I was loved. But then there were things that hit me too close to the bone. The black man squatting on the sidewalk in West Philadelphia, or the beautiful boys at Penn, throwing a Frisbee, the bright orange disc arcing up and down into my path. I stopped abruptly, and one of the boys ran recklessly to pick it up. As he stood back up, he caught sight of my face. "Shit," he said, looking at me, stunned for a moment, distracted from the game.

What you have after that is a family. Your sister has a dorm room for you to see. Your mother a panic attack to attend. Your father, well, he's being ignorant, and you can shoulder the burden of educating him. It is not all blacks, you will begin. These are the things you do instead of collapsing in the bright sun, in front of the beautiful boys, where, rumor has it, Marcie pulled a train.

The four of us drove home. I rode with my father this time. Now I realize that my mother must have been telling my sister everything she knew, the two of them bracing for what might be ahead.

Mary brought her essentials inside the house, and went up to her bedroom to unpack. The idea was that we would all have an informal meal, what my mother called "seek and ye shall find," and afterward my father would go back into his study to work, and I could spend time with my sister.

But when my mother called for Mary to come down, she didn't answer. My mother called again. Bellowing family names upstairs from the front hall was common practice for us. Even having to do it several times wasn't unusual. Finally, my mother went upstairs, only to come back down a few minutes later.

"She's locked herself in the bathroom," she told my father and me.

"Whatever for?" my father asked. He was slicing off hunks of provolone and feeding them, slyly, to the dog.

"She's upset, Bud," my mother said.

"We're all upset," I said. "Why doesn't she join the party?"

"Alice, I think it would mean a lot if you went up to talk to her."

I may have grumbled about it, but I went. It was a familiar

pattern. Mary would get upset and my mother would ask me to talk to her. I would knock on her bedroom door and sit on the edge of her bed while she lay there. I would do what I called "cheerlead for life," sometimes rallying her to the point where she would come down for dinner or at least laugh at the obscene jokes I culled for just this purpose.

But that day I also knew that I was the one she needed to see. I wasn't just the mother-appointed cheerleader; I was the reason why she had locked herself in the bathroom and wouldn't come out.

Upstairs, I knocked tentatively on the door.

"Mary?"

No answer.

"Mary," I said, "it's me. Let me in."

"Go away." I could tell she was crying.

"Okay," I said, "let's deal with this rationally. At some point I'm going to pee and if you won't let me in I'll be forced to pee in your bedroom."

There was silence and then she unlocked the door.

I opened it.

This was the "girls' bathroom." The developer had tiled it pink. If boys had moved into the house I can only imagine, but Mary and I managed to work up enough of a hatred of the pink ourselves. Pink sink. Pink tile. Pink tub. Pink walls. There was no relief.

Mary had gone to stand against the wall, between the tub and the toilet, as far away from me as she could.

"Hey," I said. "What is it?"

I wanted to hold her. I wanted her to hold me.

"I'm sorry," she said. "You're doing so well with it. I just don't know how to act."

When I moved toward her she moved away.

"Mary," I said. "I feel like shit."

"I don't know how you're being so strong." She looked at me, tears on her cheeks.

"It's okay," I said to my sister. "It's all going to be okay."

Still, she would not let me touch her. She flittered nervously from the shower curtain to the towel rack, like a bird trapped in a cage. I told her I'd be downstairs stuffing my face and that she should join me, and then I closed the door and left.

My sister had always been frailer than I was. At a YMCA day camp when we were kids, they'd passed out badges on the last day. So that every child got one, the counselors made up categories. I got an arts and crafts badge symbolized by a palette and brushes. My sister got the badge for being the quietest camper. On her badge, which they made by hand, they had glued a gray felt mouse. My sister took it on as her symbol, eventually incorporating a small mouse into the tail of the *y* in her signature.

Back downstairs, my mother and father asked after her. I told them she would be down soon.

"Well, Alice," my father said, "if it had to happen to one of you, I'm glad it was you and not your sister."

"Christ, Bud," my mother said.

"I only meant that of the two of them—"

"I know what you meant, Dad," I said, and touched my hand to his forearm.

"See, Jane," he said.

My mother felt that family, or the idea of it, should be uppermost in everyone's mind during those first few weeks. This was a hard sell to four solitary souls, but that summer I watched more bad television in the company of my family than I have ever seen before or since.

Dinnertime became sacred. My mother, whose kitchen is decorated with pithy signs that, loosely translated, all say, in one form or another, "The Cook Is Out," made supper every night. I remember my sister attempted to restrain herself from accusing my dad of "smacking." We were all on our best behavior. I cannot imagine what was going on in their minds. How tired they all probably were. Did they buy my strong-woman act, or just pretend to?

In those first weeks I wore nothing but nightgowns. Lanz

nightgowns. Specially bought by my mother and father. My mother might suggest to my father, when he was going out to the grocery, that he stop by and get me a new nightgown. It was a way we could all feel rich, a rational splurge.

So while the rest of the family sat at the dinner table wearing the normal clothes of summer, I sat in my chair wearing a long white nightgown.

I can't remember how it first came up but, once it did, it took over the conversation.

The topic was the rapist's weapon. I may have been talking about how the police had found my glasses and the rapist's knife in the same area out by the brick path.

"You mean he didn't have the knife in the tunnel?" my father asked.

"No," I said.

"I don't think I understand."

"What's there to understand, Bud?" my mother asked. Perhaps, after twenty years of marriage, she knew where he was leading. Privately, she may already have defended me to him.

"How could you have been raped if he didn't have the knife?"

Our dinner table could be loud concerning any topic. A favorite point of contention was the preferred spelling or definition of a certain word. It was not uncommon for the *Oxford English Dictionary* to be dragged into the dining room, even on holidays or with guests present. The poodle-mix, Webster, had been named after the more portable mediator. But this time the argument consisted of a clear division between male and female—between two women, my mother and my sister, and my father.

I became aware that I would lose my father if he was ostracized. Though in my defense, my sister and mother shouted at him to be quiet, I told the two of them I wanted to handle it. I asked my father to come upstairs with me, where we could talk. My mother and sister were so angry at him they were red in the face. My father was like a little boy who, thinking that he understood the rules of the game, is frightened when the others tell him he is wrong.

We walked upstairs to my mother's bedroom. I sat him down on the couch and took up a position across from him on my mother's desk chair.

"I'm not going to attack you, Dad," I said. "I want you to tell me why you don't understand, and I'll try to explain it to you."

"I don't know why you didn't try to get away," he said.

"I did."

"But how could he have raped you unless you let him?"

"That would be like saying I wanted it to happen."

"But he didn't have the knife in the tunnel."

"Dad," I said, "think about this. Wouldn't it be physically impossible to rape and beat me while holding a knife the whole time?"

He thought for a second and then seemed to agree.

"So most women who are raped," I said, "even if there was a weapon, when the rape is going on, the weapon is not there in her face. He overpowered me, Dad. He beat me up. I couldn't want something like that, it's impossible."

When I look back on myself in that room I don't understand how I could have been so patient. All I can think is that his ignorance was inconceivable to me. I was shocked by it but I had a desperate need for him to understand. If he didn't—he who was my father and who clearly wanted to understand—what man would?

He did not comprehend what I had been through, or how it could have happened without some complicity on my part. His ignorance hurt. It still hurts, but I don't blame him. My father may not have fully understood, but what was most important to me was that I left the room knowing how much it had meant to him that I took him upstairs and tried, as best I could, to answer his questions. I loved him and he loved me and our communication was imperfect. That didn't seem so bad to me. After all, I had been prepared for the news of the rape to destroy everyone in my life. We were living, and, in those first weeks, that was enough.

* * *

Although TV was something I could share with my family while we each remained in our individual islands of pain, it was also problematic.

I'd always liked Kojak. He was bald and cynical and talked curtly out of the side of his mouth while sucking on a lollipop. But he had a big heart. He also policed a city and had a bumbling sibling he got to kick around. This made him attractive to me.

So I watched *Kojak* as I lay in my Lanz nightgown and drank chocolate milk shakes. (At first, I had difficulty with solid food. Initially my mouth was sore from the sodomy and, after this, having food in my mouth reminded me too much of the rapist's penis as it lay against my tongue.)

Watching *Kojak* alone was endurable, because even though violent, it was so obviously fictional in this violence (Where was the smell? The blood? Why did all the victims have perfect faces and bodies?). But when my sister or father or mother came in to watch television with me, I grew tense.

I have memories of my sister sitting in the rocker in front of where I was positioned on the couch. She would always ask me if a given program was all right before turning it on. She would be vigilant throughout the hour or two hours it was on. If she worried, I would see her head start to turn around to check on me.

"I'm okay, Mary," I began saying, able to predict when she might grow concerned.

It made me angry with her and with my parents. I needed the pretense that inside the house I was still the same person I'd always been. It was ridiculous but essential, and I felt the stares of my family as betrayals, even though intellectually I knew otherwise.

What took me a bit longer to put together was that those television shows were more upsetting to them than they could ever have been to me. They had no idea, because I had not told them, what had happened to me in that tunnel—what the particulars were. They were fitting together the horrors of imagination and nightmare and trying to fashion what had been their sister's or child's reality. I knew exactly what had happened. But can you speak those sentences to the people you love? Tell them you were urinated on or that you kissed back because you did not want to die?

That question continues to haunt me. After telling the hard facts to anyone from lover to friend, I have changed in their eyes. Often it is awe or admiration, sometimes it is repulsion, once or twice it has been fury hurled directly at me for reasons I remain unsure of. Some men and lesbians see it as a turn-on or a mission, as if by sexualizing our relationship they can pull me back from the wreckage of that day. Of course, their best efforts are largely useless. No one can pull anyone back from anywhere. You save yourself or you remain unsaved.

FIVE

My mother was warden of the vestry at St. Peter's Episcopal Church. We had been members of this church ever since my family moved to Pennsylvania when I was five. I liked the pastor, Father Breuninger, and his son, Paul, who was my age. In college, I would recognize Father Breuninger in the work of Henry Fielding; he was an amiable if not overly insightful man, and he stood in the center of a small, devoted congregation. Paul sold Christmas wreaths to the parishioners each year, and his wife, Phyllis, was tall and high-strung. This last quality made her a target for sympathetic, but competitive, commentary from my mother.

I liked to play in the graveyard after service; I liked my parents' pre- and post-commentary in the car; I liked being doted on by parishioners; and I loved, absolutely was infatuated with, Myra Narbonne. She was my favorite old lady—my mother's favorite too. Myra liked to say she "got old before it was popular." Often her large stomach was a punch line, or her thinning angel hair. Among a congregation filled with distinguished Main Line types, where the same outfits, perfectly tailored but within an inch of appearing downright shabby, were worn each and every Sunday, Myra was a breath of fresh air. She had all the blue blood she needed, but she wore large seventies wraparounds that were, in her words, "as tacky as tablecloths." Often her shirt didn't come together all the way, as her chest sloped closer and closer to the earth. She tucked Kleenex in her bra, which my own East Tennessee grandmother did, and she slipped me extra cookies when I came in from playing in the graveyard. She was married to a man named Ed. Ed didn't come often to service, but when he did he appeared to be thinking of how soon he could leave.

I had been to their house. They had a pool and liked to have young people swim in it. They had a dog they'd named Freckles, because of his spots, and a few cats, including the fattest calico I had ever seen. During junior high and high school, Myra nurtured my desire to be a painter. She painted herself, and had turned their greenhouse into her studio. I think she also understood, without ever discussing it with me, that I wasn't very happy at home.

During my freshman year, while I was in Syracuse going out with Mary Alice to the college bars along Marshall Street, things happened back home that were alien to me.

Myra left doors unlocked. She went in and out of the house to garden. Freckles needed putting out. They had never had any trouble, and although their house was positioned far back from the road and hidden by a veil of trees, they lived in a neighborhood of gentlemen farmers. So Myra couldn't have imagined a day when three men in black stocking masks would cut her phone lines before forcing their way in.

They separated Myra and Ed, and tied Myra up. They were unhappy with the lack of cash in the house. They beat Ed badly enough that he fell backward down the stairs to the basement level below. One man went down after him. One cased the house. One, whom the others called Joey, stayed with Myra, calling her "old woman," and hitting her with open-handed blows.

They took what they could. Joey told Myra to stay put, not to go anywhere, that her husband was dead. They left. Myra lay on the floor and struggled free of the rope. She could not get down the stairs to check on Ed because she felt something broken in her foot. They had also, though she didn't know it then, broken her ribs.

Defying Joey's orders, Myra left the house. She was too afraid to go out onto the road. She crawled through the underbrush behind the backyard—half a mile or so—before reaching another, less frequented road. She stood up, barefoot and bleeding. Finally a car approached and she flagged it down.

She went to the car window.

"Please get help," she said to the lone driver. "Three men broke into our house. I think they killed my husband."

"I can't help you, lady."

She realized who was in the car. It was Joey, and he was alone. It was his voice. She got a good look at him; there was no stocking mask.

"Get off me," he said, as she grabbed, in recognition, at his arm.

He sped away and she fell down in the road. But she kept going and reached a house, where she phoned for help. Ed was rushed to the hospital. If she had not left the house when she did, the doctors later told her, he would have bled to death.

Then, that winter, St. Peter's was rocked by Paul Breuninger's arrest.

Paul had stopped selling Christmas wreaths in junior high school. He grew his curly red hair long, and didn't come to church much anymore. My mother told me that Paul had a separate entrance to the house. That Father Breuninger felt he had lost control over him. In February, high on acid, Paul walked into a florist shop on Route 30 and asked a woman named Mrs. Mole for a single yellow rose. He and his partner, waiting in the car, had cased the joint for a week. Paul had asked for a single rose each time, watching the register as Mrs. Mole rang it up.

But they picked the wrong day to rob her. Her husband had left moments before with the week's cash. Mrs. Mole had less than four dollars in her cash drawer. Paul flew into a rage. He stabbed Mrs. Mole fifteen times in the face and neck, yelling, "Die, bitch, die," over and over again. Mrs. Mole did not obey. She made her way out of the shop, collapsing in a bank of snow outside. A woman saw the blood, which had slowly trickled down the rise of the bank. She followed the trail and found Mrs. Mole unconscious in the snow.

* * *

That May, after my rape, I arrived back to a congregation that was traumatized, no one more so than Father Breuninger himself. As the warden to the vestry, my mother had been privy to his pain that spring. Paul had been arrested, and though still a minor at seventeen, would be tried as an adult. Father Breuninger had no idea that his son had been drinking a fifth of whiskey a day since the age of fifteen. He knew nothing about the drugs found in Paul's room and little about his truancy at school. Paul's insolence Father Breuninger had chalked up to being part of an adolescent stage.

Because she was warden, and because she trusted him, my mother told Father Breuninger that I'd been raped. He announced it to the church. He did not use the word *raped* but he said "assaulted brutally in a park near her campus. It was a robbery." Those words meant only one thing to any old-timer worth her salt. As the story made the rounds, they realized I had no broken bones, how brutal could it be? Oh . . . *that* . . .

Father Breuninger showed up at the house. I remember the pity in his eyes. Even then, I sensed he thought of his son in the same way he did me: as a child who, on the precipice of adulthood, had lost it all. I knew through my mother that Father Breuninger had trouble holding Paul accountable for the stabbing of Mrs. Mole. He blamed drugs, he blamed the twenty-two-year-old accomplice, he blamed himself. He could not blame Paul.

My family gathered in our living room, the least-used room of the house. We sat stiffly on the edges of the antique furniture. My mother got Fred—as the adults called Father Breuninger—something to drink, tea. There was small talk. I sat on the blue silk couch, my father's prized possession, from which all children and dogs were banned. (For Christmas one year I had coaxed a bassett onto the light blue silk by using a biscuit. I then snapped photos of her chowing down and had them framed, presenting them to my father as a gift.)

Father Breuninger had us stand and hold hands in a circle. He was wearing his black robes and white collar. The silk tassel, from the rope around his waist, swayed for a moment in the air, then stilled. "Let us pray," he said.

I was shocked. My family was a family of commentary and intellect and skepticism. This felt like hypocrisy to me. As he prayed, I looked up and around at Mary, my parents, and Father Breuninger. Their heads were bent; their eyes were closed. I refused to close my eyes. We were praying for my soul. I stared at Father Breuninger's crotch. Thought about what he was under all that black. He was a man. He had a dick like every man did. What right had he, I wondered, to pray for my soul?

I thought of something else: his son, Paul. As I stood there, I thought of Paul being arrested and Paul having to serve time. I thought of Paul being brought down low, and how good that must feel for Mrs. Mole. Paul was in the wrong. Father Breuninger, who had spent his life praising God, had lost his son, really lost him, more than I ever could be lost. I was in the right. I felt powerful, suddenly, and felt what my family was doing, this act of faith or belief or charity, was dumb. I was angry at them for seeing this charade through. For standing on the rug in the living room—room of special occasions, of holidays and celebrations—and praying for me to a God I wasn't sure they believed in.

Eventually Father Breuninger left. I had to hug him. He smelled of aftershave and the mothball smell of the closet at the church where he hung his vestments. He was a clean, well-meaning man. He was in his own crisis but there was no way then, via God, or otherwise, that I could be with him.

Then the old ladies came. The marvelous, loving, knowing old ladies.

As each old lady came, she was shuttled into the living room and seated in my parents' prized winged chair. This chair provided an unparalleled vantage point. From it, the seated person could see the rest of the living room (off to their right would be the blue couch) and into the dining room, where the silver tea set was placed on display. When these ladies visited, they were served tea in my parents' wedding china, and attended to by my mother as honored and unusual guests.

Betty Jeitles came first. Betty Jeitles had money. She lived in a beautiful house near Valley Forge, which my mother coveted and by which she drove very quickly, so as not to appear to be coveting it. Betty had a face full of deep Main Line wrinkles. She looked like an exotic breed of dog, sort of a cultivated sharpei, and she spoke with an aristocratic accent that my mother explained with the words "old money."

I wore a nightgown and robe for Mrs. Jeitles. Again, I sat on the blue couch. She gave me a book: *Akienfield: Portrait of a Chinese Village.* She had remembered that when I was little, I had told the ladies at coffee hour I wanted to be an archaeologist. We passed the brief time of her visit making small talk. My mother helped. She talked about the church and about Fred. Betty listened. Every few sentences she gave a nod or contributed a word or two. I remember her looking over at me on the couch while my mother was talking; how much she wanted to say something and how the word just wasn't one anyone could say.

Peggy O'Neil, whom my parents called an old maid, came next. Peggy was not Main Line money. Hers came from having taught school all her life and being scrupulous with her savings. She lived far off the road in a sweet house that my mother never lingered over. She dyed her hair the darkest black. She specialized, along with Myra, in having seasonal handbags. Bags made out of wicker with watermelons painted on them for spring, or bags made out of beads threaded with rawhide thongs for fall. Her clothes were workaday shifts—madras and seersucker. The materials seemed meant to distract the viewer from analyzing the shape of her body. Now that I've been a teacher, I recognize them as a teacher's clothes.

If Peggy brought me a gift, I don't remember it. But Peggy, who was less reserved than Mrs. Jeitles, didn't need a gift. I even had to remember to call her Miss O'Neil instead of Peggy. She cracked jokes and made me laugh. She talked about being afraid in her house. She told me it was dangerous to be a woman alone. She told me I was special and that I was strong and that I would get over this. She also told me, laughing, but in all seriousness, that it wasn't such a bad thing to grow up to be an old maid.

Myra came last.

I wish I remembered her visit. Or, I should say, I wish I could remember it in the detail of what she wore or how we sat or what she said. But what I remember is suddenly being in the presence of someone who "got it." Not just knew the facts, but—as near as she could—understood what I felt.

She sat in the winged chair. Her presence was comfort and succor to me. Ed had not fully recovered from the beating. He never would. He had taken too many blows to the head. He was addled now, confused a lot. Myra was like me: People expected her to be strong. Her outward traits and reputation led them to believe that if it had to happen to any of the old ladies at church, it had happened to the most resilient one. She told me about the three men. She laughed as she repeated how they hadn't known how feisty a woman her age could be. She was going to testify. They had arrested Joey based on her description. Still, her eyes clouded over when she talked about Ed.

My mother watched Myra to find evidence that I would recover. I watched Myra for proof that she understood. At one point, she said, "What happened to me is nothing like what happened to you. You're young and beautiful. No one's interested in me that way."

"I was raped," I said.

The room was still, my mother suddenly uncomfortable. The living room, where the antiques had been carefully arranged and polished, where my mother's needlepoint pillows decorated most of the chairs, where gloomy portraits of Spanish noblemen stared down from the walls, was changed now. I felt I had to say it. But I felt also that saying it was akin to an act of vandalism. As if I had thrown a bucket of blood out across the living room at the blue couch, Myra, the winged chair, my mother.

The three of us sat there and watched it drip.

"I know," Myra said.

"I needed to say the word," I said.

"It's a hard one."

"It's not 'the thing that happened to me,' or 'the assault,' or 'the beating,' or '*that*.' I think it's important to call it what it is."

"It's rape," she said, "and it didn't happen to me."

We returned to forgettable conversation. A while later, she left. But I had made contact with a planet different from the one my parents or sister lived on. It was a planet where an act of violence changed your life.

That same afternoon, a boy from our church, the older brother of a friend of mine, stopped by the house. I was on the porch in my nightgown. My sister was up in her room.

"Girls, Jonathan's here to visit," my mother called from the front hall.

Perhaps it was his sandy-blond hair, or the fact that he had already graduated from college and had landed a job in Scotland, or that his mother thought so highly of him, and as a result, we knew almost every item of his golden-boy résumé; whatever the case, my sister and I had an unspoken and mutual crush. We entered the hall at the same time, I from the back of the house, my sister descending the spiral staircase in the front hall. His eyes were on her as she stepped down. My sister did not flounce. I could not accuse her of being coy or flirtatious or otherwise unfairly competitive. She was pretty. He was smiling up at her and the initial niceties of "How are you?" "Fine. How are you?" had begun. Then he noticed me standing in the doorway of the living room. It was as if his eye landed on a thing that didn't belong.

We talked for a minute or two. My sister and Jonathan moved into the living room and I excused myself. I returned to the back of the house, shut the door to the family room, moved onto the porch, and sat with my back facing the house. I cried. The words "nice boys" entered my mind. I had seen how Jonathan looked at me and was now convinced: *No nice boy will ever want me.* I was all those horrible words used for rape; I was changed, bloodied, damaged goods, ruined.

When Jonathan left, my sister was giddy.

I moved to the doorway to the family room. They hadn't seen me, but through the window leading onto the porch I'd heard my sister's gleeful voice.

"I think he likes you," my mother said.

"Really?" asked my sister, the pitch of her voice rising on the second syllable.

"It sure looked like it to me," my mother replied.

"He likes Mary," I said, making my presence known, "because Mary wasn't raped!"

"Alice," my mother said, "don't do this."

"He's a nice boy," I said. "No nice boy is ever going to want me."

My sister was dumbfounded. Talk about sinking her ship. She had been buoyant, which she deserved. In the week following her homecoming, she had spent most of her time in her room, out of the fray and away from the limelight.

"Alice," said my mother, "that's not true."

"Yes, it is. You should have seen the way he looked at me. He couldn't deal."

My voice was raised. As a result, my father stirred from his academic lockdown in the study.

"What's all the commotion?" he asked, entering the family room. He held his reading glasses in his right hand and looked, as he frequently did, as if he had been rudely awakened from life in eighteenth-century Spain.

"Thanks for joining us, Bud," my mother said. "Stay out of this."

"No nice boy is ever going to want me," I said again.

My father, without any context, was horrified. "Alice, why would you say a thing like that?"

"Because it's true!" I yelled. "Because I was raped and now no one will want me."

"That's preposterous," he said. "You're a beautiful girl; of course nice boys will ask you out."

"Bullshit. Nice boys don't ask rape victims out!"

I was really blaring it now. My sister retreated from the room and I yelled up after her, "Fine, go write it in your journal. 'A nice boy came to see me today.' I'll never write that."

"Leave your sister out of this," my mother said.

"What makes her so special? She gets to stay up in her room while you put me on suicide watch. Dad is walking around like I'm going to fall apart if he touches me, and you're hiding in the laundry room to have your flaps!"

"Now, Alice," my father said, "you're just upset."

My mother began rubbing her chest.

"Your mother and I are doing the best we can," my father said. "We just don't know what to do."

"You could say the word for starters," I said, stilled now, my face hot with screaming, but tears making their way up again.

"What word?"

"*Rape*, Dad," I said. "*Rape.* The reason why people are staring at me, the reason why you don't know what to do, why those old ladies are coming over and Mom is flipped out, why Jonathan Gulick stared at me like a freak. Okay!"

"Calm down, Alice," my father was saying, "you're upsetting your mother."

It was true. My mother had edged over to the far end of the couch—away from us. She was bent over with one hand on her head and one rubbing the center of her chest. I openly resented her then. Resented how attention always focused on the weakest one.

The doorbell rang. It was Tom McAllister. A year older than I, he was the most handsome boy I knew. My mother thought he looked like the actor Tom Selleck. I had not seen Tom since the midnight service at Christmas Eve. We had been singing a hymn. At the close of the hymn, when I turned around in my pew, he smiled at me.

While my father answered the door to welcome him, I slipped down the back hall to wash my face in the downstairs bathroom. I splashed cold water on my face and tried to finger-comb my hair.

I arranged my robe so it covered the necklace of bruises from the rapist's hands. I cried so much each day my eyes were permanently swollen. I wished I looked better. Pretty, like my sister.

My mother and father had invited Tom out onto the porch. When I joined them, he stood up from the couch he'd been sitting on.

"These are for you," he said, and handed me a bouquet of flowers. "I got you a present too. My mom helped me pick it out."

He was staring at me. But under his scrutiny I felt different than I had with Jonathan Gulick.

My mother brought us sodas and then, after a brief exchange with Tom about his classes at Temple, she took the flowers inside to put them in water, and my father left the porch and went to read in the living room.

We sat down on the couch. I busied myself with opening the gift. It was a mug, with a cartoon of a cat holding a bunch of balloons—the kind of gift that, in another mood, I would have disdained. It seemed beautiful to me and my thanks to Tom were sincere. This was *my* nice boy.

"You look better than I thought," he said.

"Thank you."

"Reverend Breuninger made it sound like you were pretty badly beaten."

I realized that, unlike the old ladies, he saw nothing hidden in those words.

"You know, don't you?" I said.

His face was blank. "Know what?"

"What really happened to me."

"They said in church you were robbed in a park."

I watched him intently. I was unflinching.

"I was raped, Tom," I said.

He was stunned.

"You can leave if you want," I said. I stared down at the mug in my hands.

"I didn't know, nobody told me," he said. "I'm so sorry."

71

While he said this, and meant it, he also pulled away from me. His posture grew more erect. Without actually getting up to move away, he seemed to invite in as much air as could fit in the space between us.

"You know now," I said. "Does it change how you feel about me?"

He couldn't win. What could he say? Of course it must have affected him. I'm sure it did, but I didn't want the answer I know now, I wanted what he said.

"No, of course not. It's just, wow, I don't know what to say."

What I took away from that afternoon, besides his assurance that he would call me soon and we would see each other again, was that one word to my question: *no.*

Of course, I didn't really believe him. I was smart enough to know he was saying what any nice boy would. I was raised to be a good girl; I knew what to say at the right moment too. But because he was a boy my age, he became heroic in proportion to any other visitor. No old lady, not even Myra, could give me what Tom had given me, and my mother knew it. She talked Tom up all that week, and my father, who had gleefully derided a boy who had dared to ask once what country they spoke Latin in, played along. I did too, even though we all knew we were clinging to the wreckage; it was useless to pretend I hadn't changed.

There was another visit, this time a few days later and, no doubt, much harder for Tom. Again we sat on the porch. This time I listened and he spoke. He had gone home, he said, from being with me and told his mother. She hadn't seemed surprised, had even guessed as much from the way Father Breuninger spoke. That evening, or the next day, I forget the time line here, Tom's mother had called Tom and his younger sister, Sandra, into the kitchen and told them she had something to say.

Tom said she stood at the sink with her back to them. While she looked out the window, she told them the story of how she had been raped. She was eighteen when it happened. She had never told anyone about it until that day. It happened at a train station, on her way to visit her brother, who was away at school. What I remember best is how Tom said that when the two men grabbed her she had slipped out of her new coat and kept on running. They got her anyway.

I was thinking, as tears rolled down Tom's face, of how my rapist had grabbed my long hair.

"I don't know what to do or say," Tom said.

"You can't do anything," I said to him.

I wish I could go back and erase my last line to Tom. I wish I could say, "You're already doing it, Tom. You're listening." I wondered how his mother had gone on to have a husband and a family and never tell anyone.

After those visits in the early summer, Tom and I saw each other at church. By that time I was no longer fixated on gaining Tom's attention or being seen with a handsome boy. I was scrutinizing his mother. She knew I knew about her, and she certainly knew about me, but we never spoke. A distance grew between me and Tom. It would have anyway, but the story of my rape had stormed into their lives uninvited. It had catalyzed a revelation inside their home. How that revelation eventually affected them I do not know. But via her son, Mrs. McAllister gave me two things: my first awareness of another rape victim who lived in my world, and, by telling her sons, the proof that there was power to be had in sharing my story.

The urge to tell was immediate. It sprang out of a response so ingrained in me that even if I had tried to hold it back, thought better of it, I doubt I could have done so.

My family had secrets, and from an early age, I had crowned myself the one who would reveal them. I hated the hush-hush of hiding things from other people. The constant instruction to "keep it down or the neighbors will hear you." My usual response to this was "So what?"

Recently my mother and I had a discussion about saving face at her nearby Radio Shack.

"I'm convinced the clerk thinks I'm a lunatic," my mother said, on the subject of returning a portable phone.

"People return things all the time, Mom," I said.

"I've already returned it once."

"So, the clerk may think you're a pain in the ass but I doubt he'll think you're insane."

"I just can't go in there again. I can hear them now: 'Oh, there's that old lady who couldn't figure out a fork if it came with instructions.'"

"Mom," I said, "they exchange things all the time."

It's funny now, but growing up, the worry over the opinions of others meant keeping secrets. My grandmother, my mother's mother, had had a brother who died drunk. His body was discovered three weeks later by his younger brother. My sister and I were warned never to tell Grandma that Mom was an alcoholic. We also weren't supposed to talk about her flaps, and she did her best to hide them on our visits to Bethesda, where her parents lived. Although my parents cursed a blue streak, we were not supposed to curse. And even though we heard what they thought of the deacon at St. Peter's (a "supercilious moron"), what they thought of the neighbors ("He's courting a heart attack with all that fat"), what they thought of one sister when the other sister was up in her room—we were not meant to repeat it.

I seemed constitutionally unable to follow these instructions. When we moved to Pennsylvania from Rockville, Maryland, when I was five, my sister had to repeat the third grade. This was because she was too young, according to the East Whiteland school district, to be in fourth grade. So, on this basis alone, she had to stay in third grade for another year. This was traumatic for her because flunking a grade was one of the worst brands you could bear at age eight in a new town. My mother said no one had to know. She failed to say that for this to happen, they would have to wire my mouth shut and keep me from leaving the house.

A few days after settling into the new house, I was in the backyard with our basset hound, Feijoo. I met a neighbor, Mrs. Cochran, who bent down and introduced herself. She had a child my age, a boy, Brian, and no doubt wanted to get the scoop on our family. I obliged her.

"My mother's the one with the pits in her face," I said to our shocked neighbor. I was referring to my mother's acne scars. In response to the question, "Are there any more like you at home?" I said, "No, but there's my sister. She just flunked third grade."

And so it went. My mouth only got bigger as time wore on, but I won't take all the blame. I was acutely aware of my audience; the adults loved it.

Simply, the rules of revelation were too complicated for me to understand. My parents could say anything they wanted, but once outside our house, I was supposed to keep mum.

"The neighbors like to pump you for information," my mother would say. "You have to learn to be more reticent. I don't know why you insist on talking to everyone."

I didn't know what *reticent* meant. I was only following their example. If they wanted a quiet kid, I eventually told them during some screaming match in high school, maybe I should have taken up smoking. That way I would have lung cancer instead of what my mother accused me of having, which was cancer of the mouth.

Sergeant Lorenz was the first person to hear my story. But he often interrupted with the words, "That's inconsequential." He probed my story for facts that would dovetail into the more salient charges. He was what he was: a "just-the-facts-ma'am" cop.

Who could I tell these things to? I was at home. I didn't feel my sister could handle it and Mary Alice was miles away, working a job at the Jersey shore. It was not something I felt I could do over the phone lines. I tried to tell my mother.

I was privy to many things. Little asides from my mother, such as, "Your father doesn't know the meaning of affection," when I was eleven, or the discussions we had had during my grandfather's protracted illness and death. No events were hidden from me. That was a decision I think my mother made early, in direct response to her own mother. My grandmother is stoic and taciturn. In a crisis, her words of wisdom are old school: "If you don't think about it, it will go away." My mother, given her own life, knew this not to be true.

So there was a precedent for our discussion. By the time I was eighteen, she had sat me down and detailed her alcoholism, its onset and aftermath. She believed that by sharing such things I might be able to avoid them or, if need be, recognize them when they occurred. By talking about them to her children, she was also acknowledging that they were real and that they had an effect on us too, that things like this shaped a family, not just the person they happened to.

My memory says it may have been nighttime, I can't be certain, but it was a few weeks after the rape and it was at the kitchen table. If my mother and I were not alone in the house, then certainly my father was in his study and my sister in her room, so we could have heard approaching footsteps if there were any.

"I need to tell you what happened in the tunnel," I said.

Place mats were still on the table from dinner. My mother fidgeted with the corner of hers.

"You can try," she said, "but I can't promise I can do this."

I began. I told her about Ken Childs's house, about taking pictures in his apartment. I got onto the path in the park. I told her about the rapist's hands, how he grabbed me with both arms, about the fighting on the bricks. When I got into the tunnel, started taking off my clothes, when he touched me, she had to stop.

"I can't, Alice," she said. "I want to, but I can't."

"It helps me to try and talk about it, Mom," I said.

"I understand that, but I don't think I'm the one to do it with."

"I don't have anyone else," I said.

"I can make you an appointment with Dr. Graham."

Dr. Graham was my mother's psychiatrist. In reality, she was the family psychiatrist. She had begun as my sister's psychiatrist, and then wanted to see us as a family so she could see how the family dynamic affected my sister. My mother had even sent me to Dr. Graham a few times after a particularly bad spill down the spiral staircase. I was always running up or down it in sock feet and often would slip on the polished wood. Each time, I did a sort of bouncing pratfall until I reached the landing or my limbs tangled into a configuration that stopped my body just short of the flagstone floor in the front hall. My mother decided this clumsiness might be part of a desire to self-destruct. I was certain it was nothing so sophisticated. I was a klutz.

Now I had a real reason to see a psychiatrist. In the past, I prided myself on being the only member of the family who hadn't had therapy—I did not count a discussion of my pratfalls as therapy—and had tortured my sister while she was under Dr. Graham's care. Mary entered therapy the same year the Talking Heads came out with the perfect song for her little sister to use against her: "Psycho Killer." Sibling brutality with a melody. We had to scrimp to pay for her therapy. I reasoned that what my parents spent on her, they should spend on me. It wasn't my fault Mary was crazy.

Turnabout is fair play, but Mary didn't tease me that summer. I told her that Mom thought I should go to Dr. Graham and we both agreed it might be good for me. My motivation was largely aesthetic. I liked the way Dr. Graham looked. She was feminist in the flesh. She was just under six feet tall, wore large batik muu-muus on her dominant, but not heavy, frame, and she refused to shave her legs. She had laughed at my jokes in high school, and after our few sessions regarding my pratfalls, she had said to my mother, in my presence, that coming from the family I came from, I was incredibly well adjusted. Nothing, she had said at the time, was wrong with me.

My mother drove me down to her office in Philadelphia. It was a different office than the one she had had at Children's Hospital; this was her private office. She was ready for me; I walked in and sat down on the couch.

"Do you want to tell me why you've come to see me, Alice?" she asked. She knew already. My mother had told her on the phone when she called for the appointment.

"I was raped in a park near my school."

Dr. Graham knew our family. Knew both Mary and I were virgins.

"Well," she said, "I guess this will make you less inhibited about sex now, huh?"

I couldn't believe it. I don't remember whether I said, "That's a fucked-up thing to say." I'm sure I just wish I had. I do know that was the end of the session, that I got up and walked out.

What Dr. Graham had said came from a feminist in her thirties. Someone, I thought, who should have known better. But I was learning that no one—females included—knew what to do with a rape victim.

So I told a boy. His name was Steve Carbonaro. I knew him from high school. He was smart and my parents liked him—he appreciated their rugs and books. He came from a big Italian family and wanted out. Poetry was the way he chose to escape and, in this, I had more in common with him than I had with anyone else. On my parents' couch, at sixteen, we read to each other from *The New Yorker Book of Poetry*, and he had given me my first kiss.

I still have my journal entry from that night. After he left, I recorded, "Mom was kinda smirking at me." I went to my sister's room. She had yet to be kissed by a boy. In my journal I wrote, "Yuck, ick, uck, make me sick. I told Mary that French kissing is gross and I didn't know why you were supposed to like it. I told her she could talk to me anytime she wanted to, if she thought it was gross too."

In high school I was a reluctant partner for Steve Carbonaro. I would not go all the way. When he pressured me, I explained myself like this: I did not feel adamant about saying no, but I also didn't feel adamant about saying yes, so until I felt strongly one way or another, I'd stick with no.

By seventeen, in our senior year, Steve had moved on to a girl who would, in the parlance of high school, "put out." At the senior prom, while I danced with Tom McAllister, Steve drank.

When I ran into him and his girlfriend, she bitterly informed me that she was doing well, considering that that morning she had had an abortion. Later, at Gail Stuart's party, Steve showed up with another girl, Karen Ellis. He had taken his girlfriend home.

But by May 1981, none of those early fumblings mattered. Two hours in a dark tunnel made my yes-or-no struggles with the morality of sleeping with high school boys like Steve seem quaint.

Steve had gone to Ursinus College his freshman year. He returned, having discovered a new passion for the musical *Man of La Mancha*. My mother, and my more hard-to-court father, loved his investment in the myth of La Mancha. What better choice to engage a professor of eighteenth-century Spanish than a musical based on Cervantes? Give or take a century, Steve Carbonaro could not have hit his mark cleaner. He spent hours that summer on the porch with my mother and father, being served coffee and talking about the books he loved and what he wanted to be when he grew up. I believe their attention was as important to him as anything else, and his attention to me was a godsend to my parents.

The first time he visited the house that summer I told him I'd been raped. We may have gone out a few times, as friends, before I told him everything else. It was on the couch in the living room. My parents moved as silently as possible in the room above us. Whenever Steve came over, my father would duck into his study, or join my mother in her bedroom, where, in hushed whispers, they would try and conjecture what might be going on below.

I told him everything I could bear to tell. I intended to tell him all the details but I couldn't. I edited as I went, stopping at blind corners where I felt I might fall apart. I kept the narrative linear. I did not stop to investigate how I felt about having the rapist's tongue in my mouth, about having to kiss back.

He was both engaged and repulsed. Here, before him, was live performance, real tragedy, a drama he had access to that did not take place in books or in the poems he wrote.

He called me Dulcinea. He sang the songs from *Man of La*

Mancha out loud, in his white VW bug, and had me sing along. Singing these songs was vital to Steve. He cast himself as the central figure, Don Quixote de La Mancha, a man whom no one understands, a romantic who makes a crown of a barber's shaving bowl and a lady—Dulcinea—of the whore Aldonza. I was the latter.

Following a song and scene called "The Abduction," where Aldonza is kidnapped, and, it is implied, gang-raped, Don Quixote comes upon her after she has been discarded by her captors. With the force of his imagination and will, Don Quixote insists on seeing this raped and beaten woman as his sweet and lovely maiden Dulcinea.

Steve saved up and bought tickets for us to see Richard Kiley play the lead at the Philadelphia Academy of Music. This was my early birthday gift. We dressed up. My mother took photos. My father said I looked "like a real lady." I was embarrassed by the attention, but it was a night out, and with a boy, a boy who knew and had not rejected me. I fell in love with him for this.

And yet, somehow, seeing it played out onstage, with Aldonza chased by a group of men, fondled and abused, her breasts grabbed like lobes of meat, I could not sustain the illusion that Steve Carbonaro found essential to our relationship. I was not a whore who, by virtue of his imagination and sense of justice, he could raise to the height of a lady. I was an eighteen-year-old girl who had wanted to be an archaeologist when I was four, and a poet or a Broadway star when I grew up. I had changed. The world I lived in was not the world that my parents or Steve Carbonaro still occupied. In my world, I saw violence everywhere. It was not a song or a dream or a plot point.

I left *Man of La Mancha* feeling filthy.

That night, Steve was exhilarated. He had seen what he knew to be truth, the truth of a romantic nineteen-year-old played out on the stage. He drove his Dulcinea home, sang to her in the car and, at his urging, she sang back to him. We were there for a long time. The windows steamed up from the singing. I went inside. Before I did, what was precious to me that summer happened one more time: A nice boy kissed me good night. Everything was tainted. Even a kiss.

Looking back now, listening to the lyrics again, it is not lost on me, as it was then, that Don Quixote dies in the end, that Aldonza survives, that it is *she* who sings the refrain from "The Impossible Dream," *she* who is left standing to do battle.

Things between us did not end gloriously; there was no bright, shining star or quest. Ultimately, Don Quixote had a hard time loving chaste and pure from afar. He found someone who would go all the way with him. The summer ended. It was time to go back to school again. Don Quixote would transfer to Penn; my father wrote him a passionate letter of recommendation. And I, with the eventual support of my parents, went back to Syracuse. Alone.

SIX

In my senior year of high school, I had applied to three colleges: Syracuse University, Emerson College in Boston, and the University of Pennsylvania, where I was supposed to have gotten in, a cinch as a faculty child. I did not want to go to Penn, or at least that's how I remember it. I had watched my sister move in and then quickly out of a dorm on Penn's campus, bring her possessions back to my parents' house, and commute her first year. If I had to go to college—which I spent the better part of four years in high school saying I didn't want to do—I wanted it to have the benefit of being far away.

My parents humored me; they were desperate for me to go to college. They saw it as an essential gateway, the thing that had changed their own lives, particularly my father's. Neither of his parents had finished high school and the shame of this was like an ache to him; his academic achievements were fueled by a need to distance himself from his mother's bad grammar and his father's drunken dirty jokes.

In my junior year of high school, my father and I visited Emerson, where long-haired students he called "throwbacks" advised me on how to break what they saw as oppressive rules.

"You aren't supposed to have any electrical appliances," said the resident assistant of the dorm we toured. He had dark brown dirty hair and a scruffy beard. To me, he looked like John the bus driver, who had driven me to school during junior high and had dropped out of high school. Both these boys had the smell of true, authentic rebellion. They reeked of pot.

"I got a toaster oven and a hair dryer," this John boasted, pointing toward a grease-coated toaster oven wedged into a set of hand-made shelves. "Never use 'em at the same time, that's the trick."

Though amused, my father was also shocked by this boy, his mangy looks, his position of authority in the dorms. My father may have been divided. Emerson had the reputation of being an arty school in a town of monoliths like Harvard and MIT. Even Boston University, whose campus we also visited and which my father praised, was far above Emerson's place on the food chain. But I liked Emerson. I liked how when we drove up to it and saw the sign, two of the letters were missing from it. This was my kind of place. I felt I could learn not to make toast and dry my hair at the same time.

That night I had fun with my father. This is a rare event. My father does not have hobbies, wouldn't recognize a ball sport if the ball hit him in the head, and there are no cronies, there are only colleagues. The reason for relaxation of any kind is largely beyond him. "Fun is boring," he told me as a child when I attempted to coax him into playing a board game I had set up on the floor. It became one of his favorite phrases. He meant it.

But I'd always had a hint that my father could be different away from us and away from my mother. That he had fun in other countries or with his male graduate students. I liked to get my father alone, and on the trip to Emerson, he and I shared a hotel room to save money.

The night after a long day in Boston, I slipped into the twin bed nearest the bathroom. My father went down to the lobby to read and perhaps make a call to my mother. I was wound up and couldn't sleep. Earlier, I had gotten a bucket of tiny ice cubes from the hallway. I planned my attack. I took the ice cubes and put them in my father's bed, right down near the feet. I saved the remainder and placed them by my bed.

I feigned sleep when my father returned. He changed into his pajamas in the bathroom, brushed his teeth, turned out the light. I could see the outline of him as he pulled the covers back to get inside. I was elated, if a bit frightened. He might just be plain mad. I counted, and then it came. A ferocious yell followed by cursing. "For Christ's sakes, what the . . . ?"

I couldn't hold it. I started laughing uncontrollably.

"Alice?"

"Got ya," I said.

At first, he was angry, but then he threw a cube. That was all it took.

It was war. I threw back. Our beds were our bunkers. He threw great handfuls and, retrieving them, I used them as individuals, firing off rounds timed to get him just as he was coming up to strike. He was laughing and so was I. He had tried momentarily to be the parent, but he couldn't hold to it.

I got what he thought was too hysterical and reached what my mother called my hyperactive state, so we stopped. But before that, oh, to see my father joyful, laughing. At moments like this I pretended my father was the big brother I'd never had. It was up to me to instigate, but when he was that repressed kid released, my whole heart wanted him to stay that way forever.

Like a small-town girl might view Hollywood, I saw Syracuse as my big break. Compared with my sister's proximity to my parents, Syracuse was far away from home. Far enough so that I could redefine myself against what I had once been.

My roommate was Nancy Pike. She was a roly-poly, overexcited girl from Maine. In the summer, she had found out my name and written me a letter. It was six enthusiastic pages long and regaled me with what she was bringing and their attendant definitions—"I have a hot pot. It is a little pot that looks like a coffee percolator but it's really only for hot water and has a plug that you plug in. It is great for making soups and water for tea though you should never put soup directly in it."

I dreaded meeting her.

As my mother, father, and I arrived on move-in day my head was swimming. This was my new life and here were all the new people in it. A coed dorm held possibilities I dared not outline to my parents. My mother had on her Donna Reed face, which was a particularly sickly smile imbued with positive thinking, dredged up from I never understood where. My father wanted to get the stuff out of the car and get it over with. He was not made, as he pointed out many times that day, "for heavy lifting."

Nancy had gotten there first, chosen her bed, hung up a rainbow wall hanging, and begun to putter with her belongings. Her parents and siblings had stayed to meet me and my family. My mother's Donna Reed was cracking into panic. My father drew himself up to his full academic, Ivy League-professor height, the one from which he looked down on everybody who expressed interest in sports or daily life. "I was born two centuries too late," he is fond of saying, or, "I had no parents, I sprung from the Earth whole and unique." My mother could always manage a zinger: "Your father looks down on everybody because from that height, he's hoping they won't see his bad teeth."

Weird family Sebold meets excited family Pike. The Pikes filtered out and took Nancy to lunch. The word that suited them best, I think, is *crestfallen*. Their sweet daughter had drawn a superfreak.

Nancy and I didn't talk much in the first week. She would bubble and I would lie in my bunk and stare at the ceiling.

At the bright, happy orientation exercises that the resident assistants led us on—"Okay, we're going to play a game called Living Priorities. Write these down. Studying. Volunteer work. Rushing sororities. Can anyone tell me what they would choose as a priority and why?"—my roommate had hand in air. During one interminable afternoon, when the girls of our floor sat crosslegged on the grass outside the dining hall, listening to a lecture on how to do laundry, I thought I had been dropped off at a camp for morons by my parents.

I stomped into the dorm. It had been a week and I had refused to go to the dining hall with the other girls for dinner. When Nancy asked why, I said I was fasting. Later, when I was hungry, I asked her to bring me food. "It has to be white food," I said. "No colors. Erik Satie ate only white food." My poor roommate brought home mounds of cottage cheese and giant pearl tapioca.

I lay in bed, hating Syracuse and listening to Erik Satie, from whose liner notes my new regime came.

One night I heard noise in the room next to mine. Everyone else was at dinner. I went out into the hall. A door was slightly ajar.

"Hello?" I said.

It was the most beautiful girl on the floor. The one my mother had pointed out on move-in day. "Just be glad that gorgeous blonde isn't your roommate. The line of boys would be out the door."

"Hello."

I went in. She had just gotten a whole footlocker of food sent from home. It was open against the wall. After a week of white food, it was an oasis. M&M's and cookies and crackers and Starbursts and fruit leather. Products I had never even heard of or wasn't allowed to have.

But she wasn't eating. She was braiding her hair. A French braid. I expressed my admiration and told her I'd never been able to do more than simple braids.

"I'll do it for you if you want."

I sat on her bed and she stood behind me and began to take the small pinches of hair and work a skull-numbingly tight French braid down the back of my head.

She finished the braid and I thanked her and looked in the mirror. We both sat and then laid down on the two twin beds in the room. We were quiet, staring at the ceiling.

"Can I tell you something?" I asked.

"Sure."

"I hate it here."

"Oh, my God!" she said, sitting up, flushed with permission. "I hate it here too!"

We ate our way through her trunk of food. I have a memory of actually sitting in the trunk with the food but this can't be right, can it?

Mary Alice's roommate was what we called experienced. She was from Brooklyn. Her name was Debbie and her nickname was Double D. She smoked and thought little of us. She had a from-home boyfriend who was older. And I mean *older.* Early forties, but with the agelessness of Joey Ramone. He was a DJ somewhere and had a deep smoker's voice. When he visited, they went to hotels and Debbie returned to the dorm with her cheeks flushed and clearly, again, disgusted by us. Mary Alice had long toes and would feed me crackers by digging them into the box. We dressed up in stupid outfits and, with coupons from cocoa mix, sent away for a real Swiss Miss cardboard chalet.

Debbie began two-timing her boyfriend with a male cheerleader from school. Her new boyfriend's name was Harry Weiner and of course Mary Alice and I had endless fun with that. Once, on a dare, I hid inside the Swiss Miss chalet while Debbie and Harry went at it on the bed. At a certain point, dare or no, I felt too uncomfortable and crawled, on my hands and knees, with the cardboard chalet moving with me like some sort of cartoon spy's camouflage, over to the door to make my escape.

Debbie was incensed. She put in for a room transfer. Mary Alice never stopped thanking me.

Within a few weeks of the start of freshman year, a group of girls gathered in the hall outside our rooms. We sat on the floor, with our backs against the walls, our legs outstretched or Indian-style. The former homecoming queens or future flirts tucked their legs to one side, while the jocks on scholarship, like my friend Linda, didn't think twice about how they sat or looked while surrounded by their peers. Slowly the stories came out—who was and wasn't a virgin.

Some were obvious. Like Sara, who sold hash out of her black-lit room, where she had a stereo system that cost more than most of our fathers' cars, on which she played the classic stoner tracks of Traffic and Led Zep. "Some guy's in there," her assigned roommate would say, and we would throw this girl a sleeping bag and tell her not to snore.

Then there was Chippie. I had never heard the word before. Didn't know it meant whore. Thought it actually was her name, and innocently said, "Hi, Chippie, how are you?" on the way to the showers one morning. She burst into tears and never talked to me again.

There was also a girl who was a sophomore and lived at the end of the hall. She dated a townie and modeled for Joel Belfast, a semi-famous painter in the art department. The townie liked to chain her up to her bunk bed and we would see her leather and ultrasuede bras and panties as she hurried to and from the lavatory in the morning. The townie rode a motorcycle and had an atrophied left leg. Once, on the night the campus security arrived because they were making so much noise, I saw the scar that rose up out of the top of his boot and snaked up past his hip and around the back of his body. She was stoned and screaming on the bed, where she remained chained up. Soon after, she moved into off-campus housing somewhere.

These girls and Debbie were the only four on a hall of fifty that I knew for sure weren't virgins. The rest had to be, I assumed, because I was.

But even Nancy told a story. She had lost it in a Datsun to her high school boyfriend. Tree in a Toyota. Diane in the basement of a boyfriend's house. Her boyfriend's parents had knocked on the window during the act. The other stories I've forgotten, and remember only that the make of the car became a nickname for various girls. Few were the glorious cases—a boyfriend who had bought a ring, chosen a special night, and brought flowers, or had his older brother's downtown apartment for the day. When these girls spoke we didn't believe them anyway. It was better to say Datsun or Toyota or Ford; it was dues for a peer group, a way to belong.

When that evening of revelation was through, Mary Alice and I, among those outside their rooms, were the only two virgins on the hall.

These fumbled sexual exploits in the backs of cars or in the basements of someone's parents' house seem wonderful to me. Nancy was ashamed of having lost "it," as we all called virginity, in a Datsun, but it was, after all, a normal part of growing up.

In letters sent me over the breaks that year Tree and Nancy were spending every night with their high school boyfriends. For Tree there was talk of a ring being bought. These girls began to take over my landscape.

I also got letters from the boys I'd worked with at my summer job after high school, particularly an older guy named Gene. I begged Gene to send me a photo. Of course, I pretended to the other girls he was more than just a friend, and I wanted evidence to show around.

The photo he sent was clearly a few years old. He was thinner and had more hair but there was the handle-bar mustache that shouted out *man*. When I finally got the photo late in the first semester I showed it around. Mary Alice cut to the core. "Is it the seventies still? I feel a disco ball dropping down." Nancy pretended to be impressed but she and Tree were too busy keeping connected with their real boyfriends—boys they'd gone to high school with, whom they had promised to marry someday.

For her part, Mary Alice was obsessed with, in order: Bruce Springsteen, Keith Richards, and Mick Jagger. On the subject of Bruce—for he was our familiar—she was apoplectic. For her birthday I got a T-shirt made. MRS. BRUCE SPRINGSTEEN, it said, in puffy, too-big iron-on letters. She slept in it every night.

Honestly, when I look back, I can say I was in love with Mary Alice for most of my freshman year. I loved watching her get away with things and being a troop member in her carefully planned out escapades. Stealing a sheet cake from the dining hall became an operation worthy of James Bond. It involved discovering the tunnel between two dorms that led to the odd door that was always locked. There were keys that needed to be stolen and people who needed to be distracted and finally, late at night, pink cake that needed to be disguised and hustled up to our rooms.

But my dorm girlfriends were also fond of the bars on nearby Marshall Street and by spring they went regularly to fraternity keg parties. I hated fraternity parties. "We're just meat!" I yelled above the music to Tree, who was ahead of me in the line for the keg. "So what?" she shouted back. "It's fun!" Tree became a little sister. Mary Alice was always popular no matter how she felt. No fraternity house would turn away a natural blonde and her attendant friends.

I was taking a poetry class and in it, there were two boys, Casey Hartman and Ken Childs, who were unlike any in my dorm. They were sophomores, so I thought of them as mature. They were art students, taking the poetry class as an elective. They showed me the art building, a beautiful old thing that was yet to be restored. It had studios in it with carpeted platforms for the models in the life-studies classes and old couches and chairs that the students crashed in. It smelled like paint and turpentine and was open all night so that students could work because, unlike most majors, you couldn't do your homework for things like metal welding in your room.

They pointed out a decent Chinese restaurant and Ken took me to the Everson museum in downtown Syracuse. I began to wait for them outside their classes and go to the art openings they and their friends had. They were both from Troy, New York. Casey was on a creative fellowship and never had money. I would run into him and he would be having tea three times from the same bag for dinner. I only knew pieces of Casey's story. His father was in jail. His mother was dead.

It was Casey whom I had a crush on. But he didn't trust all the liberal arts girls who found him romantic, his scars from a birthmark and beatings things they wanted to cure. He talked fast, like an erupting coffeepot, and sometimes didn't make sense. I didn't care. He was a freak and so much more human, I believed, than the boys in fraternities or in my dining hall.

But Ken was the one who liked me and who, like me, liked to talk. The three of us formed a frustrated triangle. I complained about how many of the girls at Marion were so experienced and how I felt lame. Ken and Casey were quiet at first but then it came out. They felt lame too.

When there was a party at the dorm—and kegs were allowed in your room back then—I would leave and go walk on the quad. I would end up in the art building, making instant coffee in the basement, and then sit for hours reading Emily Dickinson or Louise Bogan in the spring-shot sofas and chairs spotted throughout the building. I began to think of this place as my home.

Sometimes I would walk back to Marion in hopes the party would be over, and find it had seemingly barely begun. I didn't even go inside, I just turned around. I slept in the art classrooms, on the carpeted platforms meant to warm models' feet. They weren't big enough to stretch out on, so I would curl up into a ball.

One night, I was lying in a classroom in the dark. I had closed the door and made a bed in the back. The lights in the hallways were always on and the lightbulbs were covered in mesh cages so they wouldn't break or be stolen. Just as I was nodding off, the door to the hallway opened and a man stood outlined by the light coming from behind him. He was tall and wearing a top hat. I couldn't see who it was.

He turned on the light. It was Casey. "Sebold," he said, "what are you doing here?"

"I'm sleeping."

"Welcome, comrade!" he said, and tipped his hat. "I will be your Cerberus for the night."

He sat in the dark and watched me sleep. I remember, before I nodded off, wondering if Casey could ever find me pretty enough to kiss. It was the first night I'd ever spent with a boy I liked.

I look back and I see Casey as a guard dog. I want to say that under his guard I felt safe, but the person writing this is not the person who curled up on the carpeted platforms inside dark classrooms. The world was not divided for me then as it is now. Ten days later, on the last night of school, I would enter what I've thought of since as my real neighborhood, a land of subdivision where tracts are marked off and named. There are two styles available: the safe and the not safe.

SEVEN

The burden of being father and mother to a rape victim fell very heavily on my parents during the summer of 1981. The immediate question that loomed over them was what to do with me. Where should I go? How could I be least damaged? Was it even a consideration for me to return to Syracuse?

The option most discussed was Immaculata College.

It was too late in the game for me to enter any normal college, which had already accepted its students, both freshmen and transfers, for the following year. But my mother was sure Immaculata would take me. It was a girls' school and it was Catholic and she said a major advantage was that I could live at home. My mother or father could drive me the five miles down Route 30 each day and then pick me up when classes were over.

My parents' priorities were my safety and the chance not to miss a year of college. I did my best to listen to my mother. My father was so clearly disheartened by her plan that he could barely muster the requisite endorsement (but then, he had no other options). From the very beginning I saw Immaculata as one thing and one thing only. It was a prison. I would be attending it for one reason alone: because I had been raped.

It was also ludicrous. The idea of me, *me*, I said to my parents, attending a religious academy! I had picked theoretical arguments with the deacon of our church, cultivated any obscene narrative I could get my hands on, and imitated Father Breuninger's sermons to the delight of my family and even Father Breuninger himself. I think Immaculata and the threat of it inspired me, more than anything else, to come up with an airtight argument.

I wanted to return to Syracuse, I said, because the rapist had

92

already taken so much from me. I was not going to let him take anything more. If I returned home and lived in my bedroom, I would never know what my life would have been like.

Also, I had been granted admission to a poetry workshop led by Tess Gallagher, and a fiction workshop led by Tobias Wolff. If I did not go back, I would be denied both of these opportunities. Both of my parents knew the one thing I cared about was words. No one of Gallagher's or Wolff's caliber would be teaching at Immaculata. There were no creative-writing workshops offered at the school.

So they let me go back. My mother still refers to it as one of the hardest things she ever had to do, much harder than any long drive she had to take over many bridges and through countless tunnels.

That's not to say I wasn't scared. I was. So were my parents. But we tried to work the odds. I would stay out of the park and my father would get on the phone and write letters to get me a single in Haven Hall, the only all-girls' dorm. I would have a private phone installed in my room. I would ask to be escorted by campus security guards if I had to walk after dark. I would not go to Marshall Street alone after 5:00 P.M. or hang out. I would stay out of the student bars. This didn't sound like the freedom college was supposed to promise, but then, I wasn't free. I had learned it, as my mother said I learned everything, the hard way.

Haven Hall had a reputation. Large and circular, set on a concrete base, it was an oddity among the other square or rectangular buildings that comprised the dorms on the hill. The dining hall, which had better food than many others, sat up off the ground.

But the weird architecture and the good food were not at the heart of Haven's campuswide rep. It was the residents. Rumor had it that only virgins and horse lovers (read: lesbians) lived in the single rooms of Haven Hall. Soon I knew the "tights and dykes" moniker to include a variety of female freaks. Haven was home to virgins, yes, and to lesbians, but it was also home to jocks on schoolarship, rich kids, foreign girls, nerds, and

[handwritten margin note: ground rules set by parents]

minority girls. There were professionals—those students who traveled a lot and had things like a commercial contract with Chap Stick that necessitated flying to the Swiss Alps on the random weekend. There were children of minor celebrities and sluts on the mend. Transfer students and older students and girls that for a variety of reasons didn't fit in.

It was not a particularly friendly place. I don't remember who lived on one side of me. The girl on the other—an Israeli from Queens who was attending the S. I. Newhouse School of Communications and who practiced her radio voice incessantly—was not my friend. Mary Alice and the girls from freshman year, Tree, Diane, Nancy, and Linda, all lived in Kimmel Hall, sister to Marion Hall.

I moved into Haven, said good-bye to my parents, and stayed in my room. The next day, I traversed the road from Haven to Kimmel, my skin on fire. I was taking in everyone, looking for Him.

Because Kimmel was a sophomore dorm and many of the people from Marion had naturally ended up in Kimmel, I knew most of the girls and boys who lived there. They knew me too. It was as if, when they caught sight of me, they had seen a ghost. No one expected I would come back to campus. The fact that I did made me weirder still. Somehow my return licensed them to judge me—after all, by returning, hadn't I asked for this?

In the lobby of Kimmel I ran into two boys who had lived below me the year before. They stopped dead when they saw me but didn't speak. I looked down, stood in front of the elevator, and pressed the button. A few other boys came in the front door and greeted them. I didn't turn around, but when the elevator arrived I stepped in and turned to face the front. As the doors closed, I saw five boys standing there, staring at me. I could hear it without needing to stick around. "That's the girl that got raped the last day of school," one of the boys who knew me would say. What else they said, and what they wondered, I've kept myself from imagining. I was having enough trouble just walking paths and riding elevators.

But the second floor was a girls' hall, so I thought the worst was over. I was wrong. I got off the elevator and someone rushed to me, a girl I had barely known from freshman year.

"Oh, Alice," she said, her voice dripping. She took my hand without asking and held it. "You've come back."

"Yes," I said. I stood there and looked at her. I had a memory of borrowing her toothpaste once in the bathroom.

How can I describe her look? She was oozing, she was sorry for me and thrilled to be talking to me. She was holding the hand of the girl who had been raped on the last day of school freshman year.

"I didn't think you'd return," she said. I wanted my hand back.

The elevator had descended and risen again. A crowd of girls got off.

"Mary Beth," the girl standing with me said. "Mary Beth, over here."

Mary Beth, a plain, homely girl whom I didn't recognize, came over.

"This is Alice; she lived on the hall in Marion with me last year."

Mary Beth blinked.

Why didn't I move? Walk down the hall and get away? I don't know. I think I was too stunned. I was understanding a language I'd never keyed into before. "This is Alice" translated to "the girl I told you about, you know, the raped one." Mary Beth's blink told me that. If it hadn't, her next comment sure did.

"Wow," this homely girl said, "Sue's told me all about you."

Mary Alice interrupted this exchange, coming out of her room nearby and seeing me. Often, because of Mary Alice's beauty, people thought of her as a snob if she didn't go out of her way with them. But for me, in a moment like this, people's reactions to her were a plus. I was still in love with her and now my adulation included everything she was that I no longer was: fearless, faith filled, innocent.

She took me to her room, which she was sharing with Tree.

All the girls of freshman year, save Nancy, were there. Tree tried with me, but we would never recover from that moment in the shower after the rape. I was uncomfortable. Then there was Diane. She was patterning herself so heavily after Mary Alice— imitating her language and trying to compete in coming up with dopey schemes—that I didn't trust her. She greeted me kindly if eagerly, and watched our mutual idol for her cues. Linda stayed by the window. I had liked Linda. She was muscular and tan and had close-cropped black curls. I liked to think of her as the jock version of me—an outsider who got along by having something that distinguished her in the group. She was a top-rung athlete; I was a weirdo, just funny enough to fit in.

Perhaps it was a kind of guilt at the memory of passing out that accounted for Linda's inability to meet my gaze for very long. I don't remember who it was that day, or how it got around to this, but someone asked me why I had even come back.

It was aggressive. The tone it was asked in implied that in having come back I had done something wrong—something not normal. Mary Alice caught the tone and didn't like it. She said something short and sweet, like "Because it's her fucking right," and we left the room. I counted my blessing in Mary Alice and didn't stop to count my losses. I was back in school. I had classes to attend.

Some first impressions are indelible, like mine of Tess Gallagher. I was registered for two of her classes: her workshop, and a sophomore-level survey course of literature. The survey course was at 8:30 A.M. two days a week, not a popular time slot.

She walked in and strode to the front of the room. I was sitting in the back. The first-day sizing-up ritual began. She was not a dinosaur. This was good. She had long brown hair held back by combs near her temples. This hinted at an underlying humanity. Most noticeable, though, were her highly arched eyebrows and Cupid's-bow lips.

I took this all in while she stood silent in front of us and waited for the stragglers to settle and for backpacks to be zipped or unzipped. I had pencils ready, a notebook out.

She sang.

She sang an Irish ballad a cappella. Her voice was at once lusty and timorous. She held notes bravely and we stared. She was happy and mournful.

She finished. We were stunned. I don't think anyone said anything, no dumb questions about whether they were in the right class. My heart, for the first time back in Syracuse, filled up. I was sitting in the presence of something special; that ballad confirmed my choice to return.

"Now," she said, looking at us keenly, "if I can sing a ballad a cappella at eight-thirty in the morning, you can come to class on time. If you think that's something you can't manage, then drop."

Yes! I said inside my head. Yes!

She told us about herself. About her own work as a poet, about her early marriage, her love of Ireland, her involvement in Vietnam War protests, her slow path toward becoming a poet. I was rapt.

The class ended with an assignment out of the *Norton Anthology* for the next class. She left the room as the students packed up.

"Shit," a boy in an L. L. Bean T-shirt said to his female companion in a ΔΦΣ T-shirt, "I'm out of here, this lady's a fruitcake."

I gathered my books with Gallagher's reading list on top. Besides the required sophomore *Norton*, she recommended eleven books of poetry that were available at an off-campus bookshop. Elated by this poet, and having hours to pass before my first fiction workshop with Wolff, I bought tea in a place underneath the chapel and then crossed the quad. It was sunny out and I was thinking of Gallagher and imagining Wolff. I liked the name of one of the books she'd listed, *In a White Light* by Michael Burkard. I was thinking of that, and reading the *Norton* while I walked, when I ran into Al Tripodi.

I didn't know Al Tripodi. As was becoming more and more common, Al Tripodi knew me.

"You came back," he said. He took two steps forward and hugged me.

"I'm sorry," I said, "I don't know you."

"Oh, yeah," he said, "of course, I'm just so happy to see you."

He had startled me but he *was* happy, truly so. I could see it in his eyes. He was an older student, balding, and with a vibrant mustache that struggled for attention with his blue eyes. His face may have seemed older than he was. The lines and creases in it reminded me of those I later saw on men that thrilled in riding motorcycles cross-country with no helmets on.

It came out that he had something to do with campus security and was around the night I was raped. I felt awkward and exposed, but I liked him too.

It also made me mad. I couldn't get away from it. I began to wonder how many people knew, how far the news had spread and who had spread it. My rape had made the city paper but my name wasn't used—just "Syracuse coed." Yet I reasoned my age, and even the name of my dorm, could still make me one of fifty. Naively, perhaps, I hadn't known I would have to deal with this question every day: Who knew? Who didn't know?

But you can't control a story and mine was a good one. People, even naturally respectful ones, felt emboldened in the telling because the assumption was that I would never choose to return. The police had placed my case in the inactive file when I left town; my friends, save Mary Alice, had done the same. Magically I became story, not person, and story implies a kind of ownership by the storyteller.

I remember Al Tripodi because he saw me not merely as "the rape victim." It was something in his eyes—the way he placed no distance between the two of us. I developed a sensing mechanism, and it would register immediately. Does this person see me or rape? By the close of the year, I came to know the answer to that question, or so I thought. I got better at it, at least. Often, because it was too painful, I chose not to ask it. In these exchanges, where I shut off so I could order a coffee or ask another student for a pen, I learned to close a part of myself down. I never knew exactly how many people connected what had been in the paper or the rumors that had come out of Marion Dorm with me. I heard about myself sometimes. I was told my own story. "You lived in Marion?" they would ask. "Did you know that girl?" Sometimes I listened to see what they knew, how the game of Telephone had translated my life. Sometimes I looked right at them and said: "Yes, that girl was me."

In class, Tess Gallagher was keeping my pencil busy. I wrote down in my notebook that I should be writing "poems that mean." That to tackle the hardest things, to be ambitious, was what Gallagher expected of us. She was tough. We were to memorize and recite, because she had had to as a student, a poem a week. She made us read and understand forms, scan lines, had us write a villanelle and a sestina. By shaking us up, using a rigorous approach, she hoped to both encourage us to write poems that meant, and to dispel any belief that feigning despond was what created good poetry. It got so you knew, very quickly, what would get Gallagher riled. When Raphael, who had a pointed goatee and a waxed mustache, said he hadn't a poem to turn in because he was happy and he could only write when he was depressed, Gallagher's Cupid's-bow lips pursed, her preternaturally raised eyebrows raised farther, and she said, "Poetry is not an attitude. It is hard work."

I had not written anything about the rape except journal entries in the form of running letters to myself. I decided to write a poem.

It was awful. As I recall it now, it ran five pages and rape was only a muddled metaphor that I tried to contain inside a wordy albatross that purported to be about society and violence and the difference between television and reality. I knew it wasn't my best but I thought it showed me to be smart, to be able to write poems that meant but also had format (I divided it into four sections using Roman numerals!).

Gallagher was kind. I hadn't turned the poem in to be work-shopped, so we met in her office for a conference. Her office, like Tobias Wolff's across the hall, was small and crowded with books and reference materials, but whereas Wolff's looked like he hadn't quite settled in, Gallagher's seemed like she had been there for years. Her office was warm. She had tea in a mug on her desk. A colorful Chinese silk shawl was draped across the back of her chair, and that day her long, wavy hair was held back by sequined combs.

"Let's talk about this poem you've given me, Alice," she said. And somehow I ended up telling her my story. And she listened. She was not bowled over, not shocked, not even scared of the burden this might make me as her student. She was not motherly or nurturing, though she was both those things in time. She was matter-of-fact, her head nodding in acknowledgment. She listened for the pain in my words, not to the narrative itself. She was intuiting what it meant to me, what was most important, what, in that confused mass of experience and yearning she heard in my voice, she could single out to give back.

"Have they caught this guy?" she asked after listening to me for some time.

"No."

"I have an idea, Alice," she said. "How about you start a poem with this line." And she wrote it down. *If they caught you . . .*

If they caught you,
long enough for me
to see that face again,
maybe I would know
your name.

I could stop calling you 'the rapist,'
and start calling you John or Luke or Paul.
I want to make my hatred large and whole.

If they found you, I could take
those solid red balls and slice them
separately off, as everyone watched.
I have already planned what I would do
for a pleasurable kill, a slow, soft, ending.

LUCKY

First,
I would kick hard and straight with a boot,
into you, stare while you shot quick and loose,
contents a bloody pink hue.
Next,
I would slice out your tongue,
You couldn't curse, or scream.
Only a face of pain would speak
for you, your thick ignorance through.
Thirdly,
Should I hack away those sweet
cow eyes with the glass blades you made
me lie down on? Or should I shoot, with a gun,
close into the knee; where they say
the cap shatters immediately?

I picture you now,
your fingers rubbing sleep from
those live blind eyes, while I rise restlessly.
I need the blood of your hide
on my hands. I want to kill you
with boots and guns and glass.
I want to fuck you with knives.

Come to me, Come to me,
Come die and lie, beside me.

When I finished this poem I was shaking. I was in my room
at Haven Hall. Despite its wobbles as a poem, its heavily Plath-
influenced rhymes, or what Gallagher later called "overkill" in
many places, it was the first time I'd addressed the rapist directly.
I was speaking to him.

Gallagher loved it. "Now that's the ticket," she said to me. I
had written an important poem, she told me, and she wanted it
to be workshopped. This was a big step. This meant sitting in a
room with fourteen strangers—one of them, as it happened, Al

Tripodi—and basically telling them I had been raped. Buoyed by Gallagher, but still afraid, I agreed to do it. I worried over a title. Finally, I made up my mind: "Conviction."

I passed the poem out and then, as was standard practice, I read it aloud to my fellow students. I was, as I read it, hot. My skin blushed and I could feel the blood rush to my face, prickle along the tops of my ears and the ends of my fingers. I could feel the class around me. They were riveted. They were staring at me.

When I was done, Gallagher had me read it again. Before she did this, she told the class that she expected everyone to comment. I read it again, and this time it felt like torture, an instant replay of something that had been hard enough the first time. I still question why Gallagher was so insistent that I workshop "Conviction" and that each and every student—this was not standard—respond to it afterward. It was an important poem by her standards, in that it dealt with important material. Perhaps, by her actions, she meant to emphasize this not only to the class, but to me as well.

But the eyes of most of my peers had a hard time meeting mine.

"Who wants to start?" Gallagher asked. She was direct. By her example she was telling the class: This is what we do here.

Most of the students were shy. They buried their response in words like *brave*, or *important*, or *bold*. One or two were angry that they had to respond, felt the poem, combined with Gallagher's admonition that they react, was an act of aggression on her part and mine.

Al Tripodi said, "You don't really feel that way, do you?"

He was looking right at me. I thought of my father. Suddenly, there was no one else in the room.

"Like what?"

"You don't want to shoot him in the knees and that other stuff with the knives. You can't feel that way."

"Yes, I do," I said. "I want to kill him."

The room was still. Only Maria Flores, a quiet Latina girl, had yet to speak. When Gallagher told her it was her turn, she passed. Gallagher pressed. Maria said she could not speak. Gallagher said she could formulate her thoughts during the break and then speak. "Everyone must comment," she said. "What Alice has given you is a gift. I think it's important that everyone recognize this and respond to her. You are joining her at the table by speaking."

We took a break. Al Tripodi quizzed me further out in the flagstone hall near the display case where faculty publications and awards sat on dusty glass shelves. I stared down at the dead bugs that had gotten stuck inside.

He could not understand how I could write those words.

"I hate him," I said.

"You're a beautiful girl."

Presented with this for the first time, I was unable to recognize something I would come up against time and time again. You could not be filled with hate and be beautiful. Like any girl, I wanted to be beautiful. But I *was* filled with hate. So how could I be both for Al Tripodi?

I told him about a dream I had over and over again those days. A daydream. Somehow, I wasn't sure how, I could get at the rapist and do anything to him that I wanted. I would do those things in my poem, I told Tripodi, and I would do worse.

"What is there to gain by that?" he asked me.

"Revenge," I said. "You don't understand."

"I guess I don't. I feel sorry for you."

I scrutinized the dead bugs on their backs, how their legs went out and then shot back in at sharp angles, how their antennae fell in stilled fragile arcs like lost human eyelashes. Tripodi could not see it because I didn't move a muscle, but my body was a wall of flames. I would not take pity, anybody's.

Maria Flores did not come back to class. I was infuriated. They just couldn't deal, I thought, and this made me angry. I knew I was not beautiful and in Gallagher's presence, for three hours that day, I didn't have to care about being beautiful. She, by writing that first line down, by workshopping the piece, had given me my permission slip—I could hate.

Exactly one week later, Gallagher's *If they caught you* would turn out to be all too prescient. On October 5, I ran into my rapist on the street. By the end of that night, I could stop calling him "the rapist," and start calling him Gregory Madison.

I had workshop that day with Tobias Wolff.

Wolff, whom I met the same day I did Gallagher, was a harder sell. He was a man, and at the time men had to surprise me before I even so much as thought about trusting them. He was not a performer. He made it clear that his personality was not the issue—fiction was. So I, who had decided to be a poet and had lucked into this fiction thing, took a wait-and-see attitude. I was the only sophomore in Wolff's class and the only one to wear weird clothes. The fiction writers wore a lot of starch and denim, shirts emblazoned with sports teams or upright plaids. Poets flowed. They did not, most certainly, wear shirts emblazoned with the logos of sports teams. I saw myself as a poet. Tobias Wolff, with his military posture and never indirect analysis of a story, was not my bag.

Before class I needed to get something to eat. I walked down to Marshall Street from Haven. I had been in Syracuse for a month and begun to make quick trips to Marshall Street, as everyone did, for snacks and school supplies. There was a mom-and-pop store that I liked. It was run by a Palestinian man in his sixties, who often told stories and who had an emphasis, when he said "Good day," that told me he meant it.

I was walking down the street when I saw, up ahead, a black man talking to a shady-looking white guy. The white guy stood in an alleyway and talked over the top of the fence. He had long brown hair, to his shoulders, and a few days' growth of beard. He wore a white T-shirt whose sleeves were rolled up to accentuate the small bellies of his biceps. The black guy I could see only from the back, but I was hyperaware. I went through my checklist: right height, right build, something in his posture, talking to a shady guy. Cross the street!

I did. I crossed the street and walked the rest of the way to the mom-and-pop store. I did not look back. I crossed the street again to walk directly into the store. Time slowed down here. I remember them ber things in the way one rarely does. I knew I had to go back outside and I tried to calm myself. Inside the store I chose a peach yogurt and a Teem soda—two items, if you knew me, that testified to my faltering composure. When the Palestinian man rang them up, he was brusque and hurried. There was no "Good day."

I left the store, crossed directly back to the safety of the other side of the street, and shot a quick glance over to the alleyway. Both men were gone. I also noticed a policeman to my right, on my side of the street. He was getting out of his patrol car. He was very tall, over six feet, and had bright, carrot-orange hair and a mustache. He seemed in no hurry. I assessed my surroundings and decided I was okay. It had been just a more intense version of the fear I had felt around certain black men ever since the rape. I checked my watch and quickened my step. I did not want to be late for Wolff's workshop.

Then, as if out of nowhere, I saw my rapist crossing toward me. He walked diagonally across the street from the other side. I did not stop walking. Or scream.

He was smiling as he approached. He recognized me. It was a stroll in the park to him; he had met an acquaintance on the street.

I knew him but I could not make myself speak. I needed all my energy to focus on believing I was not under his control again.

"Hey, girl," he said. "Don't I know you from somewhere?" He smirked at me, remembering.

I did not respond. I looked directly at him. Knew his face had been the face over me in the tunnel. Knew I had kissed those lips, stared into those eyes, smelled the crushed-berry smell on his skin.

I was too afraid to yell out. There was a cop behind me but I could not scream: "That's the man who raped me!" That happens in movies. I put one foot in front of the other. I heard him laughing behind me. But I was still walking.

He had no fear. It had been nearly six months since we'd seen each other last. Six months since I lay under him in a tunnel on top of a bed of broken glass. He was laughing because he had gotten away with it, because he had raped before me, and because he would rape again. My devastation was a pleasure for him. He was walking the streets, scot-free.

I turned the corner at the end of the block. Over my shoulder I saw him walking up to the redheaded policeman. He was shooting the breeze, so sure of his safety that he felt comfortable enough, right after seeing me, to tease a cop.

I never question why I went to tell Wolff I couldn't attend his class. It was my duty. I was his student. I was the only sophomore in the class.

I walked to the Hall of Languages at the top of the hill and checked my watch. I had time before Wolff's class to make two phone calls from the phone booth on the bottom floor. I called Ken Childs, told him what had happened, asked him to meet me at the library nearby in half an hour. I wanted to make a sketch of the rapist and Ken was in art school. Then, as soon as I hung up the phone, I called my parents collect.

They both got on the phone.

"Mom and Dad," I said, "I'm calling from the Hall of Languages."

My mother was attuned now to any waver in my voice.

"What is it, Alice?" she asked.

"I just saw him, Mom," I said.

"Saw who?" my father asked, as always two beats back.

"The rapist."

I don't remember their reaction. I couldn't. I was calling because I needed them to know, but, once I told them, I did not wait, I rushed at them with facts. "I'm going to tell Professor Wolff I can't come to class. I've called Ken Childs, he's meeting me to walk me home. I want to make a sketch."

"Call us when you get there," my mother said. I remember that. "Have you called the police?" my father asked.

I did not hesitate. "Not yet," I said, which meant to all of us that it was not a yes-or-no question. I would call them. I would pursue this.

I went up the stairs to where my workshop was held, and ran into Wolff as he was about to enter the English office.

The other students were filtering inside. I approached him. "Professor Wolff," I said, "can I talk to you?"

"It's class time, we'll talk after."

"I can't make it to class, that's what it's about."

I knew he would not be happy. I did not know how *not* happy he would be. He proceeded to tell me how lucky I was to be in the class, and that missing this one class was equivalent to missing three classes of a regular undergraduate course. All this I knew. All this had been why I walked blindly up to Humanities Hall instead of returning directly to my dorm.

I begged Wolff to give me just two minutes of his time. To talk to me in his office, not the hall. "Please," I said. Something in the way I said it called to that place inside him beyond the formal rules of the classroom, which I knew he valued. "Please," I said, and he responded—still it was a concession—with, "It will have to be brief."

I followed him down the short hall, turned the corner after him, and stood there while he unlocked the door. Looking back, I can't believe how calm I remained from the moment I saw my rapist on the street to that moment, inside Wolff's office, with the door closed. Now I was with a man I knew would not hurt me. For the first time, I thought it was safe to exhale. He sat facing me while I hovered over and then sat in the student chair.

I burst.

"I can't come to class. I just saw the man who raped me. I have to call the police."

I remember his face and I remember it vividly. He was a father. I knew this vaguely at the time. He had little boys. He came near me. He wanted to comfort, but then, instinctually, he pulled back. I was a rape victim; how would I interpret his touch? His face fell into the recesses reserved for the pure confusion one expresses when there is nothing on this earth that he or she can do to make something better.

He asked if he could make a call, if I had a way home, what, if anything, he could do. I told him I had called a friend who would meet me at the library and walk me home, where I would phone the police.

Wolff walked me back out into the hall. Before he let me go— my mind already working on putting one foot in front of the other, thinking of the phone call to the police, repeating over and over again in my head *maroon windbreaker, blue jeans rolled at cuffs, Converse All-Star sneakers*—Wolff stopped me and put both hands on my shoulders.

He looked at me and when it was clear to him that for that second he held my attention, he spoke.

"Alice," he said, "a lot of things are going to happen and this may not make much sense to you right now, but listen. Try, if you can, to remember everything."

I have to restrain myself from capitalizing the last two words. He meant them to be capitalized. He meant them to resound and to meet me sometime in the future on whatever path I chose. He had known me for two weeks. I was nineteen. I sat in his class and drew flowers on my jeans. I had written a story about sewing dummies that came to life and sought revenge on dressmakers.

So it was a shout across a great distance. He knew, as I was later to discover when I walked into Doubleday on Fifth Avenue in New York and bought *This Boy's Life*, Wolff's own story, that memory could save, that it had power, that it was often the only recourse of the powerless, the oppressed, or the brutalized.

The walk to the library, only two hundred yards across the front of the quad and on the other side of the street fronting the Hall of Languages, was a walk I made on automatic. I became a machine. I think it must be the way men patrol during wartime, completely attuned to movement or threat. The quad is not the quad but a battlefield where the enemy is alive and hiding. He waits to attack the moment you let your guard down. The answer—never let it down, not even for a second.

With every nerve ending pushing out against the edges of my skin, I reached Bird Library. Although I was still wary, I allowed myself to exhale here. I walked through the fluorescent light. It being still early in the semester, the library was not busy. The few people I passed, I did not look at. I didn't want to meet anyone's eyes.

I could not wait for Ken; I was too afraid to stop. I kept walking. Bird was constructed so that by walking through the building, I could exit on the other side of the block, no man's land. It was a street populated by old wood frame houses, many of them used by fraternities and sororities, but it was no longer the sanctified quad. The streetlights were fewer here and in the time it had taken me to walk from Marshall Street to tell Wolff I couldn't come to class, it had grown dark. I had only one goal: to get back to my dorm without injury and to write down everything he'd worn, to detail the features of his face.

I got there. I don't remember seeing anyone. If I did, I brushed by them without comment. Inside my small single, I called the police. I explained my situation. I had been raped in May, I said, I was now back on campus and had seen my assailant. Would they come?

Then I sat down on my bed and made a sketch. I had written out details. I started with his hair, went next to height, build, nose, eyes, mouth. Then there were comments on his face structure: "Short neck. Small but dense head. Boxy jawline. Hair slightly down in front." And his skin: "Pretty dark but not black black." At the bottom of the sheet, in the left-hand corner, I did a sketch of him and beside this noted his clothing: "Maroon jacket—windbreaker-style but with down. Jeans—blue. White sneakers."

Then Ken showed up. He was out of breath and nervous. He was a small, fragile man—the year before, I had romantically compared him to a pint-size David. So far, he had not shown much ability to handle my situation. Over the summer he had written once. He explained, and at the time I accepted it, that he had reinvented what had happened to me so it wouldn't hurt him as much. "I have decided it is like a broken leg and like a broken leg, it will heal."

Ken tried to improve on my sketch, but he was too nervous—his hands shook. He sat on my bed and looked very small to me, frightened. I decided he was a warm body who knew me, who meant well. That had to be enough. He made several attempts to draw the head of the rapist.

There were sounds in the hall. Walkie-talkies tuned to a self-important pitch, the sound of heavy footsteps. Fists thumped against the door and I answered them as girls came out into the hall.

Syracuse University Security. They had been alerted by the police. They were amped. This was the real shit. Two of them were quite wide and, in my tiny studio, their size was accentuated.

Within seconds, the Syracuse City Police arrived. Three of them. Someone shut the door. I relayed my story again and there was a slight squabble about jurisdiction. The SU Security seemed personally disappointed that since the original incident had happened in Thorden Park and the sighting was on Marshall Street, it was clearly a City of Syracuse matter and not a campus one. On a professional level, this reflected well on them, but they were not as much university representatives that night as they were hunters with a fresh scent.

The police looked at my sketches and Ken's. They repeatedly referred to Ken as my boyfriend, though I corrected them each time. They eyed him suspiciously. In his slight physique and nervousness, he stood out as a freak in a room populated by large men armed with guns and billy clubs.

"How long ago did you see the suspect?"

I told them.

They decided there was still some chance, since I hadn't acknowledged him, that the rapist would be loitering in the area of Marshall Street. It was worth a ride in a squad car.

Two of the city police took my sketch, leaving Ken's behind. "We'll make copies of this and send out an APB. Every man in the city will keep this in his car until we find him," one said.

As we readied to leave, Ken asked, "Do you need me to come?" The looks from the police must have burned into him. He came.

With six men in uniform escorting us, we left the building. Ken and I got in the back of a squad car with one officer in the front. I don't remember this man's name, but I remember his anger.

"We're gonna get this puke," he said. "Rape is one of the worst crimes. He'll pay."

He started the engine and turned on the red-and-blue flashing lights of his squad car. We roared down to Marshall Street, only a few blocks away.

"Look carefully," the officer said. He maneuvered his squad car with a manhandling agility I would later recognize in New York cabbies.

Ken was slumping down in the seat beside me. He said the flashing lights hurt his head. He shielded his eyes. I looked out. While we drove up and around Marshall Street a few times, the officer told me about his seventeen-year-old niece, just an innocent girl. She had been gang-raped. "Ruined," he said. "Ruined." He had his billy club out. He started smacking the empty seat with it. Ken winced each time it hit the vinyl. Having thought this mission was probably futile from the start, I began to be afraid of what this policeman might do.

I saw no rapist. I said this. I suggested leaving, looking at mug shots down at the station. But this officer wanted release and he was going to get it. He braked hard on the final pass down Marshall Street.

"There, *there*," he said. "What about those three?"

I looked and knew immediately. Three black students. You could tell by the way they were dressed. They were also tall, too tall to be my rapist.

"No," I said. "Let's just go."

"They're troublemakers," he said. "You stay here."

He got out of the squad car in a hurry and chased after them. He had his billy club in his hand.

Ken began to suffer some version of the panic I was familiar with from my mother. His breathing was labored. He wanted to get out.

"What's he going to do?" he said. He tried the door. It had

111

been locked automatically. This was where criminals as well as victims rode.

"I don't know. Those guys aren't even close."

The lights were still flashing overhead. People began to come up to the car to stare in. I was mad at this policeman for leaving us there. I was mad at Ken for being a wimp. I knew no good would come of an angry man, speeding on adrenaline, looking for revenge for his raped niece. I was in the center of it all and simultaneously I realized I didn't exist. I was just a catalyst that made people nervous, guilty, or furious. I was frightened, but more than anything, I was disgusted. I wanted the policeman to come back and I sat in the car with Ken whimpering beside me, put my head between my knees so the people on the outside of the car looking in would be met with "the back of the victim," and I listened for the sounds I knew were taking place in the alley. Someone was being beaten, I knew that as surely as I knew anything. It was not Him.

The officer returned. He swooped into the driver's side and laid his billy club firmly against the palm of his hand.

"That'll teach 'em," he said. He was sweating, exhilarated.

"What did they do?" Ken ventured. He was horrified.

"Open container. Never talk back to an officer."

I did not overlook what happened on Marshall Street that night. *Everything* was wrong. It was wrong that I couldn't walk through a park at night. It was wrong that I was raped. It was wrong that my rapist assumed he was untouchable or that as a Syracuse coed I was most certainly treated better by the police. It was wrong that the niece of that officer was raped. It was wrong of him to call her ruined. It was wrong to put the lights on and strut that car down Marshall. It was wrong to hassle, and perhaps physically hurt, three innocent young black men on the street.

There is no *but*, there is only this: That officer lived on my planet. I fit into his world in the way I never again would fit into Ken's. I can't remember whether Ken asked to be dropped at home or whether he came with me to the station. Whatever the case, I shut him off after the search on Marshall Street.

* * *

We reached the Public Safety Building. It was now after eight. I had not been back to the station since the night of the attack, but that night, the police station felt safe to me. I loved the way the elevators let out onto a waiting area at the end of which was a huge door that locked, automatically, behind us. Through the bulletproof glass you could see out into the lobby but no one could get at you.

The officer led me in and I heard the smooth, hydraulic hush and firm click of the door behind us. To our left was the dispatcher sitting at the command center. There were three or four uniformed men standing nearby. Some held coffee mugs. When we entered, they quieted down and stared at the ground. There were only two kinds of civilians: victims and criminals.

My officer explained to the man at the front desk that I was the rape case out of the East Zone. I was there to look at mug shots.

He set me up in a small file room across from the dispatcher. He left the door open and began to pull large black binders off the surrounding shelves. There were at least five such binders and each was filled with small, wallet-size mug shots. These five books were of black males only, and only those near the age that I thought my rapist would be.

The room seemed more a storage area for these books than a place for victims to sit and pore over the photos. The only surface was an old metal typing table, and I had difficulty balancing the books in my lap and on the rickety table, whose flyleaf kept collapsing under the weight. But I was a good student, when I needed to be, and I studied those books page by page. I saw six photos that reminded me of my rapist, but I was beginning to believe the process of mug shots would turn out to be fruitless.

One of the officers brought me some weak but still-hot coffee. It was an island of comfort in an otherwise alien environment.

"How you doing? See anything?" he asked.

"No," I said, "they all just blur together. I don't think he's here."

"Keep trying. He's fresh in your mind."

I was coming to the end of Book 4 when the call came in.

"POP Clapper just called in," the dispatcher called over to my officer. "He knows your man."

The officer left me in the room and went out to the front desk. The uniforms who'd been waiting for assignment surrounded him. I listened to the Abbott and Costello—like routine that followed.

"Says it's Madison," the dispatcher said.

"Which Madison?" asked my officer. "Mark?"

"No," said another, "he's up on a charge already."

"Frank?"

"No, Hanfy tagged him last week. It must be Greg."

"I thought he was already in."

And so it went. I remember one of the men said something about pitying Old Man Madison—how it was hard raising sons alone.

Then my officer returned. "I've got some questions to ask you," he said. "Are you ready?"

"Yes."

"Describe again that policeman you saw."

I did.

"And where did you see his car?"

I said he'd parked in the Huntington Hall lot.

"Bingo," he said. "It looks like we may have our man."

He left again and I closed the mug book lying open on the typing table. All of a sudden, I didn't know what to do with my hands. They were shaking. I placed them under my legs and sat on them. I started to cry.

A few minutes later I heard the dispatcher say, "Here he is!" and those inside the locked door cheered.

I stood up and frantically searched the room for a place to hide. I chose the corner that shared the wall with the door. My face was pressed up against the metal shelving that held the mug books for years past.

"Great work, Clapper!" someone said, and the air rushed out of me. Could it just be the officer, without my rapist in tow?

"We'll get a statement from the victim and then make out the warrant for an arrest," someone said.

Yes, I was safe. But I still didn't know what to do. I wasn't able to join them. I was a victim, not really a person. I sat back down in the typing chair.

The men outside were happy. Slapping backs and teasing Officer Clapper for his red hair. He was a "beanpole," a "carrottop," and "young stuff."

He ducked his head in the room.

"Hi, Alice," he said. "Remember me?"

I smiled ear to ear. "Yes, I do."

The men outside roared.

"Remember you? How could she forget you? You're the next best thing to Santy Claus!"

Things settled down. A call came in. Two of the men left to respond. Officer Clapper had to go write up a report. My officer brought me back into the room where I had met Sergeant Lorenz three days short of exactly six months before. He took my affidavit, quoting heavily from the detailed description I had written down.

"Are you ready for this?" the officer asked me at the end of the affidavit. "We'll arrest. You have to be willing to testify."

"I am," I said.

I was driven back to Haven Hall in an unmarked car. I called my parents and told them I was fine. The officer filed his final report on case F-362 before it was transferred back to Sergeant Lorenz.

Rape 1st
Sodomy 1st
Robbery 1st

While I was still in the CID Office with the victim the Gen Mess. was broadcast and immediately upon the broadcast there was a response from Car #561 P.O.P. Clapper, who stated that he had spoken to a person who fit the rape suspect's description at approx 1827 hrs on Marshall St. He informed me that the person whom he had spoken to was one Gregory Madison. Madison has a record and has done time in Prison. A photo line-up was to be conducted in CID Office by P.O.P. Clapper but there was no negative. It is almost certain that the suspect in question is Gregory Madison. An affidavit was taken from the victim and P.O.P. Clapper. Arrest is imminent.

Description broadcast to both 3rd and 1st shift coming on. If located observe and ask for assistance. Suspect considered armed and dangerous.

That night I had a dream. Al Tripodi was in it. In a prison cell, he and two other men held my rapist down. I began to perform acts of revenge on the rapist but to no avail. He wrested loose from Tripodi's grasp and came at me. I saw his eyes as I had seen them in the tunnel. Close up.

I woke screaming and held myself upright in my damp sheets. I looked at the phone. It was 3:00 A.M. I couldn't call my mother. I tried to sleep again. I had found him. Again, it would be just the two of us. I thought of the last lines in the poem I had turned in to Gallagher.

Come die and lie, beside me.

I had issued an invitation. In my mind, the rapist had murdered me on the day of the rape. Now I was going to murder him back. Make my hate large and whole.

EIGHT

In the first month at school, I had kept largely to myself, focusing intently on my two writing workshops. I called Mary Alice the day after seeing the rapist on the street and told her about it. She was thrilled but frightened for me. She was also busy. She, Tree, and Diane were rushing sororities. She had her sights set on Alpha Chi Omega. It was a sorority for good girls who were both athletic and academic. It was all white. Mary Alice was a shoo-in.

Her pursuit of such things, despite the running cynical commentary she provided on the rituals and idiocies of the rush process, divided us. I did not spend day-to-day time with her.

Tentatively, I made one new friendship. Her name was Lila and she came from Massachusetts by way of Georgia. But unlike my mother, who approved of all things Southern, Lila had no accent. They had drummed it out of her, she said, when she enrolled in high school in Massachusetts. To my ear, she'd done a fine job. My mother swore any Southerner would know better, could pick up the slight lilt and drawl in her words.

She lived on my hall at Haven, six doors down. She was blond and we both wore glasses. We were the same size, that is to say, slightly overweight. She considered herself a grind, a "social retard." I saw it as my duty to draw her out. I could sense she had a zany side. Lila was also, as Mary Alice still was, a virgin.

Lila was a perfect audience of one. Unlike my pairing with Mary Alice, I was not the oddball sidekick of the popular girl. I was the slightly thinner one, the louder one, the braver one.

One night I told her she needed to find her inner animal and said, "Watch me!" I took a box of raisins and stabbed it with a knife, grimacing and mugging for the camera she held. I made her switch places and stab the raisins. In the pictures from that day, I mean it. I'm after those raisins. Lila couldn't quite get into the role I'd made for her. Her blade is poised delicately over the already perforated box. Her eyes are sweet and her face a schoolgirl trying her best to appear passionately dismayed.

We specialized in getting the giggles. I anticipated her scheduled study breaks and tried to cajole her into making them longer, making them arc over a whole evening in my room, where, in laughing with her, I wouldn't have to think about anything outside.

On October 14, I was on campus. Downtown, Investigator Lorenz called Assistant District Attorney Gail Uebelhoer, who had been assigned to review the case prior to presentation to the judge for warrants. ADA Uebelhoer wasn't in. Investigator Lorenz left a message.

"Gregory Madison was arrested at two P.M."

I made the papers for the second time. VICTIM POINTS FINGER was the headline for the small, five-paragraph item in the *Syracuse Post-Standard* of October 15. Tricia, from the Rape Crisis Center, mailed this to me, as she would all subsequent articles.

A preliminary hearing was scheduled for October 19 at Syracuse City Court. The defendant was Gregory Madison, the plaintiff the People of the State of New York. It was a hearing held to determine if there was enough evidence in the case to support a grand jury. I was told that witnesses being called might range from the medical doctors who had completed the serology report the night of my rape, to Officer Clapper, who had seen Madison on the street. I would testify. So might Madison.

I needed someone to go with me to the hearing, but Mary Alice was busy, and Ken Childs was obviously not the right choice. Lila was my new friend; I didn't want to ruin that. I approached Tess Gallagher and asked her if she'd come. "I'm honored," Gallagher said. "We'll have lunch in a good restaurant. My treat."

I don't remember what I wore, only that Gallagher, who was

known on campus for flamboyant dress and just the right hat, wore a tailored suit and sensible shoes. Seeing her hemmed in this way, literally, made me know she had prepped for battle. She knew how the outside world judged poets. I know I wore something appropriate. In the halls of the courthouse we looked like what we were: a coed and her youthful mother figure.

My greatest fear was the possibility of seeing Gregory Madison. Tess and I walked through the halls of the Onondaga County Courthouse with a detective from the Public Safety Building. He was meant to guide us to the correct courtroom, where I would meet the attorney chosen to represent the State. But I had to use the ladies' room and he had only a vague idea where it was. Tess and I went off in search of it.

The old part of the courthouse was marble. Tess's low heels clicked against this in a staccato beat. We finally found the bathroom, where, fully clothed, I sat in a stall and stared at the wooden door in front of me. I was alone, however briefly, and I tried to calm down. The walk from the Public Safety Building and into the courthouse had left my heart in my throat. I had heard the phrase before but now I literally felt as if something thick and vital were jammed in my throat and thumping. Blood rushed to my brain and I put my head down, trying not to heave.

When I emerged I was pale. I did not want to look at myself in the mirror. I looked at Tess instead. I watched her readjust two decorative combs on either side of her head.

"There," she said, happy with the way they set. "Ready?"

I looked at her and she winked back at me.

Tricia was standing with the detective when we returned. Tricia and Tess were a study in opposites. Tricia, who represented the Rape Crisis Center and signed her notes to me "In sisterhood," was the one I didn't quite trust. Tess was my first experience of a woman who had inhabited her weirdness, moved into the areas of herself that made her distinct from those around her, and learned how to display them proudly. Tricia was too interested in drawing me out. She wanted me to *feel*. I didn't see how feeling was going to do me any good. Onondaga County Courthouse was not a place to open up. It was a place to hold fast to what I knew to be the truth. I had to work at keeping every fact alive and available. What Tess had was mettle. I needed this more than an anonymous sisterhood; I told Tricia she could go.

Tess and I sat on a wooden bench outside the courtroom. It reminded me of the benches in the closed-in pews at St. Peter's. We waited for what seemed like hours. Tess told me stories about growing up in Washington State, about the logging industry, about fishing, and about her partner, Raymond Carver. My hands were sweating. I had a short bout of uncontrollable shaking. I heard less than half of the words Tess said. I think she knew this. She wasn't actually speaking to me, she was singing a kind of lullaby of talk. But, eventually, the lullaby stopped.

She was irritated. Looked at her watch. She knew she couldn't do anything. A diva on campus and in the poetry world, she was just a small woman with no power now. She had to wait it out with me. Our lunch treat seemed very far away.

Since that day, if I am made to wait long enough for something I dread, my nervousness dissipates into a steely boredom. It is a mind-set and it goes like this: If hell is inevitable, I enter what I call trauma Zen.

So by the time ADA Ryan, assigned to the case that day because ADA Uebelhoer was in court with another matter, walked up to introduce himself, Tess was silent and I was staring at the elevator six feet away.

Ryan was a young man in his late twenties or early thirties. He had reddish-brown hair in need of a comb. He wore a sort of nubby sport coat with suede elbow patches, which seemed more in place on the campus I'd just left than inside a courtroom.

He called Tess "Mrs. Sebold," and, after being corrected and informed that she was one of my professors, he grew flustered. He was embarrassed and impressed. He stole little looks at her, trying both to include her and figure her out at the same time.

"What do you teach?" he asked her.

"Poetry," she said.

"Are you a poet?"

"Yes, actually," Tess said. "What do you have for our girl here?" she asked. I wouldn't understand it until later, but the ADA was flirting with Tess and she, swiftly and with a skill developed from experience, deflected him.

"First up, Alice," he said to me, "you'll be happy to know that the defendant has waived his right to appear."

"What does that mean?"

"It means that his attorney has agreed not to contest identification."

"Is that good?"

"Yes. But you still have to answer any questions his attorney has."

"I understand," I said.

"We're here to prove it was a rape. That the act with the suspect was not consensual but forcible. Understand?"

"Yes. Can Tess come with me?"

"Quietly. Don't speak once you walk through that door. The professor will slip into one of the seats in the back near the bailiff. You'll approach the stand and I'll take it from there."

He went into the courtroom doors to our right. Across from us, a group of people got off the elevator and started walking toward us. One man, in particular, took a good, long look at both of us. This was the defense attorney, Mr. Meggesto.

A while later, a bailiff opened the door of the courtroom.

"We are ready for you, Miss Sebold."

Tess and I did as Mr. Ryan had instructed. I walked to the front of the courtroom. I could hear papers shuffling and someone clearing his throat. I stepped into the witness stand and turned around.

There were only a few people in the room and only two rows near the back, which composed a gallery. I saw Tess to my right. I looked at her once. She gave me a "go get 'em" smile. I didn't look her way again.

Mr. Ryan approached me and established my name, age, address, and other vitals. This gave me time to adjust to the sound of the court reporter's machine and to the idea that all of this was being written down. What happened to me in that tunnel was now something I would not only have to say aloud, but that others would sit and read and reread.

After asking a few questions about how the light was that night and where the rape took place, he asked me the question he had warned me I would have to answer.

"Can you tell us in your own words what happened at that time?"

I tried to take my time. Ryan frequently interrupted my account. He asked about the lighting again, whether there was a moon out, whether I struggled. He wanted details of whether blows struck were open-handed or close-fisted, asked whether I feared for my life, and questioned me about how much money the rapist had taken from me, and whether I had given it willingly or not.

After I described the fight outside the tunnel, his questions turned to the events inside the amphitheater.

"Describe to me, from the time he took you into the theater, what force he used and what you did prior to the act of sexual intercourse that occurred."

"First he brought me up to his face with his hands around my neck and kissed me a couple of times and then said to take my clothes off. He tried to take my clothes off first. He couldn't get my belt undone. He told me to do it and I did."

"When he told you to take your clothes off, was that before or after he told you he would kill you if you didn't do what he told you?"

"After—and I was bleeding at the time—my face wasn't in the best of shape."

"You were bleeding?"

"Yes."

"From falling down?"

"From falling down and him hitting me and smashing my face."

"Prior to the act of sexual intercourse you described, he struck you?"

"Umm-hmm."

"Where did he strike you?"

"In the face. I couldn't breathe for a while. He kept his hands around my neck, he scratched my face. Also, he just generally punched me around when I was on the ground and he was sitting on me to keep me from going anywhere."

"All right," Ryan said, "and after this you mentioned he was having some difficulty having an erection for some period of time, is that right?"

"Umm-hmm." I had forgotten the instructions from the judge. I was supposed to clearly enunciate a yes or a no.

"What happened after that?"

"He wasn't able to have an erection. I didn't really know if he had or not—I'm not familiar with that. But, then, before he came into me and had intercourse, he stopped once and made me get on my knees and he was standing up and he told me to give him a blow job."

"Did there come a time after this you eventually did get away from him?"

"Yes."

"How did that come about?"

"After he did come in me, he got me up off the ground and started dressing and found some of my clothes and gave them to me and I put those on, and he said, 'You're going to have a baby, bitch—what are you going to do about it?'"

I detailed how the rapist hugged me, apologized, then let me go, only to call after me.

Ryan paused. His next few questions were my only rest period. What was taken from me during the incident? What was the rapist wearing? His size? His appearance?

"I don't recall whether you mentioned whether he was white or black," Ryan said before closing.

"He was black," I said.

"That is all, Your Honor."

Ryan turned to sit down. The judge called, "Cross," and Mr. Meggesto stood and approached.

Both defense attorneys who represented Madison over the

course of the year shared certain traits. They were shortish, balding, and had something fetid going on on their upper lips. Whether it was an unkempt mustache as in Meggesto's case, or grainy beads of sweat, it was an ugliness I focused on as each one cross-examined me.

I felt if I was going to win, I had to hate the attorneys representing him. They may have been earning a paycheck, or randomly assigned to the case, had children they loved or a terminally ill mother to take care of. I didn't care. They were there to destroy me. I was there to fight back.

"Is it Miss *See*-bold—is that the way it is pronounced?"

"Yes."

"Miss Sebold, you said you were at 321 Westcott Street on the night of the incident?"

"Umm-hmm."

The tone of his voice was condemning, as if I had been a bad little girl and told a lie.

"How long had you been there on this evening?"

"From approximately eight to midnight."

"Did you have anything to drink while there?"

"I had nothing at all to drink."

"Did you have anything to smoke while you were there?"

"Nothing at all to smoke."

"Did you have any cigarettes?"

"No."

"You didn't smoke that evening?"

"No."

"You had nothing to drink that evening?"

"No."

That tack not having worked, he moved on to his next.

"How long have you worn glasses?"

"Since I was in the third grade."

"Do you know what your vision is without glasses?"

"I am nearsighted and can see very well close up. I don't know exactly, but it isn't that bad. I can see road signs and such."

"Do you have a driver's license?"

124

"Yes, I do."

"Do you need your license?"

"Yes, I do."

"You maintain your driver's license?"

"Yes."

I didn't know what he was doing. It made sense to me that he might ask if my license required me to wear corrective lenses. But he didn't. Was I a better or worse person with a license? Was I firmly an adult and not a child, making it less a crime to rape me? I never figured out his reasoning.

He continued.

"Is it a fair statement to say you wear your glasses all the time to be able to see?"

"No."

"When don't you wear them?"

"When I'm reading, and basically when I am just doing most anything."

How could I explain, on the stand, a battle I had had with my eye doctor? He said I wore my glasses more than I needed to. That in my desire to be so clued in, I was ruining my vision and making my eyes, as they are now, dependent on corrective lenses.

"Did you think you needed your glasses on this evening in October?"

He meant May, but no one corrected him.

"It was night, yes."

"Do you see poorer at night?"

"No, I don't."

"Was there any special reason you brought your glasses?"

"No."

"Is it a fair statement to say you wear your glasses when you leave the dorm all the time?"

"No."

"Was there any special reason you wore your glasses that evening?"

"Probably because they were a week old and I liked them. They were new."

He jumped on this: "New prescription or just new design of frame?"

"Just new design of frame."

"Prescription the same?"

"Yes."

"Prescribed by whom?"

"Dr. Kent of Philadelphia, near my home."

"Do you recall where these—do you recall when that was?"

"December 1980, I think, was my last prescription."

"Prescribed and made in 1980, is that correct?"

Could he know that he was making his point and losing it simultaneously? That my prescription had been updated six months before the rape. I didn't know what he was doing but I was going to follow him at every turn. He wanted to back me into a maze I couldn't get out of. I was determined. I felt I had what Gallagher had—mettle. I could feel it in my veins.

"Umm-hmm," I said.

"And I believe you say that, at some point during this struggle, your glasses were knocked from you, is that correct?"

"Yes."

"It was a dark area, is that correct?"

"Yes."

"How dark would you say it was?"

"Not that dark. It was light enough so I could see physical features—face, plus the fact that his face was very close to mine and since I am nearsighted and not farsighted, my vision is good up close."

He turned to the side and looked up a moment. For a second, adrenaline pumping in my veins, I watched the court. Everyone was still. This was business as usual to them. Another prelim on another rape case. Ho hum.

"I believe you said at some point this individual kissed you?"

He was good, sweaty lip, bad mustache, and all. He went, with a keen, deft precision, right to my heart. The kissing hurts still. The fact that it was only under my rapist's orders that I kissed back often seems not to matter. The intimacy of it stings.

Since then I've always thought that under *rape* in the dictionary it should tell the truth. It is not just forcible intercourse; rape means to inhabit and destroy everything.

"Yes," I said.

"When you say, 'kissed you,' do you mean on the mouth?"

"Yes."

"Were you both standing?"

"Yes."

"In relation to your height, how tall was the individual?"

He chose the kiss to lead me to the rapist's height.

"Approximately the same height or an inch above," I said.

"How tall are you, Miss Sebold?"

"Five, five and a half."

"You would say this individual was probably the same height or maybe an inch taller?"

"Umm-hmm."

"When you were standing there, looking at him, he looked to be about the same height, is that correct?"

"Umm-hmm."

"Just about that?"

"Yes."

His tone, since questioning my vision, had changed. There was now not even a trace of respect in it. Seeing that he had not yet gotten the best of me, he had switched into a sort of hateful overdrive. I felt threatened by him. Even though, by all measures, I was safe in that courtroom and surrounded by professionals, I was afraid.

"I believe you testified that the description you gave on that night indicated he was of a muscular build?"

"Yes."

"Short and had short black hair?"

"Yes."

"Do you remember telling the police, when you made your voluntary affidavit, you thought he was about one hundred and fifty pounds?"

"Yes."

"Is that your best estimate as to the weight of this individual?"

"I am really not very good with weight," I said. "I don't know the ratio of muscle or fat in someone's body."

"You do recall telling him it was one hundred and fifty pounds?"

"The police officers gave me an estimation of what they might weigh, a man, and I said, yes, that looked approximately correct."

"Are you saying you were influenced by what the police officer told you?"

"No, he was just giving me an example to follow. It seemed approximately close."

"Based on what the police officer gave you and your physical observation, is your testimony on May eighth your best estimate of the weight of this individual is one hundred and fifty pounds?"

"Yes."

"Have you heard anything that would change your mind at this point?"

"No."

His energy zoomed. He looked just like a boy who is savoring the last bite of cake. Mr. Meggesto had gotten something back after losing on vision, but I didn't know what.

I was tired now. I was doing my best, but I felt my energy drain. I had to get it back.

"I believe you say you were struck in the face a number of times?"

"Yes."

"And that you were bleeding?"

"Yes."

"And your glasses had been knocked from you?"

In hindsight I wish I had the wherewithal to say, "None of this made me blind."

"Yes," I said.

"Did you seek any medical attention for your injuries?"

"Yes."

"When was that?"

"The same night right after I got back to the dorm, and before I arrived at the police station—I reported to the police. The police brought me to Crouse Irving Memorial Hospital and I went to the lab, where they prescribed medication for my facial cuts."

I would try and stay steady. I would give the facts.

"Were you able to find your glasses on the night of this incident?"

"The police found the glasses—"

He interrupted me.

"You didn't have them when you left the area? You did not leave with your glasses?"

"Right."

"Anything else you remember?"

"No."

I felt hushed by him now. The gloves were off.

"Can you tell me briefly what you were wearing on the night of October fifth?"

Mr. Ryan stood and corrected the date. "May eighth."

"On May eighth," Mr. Meggesto rephrased, "tell me what you were wearing."

"Calvin Klein jeans, blue work shirt, heavy beige cable-knit cardigan sweater, moccasins, and underwear." I hated this question. Knew, even on that stand, what it was all about.

"Was that cardigan sweater one that pulled on or buttoned up the front?"

"Buttons up the front."

"You didn't have to take it over your head to get it off? Is that correct?"

"Right."

I was seething. I had gotten my energy back because what my clothes had to do with why or how I was raped seemed obvious: nothing.

"I believe you testified this individual attempted to disrobe you and, failing that, ordered you to do so?"

"Right, I had a belt on. He couldn't work the belt correctly from the opposite side of me. He said, 'You do it,' so I did."

"This was the belt holding up your Calvin Klein jeans?"

He emphasized "Calvin Klein" with a sneer I was unprepared for. It had come to this.

"Yes."

"He was facing you?"

"Yes."

"Your testimony was he wasn't able to work the clasp, whatever the gimmick was, that closed that belt?"

"Umm-hmm."

"You did it on his orders?"

"Yes."

Now it was his turn to take a point. He questioned me on the rapist's knife. I had seen it only in the photos of the crime scene and in my mind's eye. I admitted to Meggesto that, though the rapist had threatened me and made gestures to retrieve it from his back pocket, because of the struggle on my part, I had never seen it.

"Is it a fair statement to say you were very frightened by all this?" Meggesto asked, moving on.

"Yes."

"When did you first become frightened?"

"As soon as I heard footsteps behind me."

"Did your pulse beat increase?"

"I imagine some, yes," I said. I didn't understand why he was asking me this.

"Do you recall?"

"No, I don't recall if my pulse beat increased."

"Do you recall becoming scared and breathing short and fast?"

"I recall becoming scared, and whatever physical things come from that, I probably had them, but I wasn't hyperventilating or anything like that."

"Do you remember anything else other than being scared?"

"Mental state?" I thought I'd say it since that's what I thought he was driving at.

"No," he said, "I mean physically. Do you remember how your body acted when you were frightened? Did you tremble, increase in pulse rate, have any change in breathing?"

"No, I don't remember any specific changes except for the fact that I was screaming. I did keep telling the rapist that I was going to vomit, because my mother gave me articles that said if you say you are going to vomit, they won't rape you."

"That was a ruse to use on this individual and might scare him off?"

"Yes."

"Did you ever learn the identity of this individual?"

"Exactly what time or—"

"Did you ever learn the identity of this individual?"

"By me, no." I wasn't quite sure of what he was asking. Interpreted him to be asking if I knew Madison's name back in May.

"Well, did you ever see this individual prior to May of 1981?"

"No."

"Did you ever see this individual after May of 1981?"

"Yes, I saw him in October."

"Did you ever see this individual between May and October of 1981?"

"No."

"Never did?"

"No."

"When did you see him after May of 1981?"

I told him of the incident on October 5. I detailed the time, location, and my sighting, at the same time, of the redheaded policeman who had turned out to be Officer Clapper. I told him I had called the police and had come back to the Public Safety Building to give a description of the rapist.

"You gave a description to whom?" he asked.

Mr. Ryan objected. "I think we have gone outside the scope of direct examination," he said. "Anything further would be for a Wade Hearing."

I had no idea what that was. The three men, Mr. Ryan, Mr. Meggesto, and Judge Anderson, debated what had been stipulated prior to the preliminary. They reached an agreement. Mr. Meggesto could continue concerning the arrest of the individual. But the judge warned that he was "going into it"—the issue of

identification. The judge's last words recorded in the transcript are "Come on." Even now I hear the fatigue in them. His major motivation, I feel certain, was to wrap it up and get to lunch.

Frantic, because I had not understood the decision or even, frankly, what the hell they had been talking about, I tried to focus back on Mr. Meggesto. Whatever was said, it gave him permission to attack again.

"After you crossed the street and went to Huntington Hall, did you ever see this individual again?"

"No."

"Were you shown any photographs?"

"No." At the time I didn't know that there was no photo lineup in my case because a mug shot of Gregory Madison did not exist.

"Ever taken to a lineup?"

"No."

"You came there and made an identification at the police station?"

"Yes."

"That is after you called your mother?"

"Yes."

"And after that you were informed someone was arrested?"

"I wasn't informed that night. I was informed, I think it was this Thursday morning, by Officer Lorenz."

"So, you didn't know of your own knowledge whether or not the individual that you saw on October fifth was the individual that was arrested?"

"There was no way I could know that unless the police who arrested him—"

"The question is, yes or no, do you know whether or not the individual—"

This time when he cut me off, it made me mad.

"As they described the man, it was the man they arrested—"

"Question is, do you know?"

"I haven't seen him since he was arrested."

"You didn't see him."

132

"The man I described on the eighth of May and the individual on October fifth is the man that raped me."

"That is your testimony, you believe the man you saw on October fifth—"

"I *know* the man I saw on October fifth is the man that raped me."

"The man you say is the man who raped you is the same man you saw on October fifth?"

"Right."

"But you don't know whether that man was arrested?"

"Well, I didn't arrest him, how would I know?"

"That is my question—you don't know?"

"All right, I don't know, then." What else could I say? He had proven, very dramatically, that I was not a member of the Syracuse Police Department.

Mr. Meggesto turned to the judge. "I don't think I have anything further," he said.

But he wasn't done. I stayed in the witness stand while the judge listened, and then debated, the point of identification with him. It turned out that Ryan's purpose had been to have Madison in the court, that by Madison's having waived his right to appear, all Ryan now had to prove was that a rape had taken place on May eighth and that I had identified a man I believed to be my assailant. There was confusion. Ryan believed that in Madison waiving his right to appear, Meggesto had forfeited the question of identification. That was not Meggesto's understanding.

"Held for action of the grand jury," the judge said finally. He was tired. I concluded from the movements of Ryan and Meggesto—they were closing up their briefcases—that I was done.

Tess and I went to lunch. We had Upstate New York food—cheese fries, that sort of thing. We sat in a restaurant booth and the smell of the grease from the kitchen filled the air. She talked. She filled the time with talk. I stared up at the lush restaurant philodendrons that adorned and softened the high shelves separating each booth. I was exhausted. Now I wonder if Tess was

133

silently asking the question I do when I reread the transcripts from that day. Where were my parents?

I want to give them an excuse. Perhaps they don't need one. At the time I felt that since it had been my decision to return to Syracuse, the outcome of this—that I had indeed run into my rapist again—was left to me. Now I'm tempted to make all the excuses available to them. My mother didn't fly. My father was teaching. Et cetera. But there was time. My mother could have driven up. My father could have canceled his classes for one day. But I was nineteen and ornery. I was afraid of their comfort, that to feel anything was to feel weak.

I called from the restaurant and told my mother the judge's decision. She was happy I had Tess with me, asked questions about when the grand jury would be held, and fretted about the lineup—any close proximity to him. She had been nervous all day, waiting for the phone to ring. I was glad to bring her good news—it was the closest I could get to straight *A*'s.

I was taking a normal course load in school. Of the five classes two were writing workshops but three were requirements. Tess's survery course. A foreign language. Classics in translation.

In the Classics class I was bored stiff. The teacher spoke less than he intoned and this, combined with the shabby, much-used textbook, made the class seem like an hour of death every other day. But in the midst of this teacher's droning on, I started to read. Catullus. Sappho. Apollonius. And *Lysistrata*, a play by Aristophanes in which the women of Athens and Sparta rebel—until the men of both nation-states agree to make peace, these women of warring cities unite in a boycott of all marital relations. Aristophanes wrote this in 411 B.C. but it translated beautifully. Our teacher insisted that it was low comedy but in its hidden message—the power of women united—the play was very important to me.

Ten days after the preliminary hearing, I returned home to my dorm after the Italian 101 class I appeared to be failing. I could not speak the words out loud the way we were required to. I sat in the back of the classroom and couldn't keep my mind on the conjugations. When I was called on, I butchered some form of what I was convinced might be a word but which the professor had trouble recognizing. Under my door at Haven, someone had slid an envelope. It was from the office of the district attorney. I was being subpoenaed to testify before the grand jury on November 4 at 2:00 P.M.

I was supposed to go down to Marshall Street with Lila after she got back from class. While I waited, I called the DA's office. Gail Uebelhoer, who would represent me, wasn't in. I had the office assistant say her name a few times slowly. I wanted to get it right. I still have the piece of paper where I wrote down, phonetically, how to say it. "You-bel-air or E-belle-air." I practiced saying it in front of the mirror, trying to make it sound natural. "Hello, Ms. You-bel-air, it's Alice Sebold from State versus Gregory Madison." "Hello, Ms. E-belle-air . . ." I worked on it. I put Italian aside.

NINE

On the morning of November 4, a county car met me at Haven Hall. I watched for it through the glass walls of the dorm's entranceway. Students had already attended breakfast in the cafeteria upstairs and gathered their books to leave for classes.

I had been up since five. I tried to linger over the rituals of hygiene. I took a long shower in the bathroom down the hall. I moisturized my face as Mary Alice had taught me to do the year before. I selected and pressed my clothes. My body alternated between stony chills and hot flashes of nerves centered near my chest. I was aware that this might be the kind of panic that ruled my mother. I swore I would not allow it to rule me.

I left the glass-walled foyer and met the detective as he was coming in. I engaged his eyes. I shook his hand.

"I'm Alice Sebold," I said.

"Right on time."

"It's hard to oversleep on a day like this," I said. I was sunny, cheery, reliable. I wore an oxford-cloth shirt and a skirt. On my feet I wore my Pappagallo pumps. I had fretted that morning because I could not find nude hose. I had black and I had red, neither of which was an appropriate choice for the virgin coed the grand jury would expect. I borrowed a pair from my resident advisor.

In the county car, marked with the seal of Onondaga on the front doors, I rode in the front beside the detective. We made small talk about the university. He talked sports teams, which I knew nothing about, and projected that the Carrier Dome, little over a year old, would bring a lot of revenue to the area. I nodded my head and tried to contribute but I was obsessively worried about the way I looked. The way I spoke. The way I moved.

Tricia, from the Rape Crisis Center, would be my company that day. We had about an hour of waiting before the lineup to be held at the Public Safety Building jail. This time the elevator of the Public Safety Building did not stop at the floor I was familiar with, where the reassuring sight of a security door and policemen with coffee mugs met you once you stepped off. The hallways the detective, Tricia, and I walked down were full of people. Police and victims, lawyers and criminals. A policeman led a man in handcuffs down the hall past us, while he barked an amiable joke about some recent party to another policeman on the hall. There was a Latina, sitting in a plastic chair in the hallway. She stared at the floor, clutching her purse and a crumpled Kleenex in her hand.

The detective brought us into a large room in which makeshift dividers no more than four feet tall separated desks from one another. There were men—policemen—sitting at most of them. Their postures were tense and temporary; they came there to fill out reports or quickly interview a witness, or make a call before going back out on patrol or, perhaps, finally going home.

We were told to sit and wait. That they were experiencing a difficulty with the lineup. His lawyer, it was intimated, was the problem. I had yet to meet Assistant District Attorney Uebelhoer. I wanted to meet her. She was a woman, and in this all-male atmosphere, this made a difference to me. But Uebelhoer was busy with whatever was holding up the lineup.

I was worried about Madison seeing me.

"He won't be able to see you," the detective said. "We lead him in and he's behind a one-way mirror. He can't see a thing."

Tricia and I sat there. She didn't talk like Tess had talked, but she was attentive. She asked after my family and classes, told me lineups were "one of the most stressful procedures for rape victims," and inquired several times whether I wanted anything to drink.

I now think what distanced me from Tricia and from the Rape Crisis Center was their use of generalities. I did not want to be one of a group or compared with others. It somehow blindsided

137

my sense that I was going to survive. Tricia prepared me for failure by saying that it would be okay if I failed. She did this by showing me that the odds out there were against me. But what she told me, I didn't want to hear. In the face of dismal statistics regarding arrest, prosecution, and even full recovery for the victim, I saw no choice but to ignore the statistics. I needed what gave me hope, like being assigned a female assistant district attorney, not the news that the number of rape prosecutions in Syracuse for that calendar year had been nil.

Suddenly, Tricia said, "Oh, my God!"

"What?" I asked, but I did not turn around.

"Cover yourself."

I had nothing to do this with. I bent over and put my face in my skirt. I kept my eyes open against the cloth.

Tricia was up and complaining. "Get them out of here," she said. "Get them out of here."

A hurried "Sorry" came from a policeman.

Moments later, I looked up. They were gone. There had been faulty communication about which way to lead the men in the lineup into the lineup room. I was out of breath. Had he seen me? I was sure if he had, he would find me and kill me. The treachery of my lies that night—that I would not report it to anyone, that I was too ashamed—would not be lost on him.

I looked up.

Gail Uebelhoer was standing in front of me. She held out her hand. I offered her mine. She shook it firmly.

"Well, that was a little scary," she said. "But I think they got them out in time."

Her hair was short and black, and she had an arresting smile. She was tall, nearly five ten, and had a real body. No emaciated waif, she was solid and female. And she had sparkling, intelligent eyes. The connection for me was immediate. Gail was what I wanted to be when I grew up. She was there to do a job. She wanted what I wanted: to win.

She explained that I was about to view a lineup and that afterward we would talk about the grand jury and she would tell me exactly what to expect, how the room would look when I walked in, how many civilians there would be in the room, and what kind of questions they might ask—questions, she warned, that might be hard to answer but that I must.

"Are you ready?" she asked.

"Yes," I said.

Led by Gail, Tricia and I approached the open door to the viewing side of the room. Inside it was dark. There were a number of men. One I recognized, Sergeant Lorenz. I had not seen him since the night of the rape. He nodded his head. There were two uniformed men and another, the attorney for the defendant, Paquette.

"I don't know why she has to be here," he said, indicating Tricia.

"I am a representative from the Rape Crisis Center," Tricia said.

"I know who you are but I think there are too many people in here already," he said. He was small and pale, balding. He would be with me through the rest of the case.

"It's common practice," Sergeant Lorenz said.

"To my knowledge she is not an official here. She has no official connection to the case."

The argument continued. Gail got involved. Sergeant Lorenz stated again that it was becoming more and more accepted in rape cases to have a representative of Rape Crisis there.

"She has her female attorney here," Paquette said. "That's enough. I refuse to have my client involved in this lineup until she is removed."

Gail consulted with Lorenz near the front of the dark room. She returned to where I stood with Tricia.

"He won't continue," she said. "We're already behind on the lineup and I have to be in court at one."

"It's okay," I said. "I'm okay."

I was lying. I felt as if the wind had been knocked out of me.

"Are you sure, Alice?" she asked. "I want you to be sure. We can delay."

"No," I said. "I'm okay. I want to do this."
Tricia was dismissed.

The lineup procedure was explained to me. How five men would be led into the area behind the mirror, and how before they were led in, the lights in that area would be turned on.

"Since it is light on their side and dark here, they won't be able to see you," Lorenz said.

He explained that I should take my time. Could ask him to have them turn to the left or the right or to speak. He repeated that I should take my time. "When you are sure," he said, "I want you to walk over and place an X solidly in the corresponding box on the clipboard I have set up over there. Do you understand?"

"Yes," I said.

"Do you have any questions?" Gail asked.

"She said yes," Paquette said.

I felt like I had as a child. The adults were not getting along and it was up to me to be good girl enough to drain the tension from the room. That tension made my breath shallow and my heart race. I could tell Meggesto my symptoms of panic now. I was thoroughly intimidated. But I had said I was ready. It was wrong to turn back.

The room itself frightened me. I was unable to take my eyes from the one-way mirror. On television shows there was always an expanse of floor on the other side of the one-way mirror, and then a platform with a door off to the side where the suspects stepped into the room, filed up two or three stairs, and took their places. There was a reassuring distance between the victims and the suspects.

But the rooms I'd seen on cop shows were nothing like this one. The mirror took up a whole wall. On the other side of the wall was a space little wider than a man's shoulders, so that when they entered and turned, the front of their bodies would be almost flush against the mirror. I would share the same square foot of floor with the suspects; my rapist would be standing right in front of me.

Lorenz gave the order over a microphone and the light was

switched on, on the other side of the mirror. Five black men in almost identical light blue shirts and dark blue pants walked in and assumed their places.

"You can move closer, Alice," Lorenz said.

"It's not one, two, or three," I said.

"You don't need to rush," Uebelhoer said. "Move closer and take a good look at each of them."

"I can have them turn to the left or right," Lorenz said. Paquette was quiet.

I did as instructed. I moved closer, even though, already, they appeared close enough to touch.

"Can you have them turn to the side?" I asked.

They were asked to turn to the left. Each of them, individually. When they faced front again, I drew back.

"Can they see me?" I asked.

"They can see a movement on the glass," Lorenz said, "but they can't see you, no. They know when someone's standing in front of them but they won't know who it is."

I took this at face value. I did not say, "Who else could it be?" There had been no one else with us in that tunnel. I stood in front of number one. He looked too young. I moved to two. He looked nothing like the suspect. Out of the corner of my eye I already knew the challenge came two men down, but I stood in front of three long enough to agree with my earlier assessment. He was too tall; his build was wrong. I stood in front of number four. He was not looking at me. While he looked toward the floor I saw his shoulders. Wide like my rapist's, and powerful. The shape of his head and neck—just like my rapist's. His build, his nose, his lips. I hugged my arms across my chest and stared.

"Alice, are you all right?" someone asked.

Paquette objected.

I felt I had done something wrong.

I moved on to number five. His build was right, his height. And he was looking at me, looking right at me, as if he knew I was there. Knew who I was. The expression in his eyes told me that if we were alone, if there were no wall between us, he would call me by name and then kill me. His eyes gripped on and controlled. I mustered all my energy and turned around.

"I'm ready," I said.

"Are you sure?" Lorenz said.

"She said she was ready," Paquette said.

I approached the clipboard while Lorenz held it for me. Everyone watched—Gail, Paquette, and Lorenz. I placed my *X* in the number-five box. I had marked the wrong one.

I was excused. I saw Tricia in the hall.

"How was it?"

"Number four and five looked like identical twins," I said, before the uniformed policeman assigned to me led me into the conference room nearby.

"Make sure she doesn't talk to anyone," Lorenz said, ducking his head in. His tone was a reprimand, now that I already had.

In the conference room I searched the eyes of the uniformed man for whether I had chosen the right one. But his face was impassive. I felt a wave of nausea hit me and paced the floor in between the conference table and a row of chairs against the wall. My throat was thick and clogged. I became convinced in those moments that I had chosen the wrong man. I told myself I had acted on impulse, not considered the two men and their postures long enough. I had been so intent on getting it over with that I hadn't been thorough. Ever since I'd been little my parents had accused me of this: not taking my time, acting rashly, jumping the gun.

The door opened and a downcast Lorenz walked in. I could see Gail out in the hallway. He closed the door.

"It was four, wasn't it?" I asked him.

Lorenz was big and burly, a sort of sitcom-father stereotype with a more gritty, Northeastern twist. I sensed immediately that I had disappointed him. He didn't need to say anything. I had chosen the wrong one. It was number four.

"You were in a hurry to get out of there," he said.

"It was four."

"I can't tell you anything," he said. "Uebelhoer wants an affidavit. She wants you to detail the lineup for her. Tell us exactly why you chose five."

"Where is she?" I was suddenly frantic. I felt myself collapsing inward. I had failed them all and this was the wrap-up. Uebelhoer would go on to other cases, better victims; she had no time to waste with a failure like me.

"The suspect has agreed to provide samples of his pubic hair," Lorenz said, and couldn't help but grin. "Counsel has elected to be present in the men's room for extraction."

"Why would he do that?" I asked.

"Because he has reason to believe that the hair found on your person the night of the incident may not match his."

"But it will," I said. "He has to know that."

"His lawyer weighed the odds and decided to do it. It looks good if they volunteer. We need to take a statement. You sit tight."

He went to find paper and to attend to things I couldn't know. The uniform left me alone in the room. "You'll be safe in here," he said.

During that time I put two and two together: I had identified the wrong man. Directly afterward, Paquette had agreed to voluntary extraction of a pubic hair from his client. Uebelhoer had told me the defense was building a case based on misidentification. A panicked white girl saw a black man on the street. He spoke familiarly to her and in her mind she connected this to her rape. She was accusing the wrong man. The lineup went directly to this.

I sat down at the conference table. I brought it all together in my mind. Thought of what had just happened to me. I had been so afraid, I had chosen the man who scared me most, the one who had been looking at me. I felt I had just caught on—too late—to a trick.

Lorenz was going to be back any minute. I needed to rebuild my case.

When Lorenz returned, he smiled while telling me that Mad-

143

ison's pubic hair had to be plucked, not cut. He was trying to be jolly in front of me.

He took an affidavit. It noted that I had entered the room at 11:05 and left at 11:11. I quickly gave my reasons for ruling out the men in positions one, two, and three. I compared four and five and noted they looked similar, with four's features being a bit "flatter and broader" than the suspect's. I said that four had been looking down the whole time and that I chose five because he was looking right at me. I added that I had felt rushed and defense counsel's refusal to allow a member of Rape Crisis in the lineup room had further intimidated me. I said that I never got a good look at four's eyes and said again that I chose five because he was looking at me.

The room was quiet for a moment, save the noise of Lorenz's hunt-and-peck typing.

"Alice," he said, "it is now my duty to inform you that you failed to pick out the suspect." He did not tell me which one was the suspect. He couldn't. But I knew.

He noted that he had informed me of my failure, and I stated, for the record, that in my opinion the men in positions four and five were almost identical.

Uebelhoer came into the room. There were other people with her. Police and Tricia now. Uebelhoer was angry, but she smiled nonetheless.

"Well, we got the hair out of the bastard," she said.

"Officer Lorenz told me I chose the wrong one," I said.

"She thinks it was four," Lorenz said.

The two of them looked at each other for a moment. Gail turned to me.

"Of course you chose the wrong one," she said. "He and his attorney worked to make sure you'd never have a chance."

"Gail," Lorenz warned.

"She has a right to know. She knows anyway," she said, looking at him. He thought I needed protection; she knew I craved the truth.

"The reason why it took so long, Alice, is because Madison

had his friend come down and stand next to him. We had to send a car to the prison to get him here. They wouldn't go ahead until he showed."

"I don't understand," I said. "He's allowed to have his friend stand next to him?"

"It's the defendant's right," she said. "And it makes good sense on a certain level. If the others in the lineup don't appear to the suspect to look enough like him, he can choose someone to stand beside him."

"Can we say that?" I was beginning to see a window of explanation here. I might still have a chance.

"No," she said, "it goes against the defendant's rights. They really worked a number on you. He uses that friend, or that friend uses him, in every lineup they do. They're dead ringers."

I listened to everything she said. Uebelhoer had seen it all, but still was passionate enough to get mad.

"So the eyes?"

"His friend gives you a look that's scary. He can tell when you're standing in front of the mirror and he psyches you out. Meanwhile, the suspect looks down like he doesn't even know where or why he's there. Like he got lost on the way to the circus."

"And we can't use that in court?"

"No. I stated a formal objection before the lineup, so it would be included in the record, but that's just a formality. It's not admissible unless he lets prior knowledge slip."

The unfairness of this seemed unconscionable to me.

"Rights are weighted on the side of the defendant," Gail said. I hungered for more facts. In those moments, where I could easily have slipped away, facts were my life. "That's why the law uses words like 'reasonable doubt.' It's his attorney's job to provide that doubt. The lineup was a risk. We knew something like this could happen, but there was no photo in the mug books and he waived the prelim. We had no choice. We can't refuse a lineup."

"What about the hair?"

"If we're lucky, it will match all seventeen points available on a hair. But even hairs taken from the same head can vary on these points. Paquette decided the gamble was worth it. He's probably going with the story that you lost your virginity voluntarily that night and were sorry about it, that eventually you would have blamed any black man that ran into you on the street. He'll do his best to make you look bad. But we're not going to let that happen."

"What's next?"

"The grand jury," she said.

I was miserable. At two, the next big leg of this journey would begin and I had to be ready for it. I'm sure I spent that time trying to clear my mind of my failure that morning, trying not to let the picture of me that Madison's attorney was building invade my mind. I did not call my mother. I had no good news, though I did have Uebelhoer. I focused on the fact that she had been present for the pubic extraction.

At two I was brought into a waiting area outside the grand jury room. Gail was inside. We had not had time, as she had wished, to talk beforehand. She had been busy working on questions through lunch and although I was scheduled for two, there were other witnesses appearing before me. Tricia, with my assurances, had left following the lineup.

While I waited, I tried to think about an Italian test I had to take the next day. I got out a worksheet of sample sentences from my knapsack and stared at them. I had made some small talk about this course to the officer who'd picked me up that morning. I wished I'd had Tess with me. I had a deep fear of alienating her and Toby by being a drain on them because of the rape, so I tried to be as assiduous in their classrooms as I was with anything concerning my case.

There was movement in the hallway. Gail was coming toward me. Quickly, she told me that she was going to ask me questions about the events of that night, that she would then lead up to my ability to identify the rapist and my identification of Officer Clapper at the same time. She wanted me to state clearly that I hadn't been sure between four and five and to say why. She told me to take as much time as I needed on each answer and not to feel hurried. "This will be easier than the preliminary hearing, Alice, just stay with me. I may seem colder to you in there than I am right now but, remember, we're in there to win an indictment and to a certain extent—well, the grand jury is made up of twenty-five civilians, and we're onstage."

She left me. A few minutes later I was led into the room. Again, I was unprepared for the room's effect on me. The witness stand was at the bottom of the room. Leading up and out from the stand were terraced levels on which swiveling orange chairs were permanently affixed. The levels spread out in a circular arc and grew larger as they ascended. There were enough seats for the twenty-five members of the jury and for the alternates who sat through all the cases but might never cast a vote.

The result of the room's design was that all eyes bore down on whoever was seated in the witness stand. There was no defense table or prosecutor's table.

Gail did as she had said she would. She used a courtroom manner. She made a lot of eye contact with the jurors, used hand gestures, and spent time enunciating key words or phrases she wanted them to note and remember. Her pattern of questioning also was meant to calm both me and the jurors. She had told me rape cases were hard for them. I saw proof of this soon enough. When she asked me where he had touched me, and, in my answer, I had to say that he had put his fist in my vagina, many of the jurors looked down or immediately away from me. But the fact that troubled them most was what came next. Uebelhoer questioned me about bleeding: how much blood, why so much? She asked me if I had been a virgin. I said, "Yes."

They winced. They felt pity. Throughout the remaining questions some of the jurors, and not all of them women, fought back tears. I was aware my loss that night was my gain today. Having been a virgin made me look good, made the crime appear worse.

I did not want their pity. I wanted to win. But their reactions pushed me to think about what I was saying, not just tally it up as a pro or con in terms of the chances for a conviction. The tears of one particular man, in the second row, felled me. I cried a little then. The reality was that this, too, made me look good.

The sketch I drew the night of October 5 was entered into evidence and marked for identification. Uebelhoer asked pointed questions about whether I had been assisted in the sketch, whether the handwriting was mine, whether anyone had influenced it.

She moved on to the lineup. Now the questioning was more heated. Like a surgeon with a probe, she brought forth each nuance of the five minutes I'd spent inside that room. Finally she asked me if I was certain I had identified the right man.

I answered: No.

Then she asked me why I had chosen number five. I explained in detail his height and his build. I talked about the eyes.

Eventually it came time for the jurors to ask their questions:

Juror: "When you saw the police officer up on Marshall Street, why didn't you go to him then?"

Juror: "You picked him out of the lineup; are you absolutely sure that this was the one?"

Juror: "Alice, why were you coming through the park alone at night; do you usually go through by yourself?"

Juror: "Didn't anybody warn you not to go through the park at night?"

Juror: "Didn't you know that you are not supposed to go through the park after nine-thirty at night? Didn't you know that?"

Juror: "Could you have definitely eliminated number four? Did he ever look at you?"

I answered all of these questions patiently. The questions concerning the lineup I answered directly and truthfully. But the questions about what I had been doing in the park, or why I hadn't gone up to Officer Clapper, made me numb. They were not getting it, that's how it felt. But, as Gail had said, we were onstage.

On television and in the movies, the lawyer often says to the victim before they take the stand, "Just tell the truth." What it was left up to me to figure out was that if you do that and nothing else, you lose. So I told them I was stupid, that I shouldn't have walked through the park. I said I intended to do something to warn girls at the university about the park. And I was so good, so willing to accept blame, that I hoped to be judged innocent by them.

That day it all got raw. If Madison stood next to his friend and played a game of eyes to psyche me out, then I would give it right back to him. I was authentic. I had been a virgin. He had broken my hymen in two places. The OB-GYN would testify to the fact. I was also a good girl, and I knew how to dress and what to say to accentuate that. That night following the grand jury testimony, I called Madison a "motherfucker" in the privacy of my dorm room while I pounded my pillow and bed with my fists. I swore the kind of bloodthirsty revenge no one thought possible coming from a nineteen-year-old coed. While still in court I thanked the jury. I drew on my resources: performing, placating, making my family smile. As I left that courtroom I felt I had put on the best show of my life. It was no longer hand to hand and I had a chance this time.

I went out to sit in the waiting area. Detective Lorenz was there. He wore a black patch over one of his eyes.

"What happened?" I asked. I was horrified.

"We chased a perp and he ran. Hit me in the eye with a mace. How'd you do in there?"

"Okay, I guess."

"Listen," he said. He began to fumble out an apology. He said he was sorry if he hadn't seemed very nice back in May. "You get a lot of rape cases," he said. "Most of them never get this far. I'm pulling for you."

I assured him that he had always been wonderful to me, that the police had all been wonderful. I meant every word of it.

Fifteen years later, when doing research for this book, I would find sentences he had written in the original paperwork.

May 8, 1981: "It is this writer's opinion, after interview of the victim, that this case, as presented by the victim, is not completely factual."

After interviewing Ken Childs later that same day he wrote: "Childs describes their relationship as 'casual.' It is still this writer's opinion that there were extenuating circumstances to this incident, as reported by victim, and [it] is suggested that this case be referred to the inactive file."

But after meeting with Uebelhoer on October 13, 1981: "It should be noted that when this writer first interviewed the victim at approx. 0800 on May 8th 1981, she appeared to be disoriented about the facts of the incident and disconcerted as she kept dozing off. This writer now realizes that the victim had been through a tremendous ordeal with no sleep for approximately 24 hours which would account for her behavior at the time. . . ."

For Lorenz, virgins were not a part of his world. He was skeptical of many things I said. Later, when the serology reports proved that what I had said was not a lie, that I had been a virgin, and that I was telling the truth, he could not respect me enough. I think he felt responsible, somehow. It was, after all, in his world where this hideous thing had happened to me. A world of violent crime.

TEN

Maria Flores, from Tess's workshop, fell from a window. That was how the *Daily Orange*, Syracuse's campus paper, reported it. They used her name and said it was an accident.

As the students filed into the English department conference room for workshop, only one or two of us had seen the item in the paper. I hadn't. Apparently, the paper said Flores, though badly injured in the accident, had miraculously survived. She was in the hospital.

Tess was late. When she came in, the room hushed. She sat down at the head of the table and tried to start class. She was clearly upset.

"Did you hear about Maria?" one of the students asked.

Tess hung her head. "Yes," she said. "It's horrible."

"Is she okay?"

"I just spoke to her," she said. "I'm going to see her at the hospital. It's always so difficult. This poetry business."

We didn't quite understand. What did Maria's accident have to do with poetry?

"It was in the paper," a student volunteered.

Tess looked at him sharply. "They used her name?"

"What is it, Tess?" someone asked.

Our question was answered the following day, when an almost identical article described it as an attempted suicide. The only other difference was that this time the paper left out her name. It didn't take a genius to put two and two together.

Tess had told me it would mean quite a bit to Maria if I went to visit her in the hospital. "That was a powerful poem you wrote," she added, but didn't say what else she knew.

151

I went. But before I did, Maria made another unsuccessful attempt. She tried to kill herself by cutting an electrical cord near her bed, unfurling the wires inside, and scoring them over and over against her wrists. She'd done this while partially paralyzed on her left side. But a nurse had walked in on her, and now her arms were strapped to the bed.

She was in Crouse Irving Memorial Hospital. A nurse led me into the room. Standing beside Maria's bed were her father and her brothers. I waved to Maria and then shook the men's hands. I said my name and that I was in her poetry class. None of them was very responsive. I attributed this to shock, and to what might have seemed the strange phenomenon of this woman visiting who appeared to have some connection with her that they, her father and brothers, didn't. They left the room.

"Thank you for coming," she said in a whisper. She wanted to hold my hand.

The two of us didn't really know each other, had just shared Tess's class, and, until recently, I had harbored a bit of resentment toward the fact that she'd walked out on my workshop.

"Can you sit?" she asked.

"Yes."

I did.

"It was your poem," she said now. "It brought it all back."

I sat there as she whispered to me her own facts. The man and the boys who had just left the room had raped her for a period of years when she was growing up.

"At a certain point it stopped," she said. "My brothers grew old enough to know what they were doing was wrong."

"Oh, Maria," I said, "I never meant to—"

"Stop. It's good. I need to face it."

"Have you told your mother?"

"She said she didn't want to hear it. She promised she would not tell my father as long as I never mentioned it again. She's not speaking to me."

I looked at all the get-well cards above her bed. She was a resident advisor and all the residents on the hall, as well as her friends, had sent cards. I was struck with what was painfully clear. By jumping but surviving, she was now completely dependent on her family to take care of her. On her father. "Have you told Tess?"

Her face lit up. "Tess has been wonderful."

"I know."

"Your poem said all the things I've been feeling inside for years. All the things I'm so afraid of feeling."

"Is that good?" I asked.

"We'll see," she said and smiled weakly.

Maria would recover from the fall and return to school. For a time she severed relations with her family.

But that day, we joked that she sure had commented on my poem by jumping, and that Tess would have to give her that. Then I talked. I talked because she wanted me to and because here, next to her, I could. I told her about the grand jury and the lineup and about Gail.

"You're so lucky," she said. "I'll never get to do any of that. I want you to go all the way."

We were still holding hands. Every moment in that room was precious to both of us.

I looked up eventually and noticed her father standing in the door. Maria couldn't see him. But she saw my eyes.

He did not leave or advance. He was waiting for me to get up and go. I felt this radiate from where he stood. He didn't know exactly what was going on between us, but there was something he seemed not to trust.

By November 16, the "known pubic hair sample from Gregory Madison" and the "Negroid pubic hair recovered from pubic combings of Alice Sebold, May 1981" had been compared. The lab found that on seventeen points of microscopic comparison, the hairs had matched on all seventeen.

On November 18, Gail drafted an inter-office letter for the files. She posted it on the twenty-third.

‹ › ›

There is no question this was a rape. Victim was a virgin and hymen was torn in two places. Lab reports show semen, and medicals show contusions and lacerations.

Identification is at issue. Rape was May 8, 1981 and victim gave detailed description to cops but no arrest made. She goes back to Pennsylvania May 9, 1981. When she returns to S.U. in the fall, she spots defendant on street, and he approaches her and says, "Hey, girl, don't I know you from somewhere?" She runs and calls cops. I had a line-up and she ID's wrong guy (who was a dead ringer for defendant and standing right next to him, and who defendant personally requested). Later she tells cops that she thought it could have been either the defendant or the other guy. Defendant's pubic hair was found to be consistent with one found in her pubic combings. There was a partial print on the weapon (knife) found at the scene, but it has insufficient ridge details to make a comparison (I had it sent to F.B.I. for more testing). Lab advises they cannot determine blood type from semen because it is too tainted with her blood.

Good luck. Victim is excellent witness.

I returned home to Pennsylvania for Thanksgiving. One day after coming back to Syracuse on Greyhound, there was a letter waiting for me at my dorm.

"Pursuant to your request," it read in part, "this is to advise you that the above-mentioned captioned defendant has been indicted by the grand jury."

I was thrilled. I stood in my single at Haven and shook with it. I called my mother and told her. I was moving forward. The trial seemed imminent. Any day now.

I was in class when Madison entered his plea on December 4, before Justice Walter T. Gorman. On an eight-count indictment, Madison pled not guilty. A pretrial hearing was scheduled for December 9. Paquette, representing Madison, admitted to one petit larceny conviction "back somewhere." The State didn't know enough to counter him, and Madison's juvenile record could not be considered. When Gorman asked Assistant DA Plochocki, who was representing the State because Gail was in another court, if he wanted to be heard on bail, Plochocki said, "Judge, I don't have the file." So bail was set at $5,000. Mistakenly, through Christmas and New Year's, I joyfully pictured my assailant in jail.

Before I went home for the Christmas holidays, I'd taken an incomplete in Italian 101, a *C*- in Classics, a *B* in Tess's survey course—my paper wasn't quite up to snuff—and two *A*'s: one in Wolff's workshop, one in Gallagher's.

I saw Steve Carbonaro. He had given up Don Quixote and taken to keeping a bottle of Chivas Regal in his apartment near Penn. He scoured flea markets for old, threadbare Oriental rugs, wore a satin smoking jacket, smoked a pipe, and wrote sonnets for a new girlfriend whose name he loved—Juliet. Through his window, with the lights turned off in his own apartment, he watched two extroverted lovers who lived in an apartment across the way. I didn't like the taste of scotch and thought the pipe was stupid.

My sister was still a virgin at twenty-two. I spent time wishing she were less pristine. I know she spent time wishing she were less pristine too. But our motivations were different. I wanted her to fall—for that was how it was seen in our household—so I wouldn't be alone. She wanted to fall so that she would have more in common with most of her friends.

We lived unhappily on either side of the word. She was one, I wasn't one. At first my mother had joked about how the rape might put an end to her lectures on virginity, so now she would lecture me on chastity. But something in this didn't work. It would appear odd if my mother emphasized to my sister the old rules but made new ones up for me. I had moved, by being raped, to a category she found unaddressable.

So I did what I did with the hardest issues: I took the fall-back position of the Sebolds—a thorough analysis of the semantics involved. I looked up all the words and versions—*virgin, virginity, virginal, chaste, chastity*. When the definitions didn't provide me with what I wanted, I manipulated the language and redefined the words. The end result was that I claimed myself still a virgin. I had not lost my virginity, I said, it was taken from me. Therefore, I would decide when and what virginity was. I called what I still had to lose my "real virginity." Like my reasons for not sleeping with Steve or for returning to Syracuse, this seemed airtight to me.

It wasn't. A lot of what I figured out and subverted wasn't airtight in the least, but I couldn't admit to that then. I also created a painful reasoning for why it was better to have been raped as a virgin.

"I think it's better that I was raped as a virgin," I told people. "I don't have any sexual associations with it like other women do. It was pure violence. This way, when I do have normal sex, the difference between sex and violence will be very clear to me."

I wonder now who bought it.

Even with classes and court appearances, I had found time to nurse a crush. His name was Jamie Waller and he was a student in Wolff's workshop. He was older—twenty-six—and friends with another student in our class, Chris Davis. Chris was gay. I thought this marked Jamie—who was straight—as a highly evolved male. If he could be so openly comfortable in the company of a gay man, I reasoned, he might be able to find a rape victim okay.

I managed to do all the things love-struck girls do. I had Lila meet me after class so she could get a look at him. Back at the dorm we discussed how cute he was. Each time I saw him I would detail for her what he was wearing. He was a master of what I called shoddy prep. He wore rag-wool sweaters with egg stains on them, and his Brooks Brothers boxers often peeked out of his wide-wale cords. He lived off campus in an apartment and had a car. He went skiing on the weekends. He had what I wanted—a life apart. I mooned over him in private; in public I pretended I was tough.

I hated the way I looked. I thought I was fat and ugly and

weird. But even if he could never find me physically attractive, he still liked a good story and he liked to get drunk. I could tell one and do the other.

Following Wolff's workshop, Chris, Jamie, and I would grab a few drinks, then Jamie would say, "Well, kids, I'm taking off. What are you two doing this weekend?" Chris and I never had good answers. We both felt lame. My weekends consisted of waiting for the grand jury and then what followed. Chris later admitted that his weekends had been committed to going to the gay bars in downtown Syracuse and trying, without success, to find a boyfriend. Chris and I both overate and drank too much coffee while reading good poetry. When we wrote a poem of our own that we didn't despise, we might call each other and read it aloud. We were lonely and hated ourselves. We kept each other laughing, bitterly, and waited for Jamie, fresh and back from a weekend at Stowe or Hunter Mountain, to fill our dismal lives.

There was the night that fall when I told the two of them about the rape. All three of us were drunk. It was after a reading or a workshop and we had gone to a bar on Marshall Street. It was a bar a bit nicer than most of the student bars, which were more like caverns.

I don't remember how it came out. It was in the day or two before the lineup and so it was all I was thinking about. Chris was stunned and the news had the effect of making him drunker. His brother, Ben, had been murdered two years before, though I didn't know this then. It was Jamie whom I cared about. Jamie I imagined myself falling in love with and marrying.

However he responded, it could not have fulfilled the rescue fantasy I had fabricated. Nothing could. There was no rescue. The table was awkward for a second and then Jamie found the answer. He ordered another round of drinks.

Jamie drove home alone in his car to his off-campus apartment. Chris, who lived in the opposite direction, walked me home. I lay on the bed and the room spun. I didn't like how drinking felt but I liked how it released me. News slipped out and the world didn't explode and eventually I could count on passing out. I had a headache in the morning and I always threw up, but Jamie, and everyone, it seemed, liked me when I was drunk. The added bonus: I often didn't remember much.

After Christmas, we drank more frequently, often without Chris. Jamie told me he had come back to finish his diploma after nursing his father through a protracted terminal illness. He confided that he owned a women's clothing store in Utica, and had to go down often to look in on it. All this made him more glamorous, but what I really liked about Jamie was his no-bullshit factor. He ate and belched. He slept around. He'd lost his virginity way before I had—he was something like fourteen and she was older. "I never had a chance," he would say, take a sip of beer from a long-neck, or wine from a glass, and snort gleefully. He joked about how many women he'd had, and told stories about being caught with married women by their husbands.

I didn't feel comfortable hearing a lot of this. His promiscuity seemed inconceivable, but it also meant that he had seen and done it all. There were no surprises. In his eyes I would not be a freak. Jamie was not a nice boy. But having a nice boy think of me as "special" was what I wanted least.

He listened patiently to what was going on in my life: about Gail, or the lineup, or my fear of going to trial. In the weeks that turned into months after the Christmas holiday, I lived in constant anticipation of the trial. Repeatedly it was pushed back. A pretrial hearing was set for January 22 and I went. It was canceled but I still had to show up, prep with the DA, Bill Mastine, and with Gail, who was now pregnant, and so handing most of the reins over to Mastine.

I saw in Jamie a recognition that the two of us were oddballs. He had gone through a lot with his father and believed that at nineteen, I was distinguished by the rape from most of my peers. But instead of making me feel my feelings, as Tricia from the Rape Crisis Center would want, he taught me how to drink. And I did.

* * *

Jamie and I talked about sex and I told a lie.

In the bar one night, Jamie asked me—it felt offhand—if I'd slept with anyone since the rape. I said no, but in that second, the expression on his face told me that was not the right answer. I rephrased, "No, don't be silly, of course I have."

"Yeesh," he responded, turning his beer glass in circles on the table, "I wouldn't have wanted to be that guy."

"What do you mean?"

"It's a pretty big responsibility. You'd be afraid of fucking up. Plus, who knows what could happen?"

I told him it hadn't been that bad. He asked me how many men I'd slept with. I made up a number. Three.

"That's a good amount. Just enough to know you're normal."

I agreed.

We continued to drink. I was alone now, I knew that. If I had told the truth he would have rejected me. The pressure I felt to "get it over with"—in my words to Lila—was overwhelming. I was afraid if I went too long, the fear involved in having sex would only increase. I didn't want to be a dried-up old woman, or become a nun, or live in the house of my parents and stare at the wall ceaselessly. These destinies were very real to me.

Just before Easter vacation, the night came.

Jamie and I went to a movie. Afterward, we got very drunk at the bar. "I've got to take a piss," he said, for not the first time that evening.

When he was in the men's room, I calculated. We had been leading up to this point for a while. He had asked the only question that would act as a restraint. I'd told a lie and it appeared I'd told it successfully. The next day he would take off for a ski weekend and I'd be alone with myself and with Lila for a few days.

He returned to the table. "If I get any drunker I can't drive home," he said. "Are you coming with me?"

I got up and we walked outside. It was snowing. The fresh bite of snowflakes pelted our booze-warmed skin. We stood and breathed in the cold air. Snowflakes gathered on the tips of Jamie's eyelashes and across the ridge of his ski cap.

We kissed. It was wet and sloppy, different from Steve, more like Madison. But I wanted this. I willed myself to want it. This is Jamie, I repeated in my head. This is Jamie.

"So, you coming home with me?" he asked.

"I don't know," I said.

"Well, it's cold as a witch's clit out here, I'm going home. Come or don't come."

"I have my contacts in," I said.

He was smooth and drunk and had done it all a thousand times before. "Well, you've got two choices. You can walk home and you can sleep alone in your bed, or I can drive you there and wait for you while you take your contacts out."

"You'd do that?"

He stayed outside in his car. I hurried up the elevator in Haven, went to my room, and removed my lenses. It was late but I woke Lila anyway. I knocked on her door. She answered it in her Lanz nightgown. Her room was dark. I had woken her up. "What is it?" she asked angrily.

"This is it," I said to Lila. "I'm going home with Jamie. I'll be back in the morning. Promise you'll have breakfast with me."

"Fine," she said, and shut the door.

I had wanted someone to be in on it with me.

It was snowing heavily now. To stay focused on the road, we were quiet. The heat rushed out of the dash onto my legs. Jamie was my guide on a mission to a place I'd never been. I had one last chance to make it before the walls closed in. His random promiscuity now seemed glorious to me. In the way he had talked about it, I knew there was as much bravado as there was real joy. I realized even then that he'd been drunk during so many of these encounters. He was drunk now. But all of this was detail work to me. Drinking. Promiscuity. An undirected life. They were all, to my mind, a product of his own choice. No one had made him drink or fuck or run. Now, I can look and see that it may have been otherwise; then, I stared out at the road. The wipers were going. Snow built up on either side of them and formed a white widow's peak in the middle of the windshield. I was going home with a normal man—by most standards an attractive one—and he was taking me there to make love to me.

I had spent time imagining his place. It was less than fabulous when we arrived. He lived in a one-bedroom apartment. The living area had no furniture, just milk crates jammed with albums and tapes, and a stereo that sat on the carpeted floor. He walked in and threw his school bag down, took a leak with the bathroom door open, from which I looked away, and reentered the kitchen. There was a let's-just-get-to-it attitude now that we were in his apartment. I stood in the hallway between the darkened kitchen area and the unfurnished living area. His bedroom was near the bathroom. I knew that was where we were going, knew that was what I had come here for, but I hesitated. I was afraid.

Jamie said he guessed I was new enough so he should offer me a drink. He had an open bottle of white wine in the fridge and two dirty wineglasses. He held the glasses under the tap and then filled both with wine. I took my dripping glass and sipped.

"You can put your bag down," he said. "Music would make this easier, huh?"

He walked into the living area and crouched down over a milk crate of tapes. He picked up, scanned, and tossed back two or three. I put my book bag near the front door. He chose Bob Dylan, the kind of slow, stalling melodies that always made me feel as if the dead were rattling their chains. I wasn't a Dylan fan, but I knew enough not to say anything.

"Don't stand there like a statue," he said, turning and coming closer. "Kiss me."

Something in my kiss displeased him.

"Look, you wanted this," he said. "Don't clam up now."

He suggested I go and brush my teeth. I said I would but I didn't have a toothbrush.

"Haven't you ever stayed over at a guy's place before?"

"Yes," I lied, sheepishly.

"What did you do then?"

"I used my finger," I said, thinking quickly. "And brushed my teeth that way."

Jamie walked past me and into the bathroom and found a toothbrush. "Use it," he said. "If you fuck someone you should be able to use their toothbrush!"

Frightened and drunk and bumbling, I grasped on to this logic. I went into the bathroom and brushed my teeth. I threw water on my face and worried, for just a second, if I looked pretty. But as soon as I looked in the mirror, I looked away. I could not watch what I was doing. I swallowed hard, breathed in, and left the bathroom.

Jamie was moving dirty laundry off the mattress on the floor of the bedroom. His sheets were soiled and various blankets lay twisted in knots and balls where they had landed when kicked away. He had turned Dylan up. His ski boots lay outside the door on their sides. He'd brought my wine into the bedroom and put it by his clock radio on the milk crate next to the mattress.

He pulled his shirt off over his head. I had seen very few men's bodies before. His seemed scrawnier than I had imagined, and freckled. The waistband of his long underwear had lost its elasticity and spilled out over the top of his pants.

"Are you planning to keep your clothes on?" he asked.

"I'm self-conscious."

"There's no time for that," he said. "I've got to get up for Spanish in the morning, and then I'm long-hauling to Vermont. Let's get the show on the road."

Somehow we did. Somehow I lay under him as he fucked me. He fucked me hard. It was what I later heard girls call "athletic sex." I held on. When he came, he came loudly and snorted and bellowed. I wasn't prepared for it. I wept. I wept louder than I ever could have imagined. I shook with it. He stopped his noises and he held tightly to me. I felt humiliated but I couldn't stop. I don't think he knew that he was what I considered my first, but he was smart enough to know where the crying stemmed from.

"Poor baby," he said. "Poor, poor baby."

Soon after, he passed out on top of me. I stayed awake all night.

In the early morning he wanted to have sex again. But first, after kissing me, he pushed me down near his penis. Once there, I didn't know what to do.

"Haven't you ever done this before?" he asked.

I tried but gagged.

"Come up here," he said, releasing me. We kissed some more and, concerned with a look he saw in my eye, he grabbed me by my hair and pulled my head away from his. "Look," he said. "Don't do that. Don't fall in love with me." I didn't know what he meant or how to respond to the reprimand. I said I wouldn't but I didn't know how not to.

He drove me back to Haven. "Take care of yourself, kiddo," he said. He didn't want responsibility. He'd had enough of it nursing his father. He went off to class and then to ski.

"Well, I did it," I wrote on Lila's memo board hanging on the outside of her door. I knew she was asleep and was thankful for it. I hadn't slept in over twenty-four hours. I went to my room. I needed time to make it sound good. When I woke in the late afternoon, it was over. I had lost my real virginity. Everything had functioned, if not exactly perfectly, and I had been accepted by a man.

Of course, I did what he told me not to do. I fell in love with him.

I did make a good story out of it. I laughed at myself, my fumbling. I got drunk. I called Chris and told him. He loved it. He screamed, "You bagged the prize!" I acted experienced and wise around Lila while we ate Swiss Almond Vanilla Häagen-Dazs. Jamie didn't call me. I reasoned I would see him after Easter, that cool people like the two of us didn't need things like rings or flowers or phone calls. I packed for the trip home to Pennsylvania. I hid a bottle of Absolut in my red bottom-of-the-line Samsonite. I was fine.

ELEVEN

In late April, a month after Easter break, I was on Marshall Street. It was midafternoon. Spring had finally come to Upstate New York in that peekaboo way that it does. There was still old snow on the ground. Each winter, the snow made Syracuse beautiful; it covered the gritty, Northeastern browns and grays of the buildings and roads. But by April, everyone had had enough of it, and the warmth was celebrated by the students. They wore shorts, despite the fact that goose bumps rose up and down their arms and legs, and the girls showed off their Florida tans. The street was crowded, and with the anticipation of the end of classes that meant the start of good times, students were smiling and laughing and buying SU paraphernalia in the stores on Marshall Street.

I had gone shopping for my sister. She was graduating magna cum laude from Penn. As I walked up Marshall, a group of fraternity boys and their girlfriends were coming my way. They were all bright spring smiles. Two of the boys flaunted their toughness by wearing white starched boxer shorts with the standard no-sock Docksiders on their feet. I looked at them because I had to; they were covering the sidewalk and begging for attention. But there was someone trying to get by them on the other side.

I grew up watching *Bewitched*, in which the Elizabeth Montgomery character was able to snap her fingers and freeze everyone but herself and her husband, Darrin. They continued talking while the frozen people stayed still in their awkward, formerly animated poses. That was how it felt that day. I saw Gregory Madison blocked by this crowd, and then, he saw me. Everything else stopped.

I don't know why I hadn't thought that this could happen.

But I hadn't. I still envisioned him in jail, or, at least, not stupid enough to come back to the university area before the trial. But there he was. In October he had been cocksure when he spotted me. Now we saw each other, recognized each other, and nodded. No words. It was a split second. The happy frat boys and girls stood between us. We passed by them on either side. His eyes told me what I needed to know. I had become his opponent now, no longer merely his victim. This he recognized.

Lila and I had begun, sometime that winter, to call each other Clone. We both gained from it. By being my clone, she could seem a bit more daring and wild than she really was; I could pretend that I was a normal college coed whose life revolved as much around my classes and food runs to Marshall Street as it did a rape trial. As Clones we decided to room together off campus. The two of us, and a friend of Lila's named Sue, found a three-bedroom apartment in an off-campus area where many students lived. We were excited about living in a real house, and, certain the trial would *have* to be over by then, I saw this as a fresh start. We would take possession in the fall.

By the first week of May, I was packing to go home for the summer. I'd gotten a *B* in my Shakespeare class and said good-bye to Jamie. I had no illusions that I would hear from him.

I had taken a course called Cervantes in English in which, for the final paper, I took my revenge on the myth of La Mancha. I reinterpreted Don Quixote as a modern urban parable and made Sancho the hero. He was street smart where Quixote was not. In my version, Quixote drowns in a curbside puddle, unable to realize it is not a lake.

Before I left, I called Gail to let her know my schedule. All spring, the office of the district attorney had given me an "any minute now" rap and this time was no different. She thanked me and asked me about my plans.

"I'll get a summer job, I guess," I said.

"I'm hoping we'll go to trial soon," she said. "You will be available, won't you?"

"It's my number-one priority," I said, not putting it together until years later: In rape cases, it was almost expected that the victim would drop out of the process even if she originally initiated it.

"Alice, let me ask you something," she said, her tone shifting a bit.

"Yes?"

"Will you have someone with you from home?"

"I don't know," I said.

I had talked to my parents about this during the Christmas holidays and then again at Easter. My mother had spoken to her psychiatrist, Dr. Graham, about it, and my father fretted that the longer the trial was postponed, the greater the chance it would ruin his annual trip to Europe.

Until recently I believed that their final decision, that he would be the one who came with me, was based on her own inability to be there—the unpredictable chances of a flap. But as it turned out, Dr. Graham had counseled her to go despite her panic.

In the phone call in which my mother told me how the decision had ultimately been made, I stayed quiet. I asked the questions a reporter would ask. Numbly, I gathered the information. My mother was peeved at Graham, she said, because, of course, Graham would "support the professional, i.e., your father."

"So Dad didn't want to come with me either?" I asked, playing out what she'd begun.

"Of course not, his precious Spain awaited."

What I came away with was the fact that neither one of them had wanted to be at the trial with me. They had their reasons; I acknowledge these.

Finally, it was decided, my father would come with me. I held out a small corner of hope, up until the moment my father and I boarded the plane, that my mother would park her car in the longterm lot and rush in. No matter how tough my pose, I both wanted and needed her.

By the close of her senior year, Mary had mastered fifteen Arab dialects and won a Fulbright Scholarship to study at the University of Damascus in Syria. I was both jealous and in awe. I made my first, but not my last, joke about our respective majors. "Yours may be Arabic," I said. "It looks like mine is rape."

Mary excelled academically in a way I never could, perhaps in a way I was too distracted to ever attempt. But the truth was, Mary had been escaping via academics for a long time. Raised in a house where my mother's problems provided the glue of family, she patterned herself after my father. Learn a language of another country and then you can go to that country: a place where the problems of your family will not follow. A language they do not speak.

I had not quite given up on the idea of the blissful sibling relationship that my mother wanted for us, but events always conspired, it seemed, to make this impossible. The City of Syracuse scheduled testimony to begin on May 17, the same day as my sister's commencement ceremony at Penn. I continually stole her spotlight whether I wanted to or not.

I talked to Gail. They could not reschedule the trial, but they would lead with the other witnesses and somehow work it so I could testify on the second day. My father and I booked a flight for the evening of the seventeenth. Directly after Mary's graduation, my mother would drop us off at the Philadelphia airport. Until then, my mother, father, and I agreed, Mary's day would be our focus.

My mother, Mary, and I went clothes shopping—Mary for a dress to wear to graduation, me for an outfit for the trial.

Both my sister and I had strayed far from the way we were dressed as children, my mother having a penchant for the colors of the flag. Mary went toward dark greens and creams, I went to black and blue. But for the trial, I ceded my Gothic tendencies to my mother. I put her firmly in control. I would wear, as it resulted, a red blazer, a white blouse, a blue skirt.

In the evening, on the sixteeth, my father and I packed. On the seventeenth, we all dressed in our separate rooms and prepared for the drive down to Penn. I took a last look in my mirror.

Whatever the trial's result, my part in it would be over by the time I saw myself there again. I was going to Syracuse and would meet and see many people, but all I thought about was the one appointment I had to keep. I had a date with Gregory Madison. As I opened the door of my bedroom I breathed deeply. I shut myself off. I turned myself on. I was Mary's little sister—excited, ebullient, alive.

At the ceremony, my father would march in his Princeton colors. Mary and he stood with us in the crowded lobby of the auditorium, where mothers and fathers fussed over the last-minute set of mortarboards, and one woman, unhappy with her daughter's mascara, spit-washed the black flecks from under her eyes. Extended families surrounded the happy graduates, flashbulbs popped, and self-conscious girls and boys tried to make mortarboards look less than nerdy by tilting them on their heads.

My grandmother, mother, and I found our seats on the main floor, to the side of the large body of graduating students. I stood on my chair to find Mary. I spotted her smiling beside another girl, a friend of hers I didn't know.

After the ceremony, we celebrated with a lunch at the Faculty Club. My mother took too many pictures of us on the concrete benches outside. My mother still has an enlargement framed and mounted from that day. I used to wish that she would take it down. But it commemorates an important day in our family: my sister's graduation, my rape trial.

I don't remember the airport. I remember the rush from a day of celebration into the onset of dread. Once in Syracuse, we were met by Detective John Murphy from the DA's office. This man, with prematurely gray hair and a friendly smile, approached my father and me as we located the signs for the main terminal.

"You must be Alice," he said, and extended his hand.

"Yes." How had he known me?

He introduced himself to my father and to me, told us his job—to act as our escort over the next twenty-four hours—and offered to carry my bag. As we walked briskly toward the exit, he explained our accommodations and that Gail would meet us in the cafe in the lobby.

"She wants to go over the testimony," he said.

Finally, I asked, "How did you know who I was?"

He looked blankly at me. "They showed me some photos."

"I would have hoped I looked better than that, if they're the photos you mean."

My father was tense; he walked at a remove from us.

"You're a beautiful girl, you can tell that even in those photos," Murphy said. He was smooth. He knew the answers to give and the things to say.

In the county car on the way to the hotel, Murphy talked over his shoulder to my father, making eye contact with him in the rearview at lights and turns.

"Follow sports, Mr. Sebold?" he asked.

My father did not.

Murphy tried fishing.

My father did his best here but had little to go on. If Murphy had gotten up at 5:00 A.M. to study Cicero, they might have had something to start with.

We ended up on Madison.

"Even in holding," Murphy said, "I might go up there and say 'thanks' to a guy, act all friendly with him. Then I leave. That gets them in trouble with the other inmates, makes them look like an informer. I'll do that to that puke if you want."

I don't remember my response, if I had any. I was aware of my father's discomfort and, in turn, aware that my own comfort with such talk had grown during the last year. I liked men like Murphy. Their quick, exact talk. Their no-bones-about-it demeanor.

"They don't like rapists," Murphy informed my father. "It can go rough on them. They hate child molesters the most, but rapists aren't much above."

My father acted interested, but I think he was scared. He found talk like this distasteful. He liked to be in control of a discussion and if he wasn't, he usually opted out. This meant his paying attention itself was something out of the ordinary.

"You know, my girlfriend's name is Alice," Murphy said.

"Really?" my father said, taking interest.

"Yep. We've been together for some time now. When I heard your daughter's name was Alice, I had a good feeling about this case."

"We're quite fond of the name ourselves," my father said.

I told Detective Murphy about how my father had wanted to name me Hepzibah. That it was only because of my mother's vehement objection that the idea died.

He liked this. It made him laugh and I repeated the name until he got it right.

"That's a doozy," he said. "You lucked out."

We turned onto the main street of Syracuse's downtown. In May, it was still light at 7:30 P.M., but the stores were closed. We passed by Foley's department store. The cursive script and old brass security gates comforted me.

Up on our left I could see the marquee for the Hotel Syracuse. It too belonged to a more prosperous past. The old lobby was bustling. John Murphy checked us in at the reservation desk and showed us where the restaurant was. He told us he would return for us at nine the following morning.

"Have dinner. Gail said she'd be by sometime around eight o'clock tonight." He handed me a blue folder. "This is material she thought it might be useful for you to go over."

My father thanked him earnestly for his escort.

"No problem, Mr. Sebold," Murphy said. "I'm off to see my own Alice now."

We parked our bags in the room upstairs and returned to the lobby. I didn't want to eat but I did want a drink. In the bar area of the restaurant, my father and I sat at a small round table. We ordered gin and tonics. "Your mother doesn't have to know," he said. Gin and tonics were my father's drink. When I was eleven, I had watched him drink an entire pitcher on the day President Nixon resigned. My father went off to call my mother. She and her own mother and my sister would be sitting tight, she said, waiting for any news.

While he was gone I opened the blue folder. On top was a copy of my testimony from the preliminary hearing. I hadn't seen it before. I read over it, covering the page as I went with the folder itself. I didn't want anyone there—the young businessmen, the older salesmen, and the sole professional woman—to see what I held in my hands.

My father returned, trying not to disturb me while I was going over my words. He pulled out a small book in Latin that he'd brought from home.

"That doesn't look like good dinner material!"

I looked up. It was Gail. She was pointing to the blue folder. At three weeks before her projected delivery date, she wore a blue maternity T-shirt, tan corduroy pants, and running shoes. She had her glasses on, which I hadn't seen before, and she carried a briefcase with her.

"You must be Dr. Sebold," she said.

Score one for Gail, I thought. I had told her once that my father was a Ph.D. and hated being called Mister.

My father stood up to shake her hand. "Call me Bud," he said.

He offered to get her a drink. She said water would be fine, and as he went to the bar, she sat down beside me, bracing her arm on the back of the chair as she lowered herself down.

"Boy, you're *really* pregnant!" I said.

"You can say that again. I'm ready for the arrival. Billy Mastine," she said, referring to the district attorney, "gets the case because the sight of a pregnant woman makes the judge nervous." She was laughing but I didn't like it. I never considered anyone else my attorney. She, not the district attorney, had driven over on her off-hours to review the case. She was my lifeline, and the idea that she was being punished for being pregnant seemed another anti-woman maneuver to me.

"You know, Husa, your GYN, she's pregnant too. Eight months. Paquette is going to bust. All us pregnant ladies surrounding him. Cross-examining us makes them look bad."

My father returned and we got down to business. She excused herself to my father, saying that she didn't mean to be rude.

171

"Billy and I think that his attorney might go with an impotency defense."

My father listened hard. He played with the two onions at the bottom of his second drink, a Gibson.

"How can they prove that?" I asked, and Gail and I laughed. We imagined them bringing a doctor in to testify to the fact.

Gail broke down the three kinds of rapists.

"In all the studies they've done it seems like Gregory fits into the most common one. He's a power rapist. The others are anger rapists and the worst, sadistic."

"What does that mean?" I asked.

"Power rapists are often unable to sustain an erection and are only able to do so once they feel they've completely physically and mentally dominated their victim. He might have a bit of the sadistic thrown in. We found it interesting that he was able to finally have an erection once he'd made you kneel in front of him and give him a blow job."

If I noticed my father at all, it was only to will myself not to worry about him.

"I told him a lot of lies," I said, "about how strong he was, and when he lost his erection, I told him it wasn't his fault, that I wasn't good at it."

"That's right," Gail said. "That would make him think he had dominated you."

With Gail, I could be completely myself—say anything. My father sat beside us as we talked. Occasionally, if Gail sensed his interest or his confusion, she made a gesture of inclusion. I asked her how much time Madison would get if convicted.

"You know we offered him a plea."

"No," I said.

"Two to six, but he didn't take it. If you ask me his attorney is too cocky. It goes tougher on them if they refuse a plea and are then found guilty at trial."

"What's the maximum he can get?"

"On the rape charge, eight and a third to twenty-five."

"Twenty-five years?"

"Right, but he's eligible for parole at eight and a third."

"In Arab countries they cut off people's hands and feet," my father said.

Gail, who was of Lebanese descent, smiled. "An eye for an eye, huh, Bud?" she said.

"Exactly," said my father.

"Sometimes it seems fairer, but we have the law here."

"Alice told me about the lineup, how he could have his friend stand next to him. That doesn't seem right."

"Oh," Gail said, smiling, "don't worry about Gregory. Whatever he was given he might manage to screw up."

"Will he testify?" I asked.

"That depends on you. If you're as strong as you were at the prelim and grand jury, Paquette will have to have him take the stand."

"What can he say?"

"He'll deny it, say he wasn't there on May eighth, doesn't remember where he was. They'll create a story for October. Clapper saw him and Paquette's not stupid enough to have his client deny speaking to a cop."

"So I say it happened and he says it didn't."

"Yes. It's your word against his, and this is a nonjury trial."

"What does that mean?"

"It means Judge Gorman serves as both judge and jury. It was Gregory's choice. They worried about the superficials swaying citizens on a jury."

By this time I knew what the superficials were and knew they stood in my favor. I was a virgin. He was a stranger. It had happened outside. It was night. I wore loose clothes and could not be proven to have behaved provocatively. There were no drugs or alcohol in my system. I had no former involvement with the police of any kind, not even a traffic ticket. He was black and I was white. There was an obvious physical struggle. I had been injured internally—stitches had to be taken. I was young and a student at a private university that brought revenue to the city. He had a record and had done time.

She checked her watch and then, suddenly, reached out and grabbed my hand.

"Feel that?" she said, putting my hand up against her belly. I felt her baby kick. "A soccer player," she said, smiling.

She told me that mine was not the only charge Gregory faced. He had an outstanding charge for an aggravated assault against a police officer. While out on bail since Christmas, she said, he had also been arrested for a burglary.

We went over the preliminary and some affidavits dating back to the night of the rape. She told me that the police had already testified.

"Clapper got up there and talked about knowing Gregory from around the neighborhood, indicating he had former knowledge of him. If Madison takes the stand, Billy will try to go after that."

Here my father was paying close attention.

"So his record could be used?" he asked.

"Nothing juvenile," she said. "That's not admissible. But we'll make an attempt to establish that Greg is no stranger to the police. If he trips up and mentions it himself, then we can ask."

I described the outfit my mother and I had bought. Gail approved. "A skirt is important," she said. "I don't go anywhere near a courtroom in slacks. Gorman is particular on this point. Billy once got thrown out of his courtroom for wearing madras plaid!" Gail stood up. "I have to get this one home," she said, indicating her stomach. "Be direct," she said to me. "Be clear, and if you're confused, look over at that prosecution table. I'll be sitting right there."

That night was one of the worst in my memory for physical pain. I had begun, during the year, to have migraine headaches, although I didn't know they were migraines at the time. I had hid the fact I'd had them from my parents. I remember standing in the hotel bathroom and realizing I was going to have one that night. I could feel the drum beating in the back of my head as I brushed my teeth and dressed for bed. Over the rush of the water

I heard my father calling my mother to report on Gail. Having met her, he was flooded with relief.

But that night, as my headache grew worse, my father became frantic. I felt the pain most acutely in my eyes. I couldn't open or close them. I was sweating intensely and alternated between sitting bent over on the edge of one of the beds, rocking my head in my hands, and pacing back and forth between the balcony window and the bed.

My father hovered. He fired questions at me. "What is it? Where is the pain? Should I get a doctor? Maybe we should call your mother."

I didn't want to talk, because it hurt. "My eyes, my eyes," I moaned. "I can't see, they hurt so much, Dad."

My father decided that I needed to cry.

"Cry," he said. "Cry."

I begged him to leave me alone. But he was convinced he'd found the key.

"Cry," he said. "You need to cry. Cry."

"That's not it, Dad."

"Yes, it is," he said. "You are refusing to cry and you need to. Now cry!"

"You just can't will me to cry," I said to him. "Crying doesn't win a trial!"

I went to the bathroom to throw up, and closed the door against him.

Eventually, out in the other room, he fell asleep. I stayed in the bathroom with the lights on and then off, trying to soothe or shock my eyes back to their normal state. In the early-morning hours I sat on the edge of the bed as the headache began to lift. I read the Bible from the drawer beside my bed as a way to test that I hadn't begun to go blind.

The nausea hung on. Gail met us in the hotel cafe at eight. John Murphy arrived and sat with my father. Gail and Murphy tag-teamed me. I drank coffee and picked at the scales of a croissant.

"Whatever you do," Murphy said, "don't look him in the eyes. Am I right, Gail?"

I sensed she didn't want to get this aggressive this fast.

"He'll look at you real mean, try and throw you off," Murphy said. "When they ask you to point him out, stare in the direction of the table."

"Agreed," Gail said.

"Will you be there?" I asked Murphy.

"Your father and I will be sitting in the gallery," he said. "Right, Bud?"

It was time to drive to the Onondaga courthouse. Gail went in her own car. We would see her there. Murphy, my father, and I went in the official county car.

Inside the building, Murphy led us toward the courtroom, but stopped us midway down.

"We'll wait here until we're called," he said. "You okay, Bud?"

"Fine, thank you," my father said.

"Alice?"

"As good as I can be," I said, but I was thinking of only one thing. "Where is he?"

"That's why I stopped you here," Murphy confided. "To avoid any run-ins."

Gail came out of the courtroom and advanced toward us.

"Here's Gail," Murphy said.

"We've got a closed courtroom."

"What's that?" I asked.

"It means Paquette is trying to do what he did in the lineup. He's closing the courtroom so you can't have family sit in."

"I don't understand," my father said.

"He wouldn't let Tricia stay in the lineup," I said to my dad. "I hate him," I said. "He's a slimy asshole."

Murphy smiled.

"How can he do that?" my father asked.

"The defendant has the right to request a courtroom be closed if he thinks it will rob the witness of support," Gail said. "Look on the bright side, Gregory's father is here too. By closing the court, he won't have his father there either."

"How could he support a rapist anyway?"

"It's his *son*," Murphy said quietly.

Gail walked back to the courtroom.

"It might be easier for you without your father there," Murphy offered. "Some of what you'll have to say is harder in front of family."

I wanted to ask why, but I knew what he was saying. No father wanted to hear the story of how a stranger shoved his whole hand up his daughter's vagina.

Detective Murphy and my father stood facing me. Murphy offered words of condolence to my father. He pointed to a bench nearby, saying they could wait right there the whole time. My father had brought a small, leather-bound book along.

In the distance I saw Gregory Madison walking toward the courtroom. He had come from the hallway perpendicular to the one where I stood. I looked at him for a second. He did not see me. He was moving slowly. He wore a light gray suit. Paquette and another white man were with him.

I waited a second and then interrupted my father and Detective Murphy.

"Do you want to see him?" I asked my dad. I grabbed his arm to make him turn. "There he is, Dad."

But it was just Madison's back now, entering the courtroom, a flash of gray polyester suit.

"He's smaller than I thought," my father said.

There was a beat. A silence. Murphy rushed in.

"But wide. Believe me, he's all muscle."

"Did you see his shoulders?" I asked my dad. I'm sure my father had imagined Madison as towering.

Then I saw another man. He had a softer version of his son's build, white hair around the temples. He hesitated, for a moment, near the courtroom door, then spotted our little group down the hall. I didn't point him out to my father. Murphy's earlier comment had made me see him differently. After a second, and a look at me, he disappeared back down the other hall. He must have realized who I was. I didn't see him again, but I remembered him. Gregory Madison had a father. It was a simple fact but it stayed with me. Two fathers, both of them helpless to control their children's lives, would sit out the trial in their separate hallways.

The courtroom door opened. A bailiff stood in the open doorway and made eye contact with Murphy.

"You're up, Alice," Murphy said. "Remember, don't look at him. He'll be sitting at the defense table. When you turn around, look for Bill Mastine."

The bailiff came to get me. He looked like a cross between a theater usher and someone in the military. Detective Murphy and he nodded to each other. The pass-off.

I reached for my father's hand.

"Good luck," he said.

I turned. I was glad for Murphy. I thought suddenly that if my father were to go to the men's room, he might bump into Mr. Madison. Murphy would keep this from happening. I let it come now, the thing that had been burning at the corners of my temples the night before and boiled beneath the surface all that year: rage.

I was frightened and shaking when I crossed the courtroom, passed the defense table, the judge at the podium, the prosecution table, and came to take the stand. I liked to think I was Madison's worst nightmare, although he didn't know it yet. I represented an eighteen-year-old virgin coed. I was dressed in red, white, and blue.

A female bailiff, middle-aged and wearing wire-framed glasses, assisted me up onto the stand. I turned around. Gail was seated at the prosecution table. Mastine was standing. I was aware of other people, but I didn't look at them.

The bailiff held a Bible in front of me.

"Place your hand on the Bible," she said. And I repeated what I had seen on TV a hundred times.

"I swear to tell the truth . . . so help me, God."

"Be seated," the judge said.

My mother had always taught us to be scrupulous when wearing a skirt by smoothing it out before sitting down. I did this and as I did, I thought of what lay beneath the skirt and slip, still visible, if I lifted up the hem, through the flesh-tone stockings. That morning, while I dressed, I had written a note to myself on my skin. "You will die" was inked into my legs in dark blue ballpoint. And I didn't mean me.

Mastine began. He asked me my name and address. Where I was from. I barely remember answering him. I was getting the lay of the land. I knew exactly where Madison sat, but I didn't look at him. Paquette cleared his throat, rustled papers. Mastine asked me where I went to school. What year I had just finished there. He took a moment to close the window, first asking permission of Judge Gorman. Then he led me back in time. Where was I living in May of 1981? He directed my attention to the events of May 7, 1981, and the early hours of May 8, 1981.

I went into minute detail and, this time, did as Gail had told me to; I took each question slowly.

"Did he say anything to you by way of a threatening nature while you were screaming, and while the struggle was taking place?"

"He said he would kill me if I didn't do what he said."

Paquette stood. "I am sorry. I can't hear."

I repeated myself: "He said that he would kill me if I did not do what he said."

A few minutes later, I began to stumble. Mastine had led me up and now into the amphitheater tunnel.

"What happened there?"

"He told me to—that he was—well, I figured out by that time that he was—didn't want my money."

It was a shaky start to the most important story I would ever tell. I began a sentence only to trail off and begin again. And this wasn't because I was unaware of exactly what had happened in the tunnel. It was saying the words out loud, knowing it was *how* I said them that could win or lose the case.

" . . . Then he made me lie down on the ground and he took his pants off and left his sweatshirt on, and he started fondling my breasts and kissing them and doing things like that, and he was very interested in the fact that I was a virgin. He kept asking me about it. So he used his hands in my vagina. . . ."

I was breathing shallowly now. The bailiff beside me became more and more alert.

Mastine did not want the fact of my virginity to go by unnoted.

"Stop for a second," he said. "Had you ever had sexual intercourse with anyone at that time of your life?"

I felt shame. "No," I said, "I had not."

"Continue," said Mastine, stepping back again.

I talked uninterrupted for nearly five minutes. I described the assault, the blow job, talked about how cold I was, detailed the robbery of $8 from my back pocket, his kiss good-bye, his apology. Our parting. ". . . and he said, 'Hey, girl.' I turned around. He said, 'What is your name?' I said 'Alice.'"

Mastine needed specifics. He asked about penetration. He asked how many times it had occurred if more than once.

"It would be ten times because—or something to that effect, because he kept putting it in there, and then it kept falling out. So that is 'in there,' right? I am sorry. That is entering, right?"

My innocence seemed to embarrass them. Mastine, the judge, the bailiff beside me.

"So in any event, he did have penetration?"

"Yes."

Next, more questions on lighting. Then the photo exhibits. Photos of the scene.

"Did you receive any injuries as a result of this attack?"

I detailed these injuries.

"Were you bleeding when you left the scene?"

"Yes, I was."

"I am showing you the photographs marked for identification thirteen, fourteen, fifteen, sixteen. Look at those, please."

He handed me the photos. I looked only briefly at them.

"Are you familiar with the person depicted in those photographs?"

"Yes, I am," I said. I placed them on the edge of the stand, away from me.

"Who is tha—?"

"Me," I interrupted him. I began to cry. By trying not to, I made it worse. I sputtered.

"Are those photographs true and accurate portrayals of how you appeared after the attack on the evening of May eighth, 1981?"

"I was uglier, yes, but they are true portrayals." The bailiff went to hand me a glass of water. I reached for it but my grasp wasn't sure and it fell.

"I'm sorry," I said to the bailiff, crying more now. I tried to dab at her wet lapels with a Kleenex from the box she held.

"You're doing fine; breathe," this steely bailiff said. This made me think of the emergency room nurse on the night of the rape. *Good, you got a piece of him.* I was lucky; people were pulling for me.

"Do you want to continue?" the judge asked me. "We can take a short break."

"I will continue." I cleared my throat and wiped my eyes. Now I held a Kleenex balled up in my lap—something I had not wanted to be reduced to.

"Can you tell us what clothing you were wearing that evening?"

"I was wearing a pair of jeans and a blue work shirt and an oxford type of shirt and a cable-knit cardigan sweater that was tan, and moccasins and underwear."

Mastine had been standing near the prosecution table. Now he stepped forward holding a clear plastic bag.

"I am showing you a large bag which is marked exhibit number eighteen. Would you take a look at the contents of that bag and tell us if you are familiar with them?"

He held the bag in front of me. I had not seen these clothes since the night of the rape. My mother's sweater, shirt, and jeans that I had borrowed that afternoon were tightly packed inside. I took the bag from him and held it to one side.

"Yes."

"What are the contents of that bag?"

"They look to be the shirt and jeans and sweater that I had on. I don't see the underwear but—"

"How about where your left hand is?"

I moved my hand. I had borrowed a pair of my mother's underwear. She wore nude, I wore white. This underwear was stained so thoroughly with blood that only one clean patch reminded me of this.

"Okay. My underwear," I said.

They were received into evidence.

Mastine finished up on the events of that day. He established that I had returned to Pennsylvania after failing to pick a photo out of the mug books at the Public Safety Building. We moved to the fall, noting my return day in September for the beginning of my sophomore year.

"I direct your attention now to October fifth, 1981, the afternoon of that day. Do you recall the events of that day, that afternoon?"

"I recall one particular event, yes."

"Is the person who attacked you in Thorden Park, is he in court here today?"

"Yes, he is."

I did what I was warned not to. I focused my attention on Madison's face. I stared at him. For a few seconds, I was unaware of Mastine or of Gail, or of the courtroom.

"Would you tell us where he is sitting and what he has on?" I heard Mastine say.

Before I spoke, Madison looked down.

"He is sitting next to the man with the brown tie and he has a gray three-piece suit on," I said. I relished pointing out Paquette's ugly brown tie and identifying Madison not by his skin color, as I was expected to do, but by his clothes.

"Let the record reflect that the witness identified the defendant," Mastine said.

For the remainder of the direct examination, I did not take my eyes off Madison for more than a second or two. I wanted my life back.

Mastine spent a long time on the events of October 5. I had to describe Madison on that day. What he looked like, what he said. Madison raised his head from the defense table only once. When he did, and saw that I was still looking at him, he turned away and to the city of Syracuse outside the window.

Mastine questioned me in detail about what Officer Clapper looked like, where he was standing. Had I seen Madison approach him? From what direction? Where did I go? Who did I call? Why the time discrepancy between seeing him and calling the police? Oh, he pointed out, the discrepancy was because I had appeared at class to tell my teacher I couldn't attend? Had naturally called my parents and told them what had happened? Had tried to wait for a friend to walk me home? All the things a good girl, he implied, might do after running into her rapist on the street.

His purpose in all this was to make anything Paquette could go after in his cross moot. That was what made Clapper so important. If I had identified Clapper and he, in turn, had identified Madison, this made my case close to airtight. This was the key point of identification Mastine emphasized. What Mastine and Uebelhoer, what Paquette, Madison, and I all knew, was that the lineup was the weak link.

I had thought long and hard about what I was going to say. This time around I would not pretend a command I did not have.

Mastine had me detail my reasoning for ruling out the men I initially had. I took my time explaining the similarities between numbers four and five and how I hadn't been sure at the time I marked the box but that I had chosen five because of the eye contact.

"At the time that you indicated it was number five, were you in fact positive it was him?"

"No, I was not."

"Why did you mark the box, then?"

This was the single most important question of my case.

"I marked the box because I was very scared, and he was looking at me and I saw the eyes, and the way the lineup is, it is not like it is on television, and you are standing right next to the person and he looks like he is two feet away from you. He looked at me. I picked him."

I could feel Judge Gorman's attention heighten. I watched Gail as I answered the questions Mastine put to me, tried to think of good things, of the baby floating inside her womb.

"Do you know to this day who that depicted?"

"Number five?"

"Yes," said Mastine.

"No," I said.

"Do you know which position the defendant was in, in the lineup?"

If I told the truth, I could say that the moment I picked number five I knew I was wrong and had regretted it. That everything after that, from the mood in the lineup room, to the relief on Paquette's face, to the dark weight I felt on Lorenz in the conference room, had only confirmed my mistake.

If I lied, if I said, "No, I do not," I knew I would be perceived as telling the truth in my confusion between four and five. "Identical twins," I had said to Tricia in the hallway. "It's four, isn't it?" were my first words to Lorenz.

I knew the man who raped me sat across from me in the courtroom. It was my word against his.

"Do you know which position the defendant was in, in the lineup?"

"No, I do not," I said.

Judge Gorman held up his hand. He had the court reporter read over Mastine's last question and my answer to it.

Mastine asked me if there was any other reason I felt scared or hurried during the lineup.

"The attorney for the defendant hadn't let me have my rape— he wouldn't allow me to have my rape center counselor with me."

Paquette objected. He believed this was irrelevant.

Mastine continued. He asked me about the Rape Crisis Center, about Tricia. I had met her on the day of my rape. He emphasized the connection. All of this went to why, in his mind, I had made my one and only mistake. This mistake, he wanted to make certain, should not invalidate what occurred on October 5 and the corroborating evidence of Officer Clapper.

"Is there any doubt in your mind, Miss Sebold, that the person that you saw on Marshall Street is the same person that attacked you on May eighth in Thorden Park?"

"No doubt whatsoever," I said. And I had none.

"That is all I have at this point, Your Honor," Mastine said, turning to Judge Gorman.

Gail gave me a wink.

"We will take about a five-minute recess," Judge Gorman said. "I caution you, Miss Sebold, don't discuss your testimony now with anyone."

This was what I had been promised—a break between direct and cross. I was assigned to the bailiff. She led me off to the right, through a door, down a short hall, and into a conference room.

The bailiff was as friendly as she could be.

"How was I?" I asked.

"Why don't you sit down," she said.

I sat at the table.

"Can you just make a signal?" I asked. Suddenly I got the idea into my head that the room was bugged—a way to make sure that the rules were followed. "Thumbs up or down?"

"I can't discuss the case. It will all be over soon."

We were quiet. I could now make out the traffic noise outside. I hadn't heard anything other than Mastine's questions while I testified.

The bailiff offered me stale coffee in a styrofoam cup. I took it and wrapped my hands around the warm outsides.

Judge Gorman entered the room.

"Hello, Alice," he said. He stood on the other side of the table from me. "How is she, bailiff?" he asked.

"She's good."

"Haven't talked about the case?"

"No," the bailiff said, "quiet, mostly."

"So what does your father do, Alice?" he asked me. His tone was more gentle than the one he used in court. The voice lighter, more circumspect.

"He teaches Spanish at Penn," I said.

"I bet you're glad he's here today."

"I am."

"Do you have any sisters or brothers?"

"An older sister. Mary," I added, anticipating his next question. He went over and stood by the window.

"I've always liked this room," he said. "What does Mary do?"

"She's majoring in Arabic at Penn," I said, suddenly happy to have questions that were so easy. "She goes there free but I didn't get in," I said. "Something my parents really regret now," I said, making a joke.

"I bet they do," he said. He had been half sitting on the radiator and now he stood and adjusted his robe. "Well, you just sit here for a little while longer," he said, "and we'll call you."

He left.

"He's a good judge," the bailiff said.

The door opened and a male bailiff poked his head in. "We're ready," he said.

My bailiff stubbed out her cigarette. We didn't speak. I was ready now. This was it.

I reentered the courtroom and took the stand. I took a deep breath and looked up. In front of me was my enemy. He would do everything he could to make me look bad—stupid, confused, hysterical. Madison could look at me now. His man had been sent in. I saw Paquette approach me. I looked right at him, took him all in: his small build, ugly suit, the sweat on his upper lip. He may have been, in some part of his life, a decent man, but what overwhelmed me now was my contempt for him. Madison had committed the crime but Paquette, by representing him, condoned it. He seemed the very force of nature I had to fight. I had no trouble hating him.

"Miss Sebold, I believe that you testified that you were headed into Thorden Park on May eighth around midnight. Is that right?"

"Yes."

"You were coming from Westcott Street?"

"Yes."

"Did you go through an entrance through the park there, like a gateway?"

"There is a bathhouse and there is pavement in front of the house, and I went on the pavement and then it continues on a brick path by the pool and I walked on that brick path."

"So that the bathhouse, then, is at the perimeter of the pool, on the Westcott side?"

"Yes."

"The path you are talking about takes you right into the center of the park and right out on the other side, would it?"

"Yes, it would."

"You started to go down that path?"

"Yes, I did."

"You testified today that the whole area was surrounded by lights and that the lighting was quite good?"

"Yes, I did."

"Do you remember testifying in a preliminary examination on this case?"

"Yes, I did." I hated these questions. Who wouldn't remember? But I held my sarcasm in check.

"Do you remember saying that there were some lights on anyway from the bathhouse but—"

"What page?" Mastine asked.

"Page four, the preliminary exam."

"Is this the preliminary exam?" Gorman asked, holding up a group of papers.

"Yes," Paquette said.

"Line fourteen. 'I think there are some lights from my way to the bathhouse I could see behind. It was dark, but not black behind me.'"

I remembered my phrase "dark but not black."

"Yes, I said that."

"Isn't that a little bit different than saying you were surrounded by lights on all sides and quite good lighting?"

I knew what he was doing.

"It may sound more dramatic to say surrounded by lights. The light was there and I saw what I saw."

"My question is, was it dark but not black the way you testified in the preliminary, or was it quite good lighting, surrounded by lights, the way you testified today?"

"When I said quite good lighting, I meant quite good lighting in the dark."

"Okay. Now, you went about how far into the park before you were first accosted?"

"I went past the bathhouse and past the gate and the fence that is along the pool and about ten feet past that fence, and then I was taken by the man."

"How many feet or yards would it be from the entrance to the park until that point that you described as ten feet beyond?"

"Two hundred feet."

"About two hundred feet? You were into the park about two hundred feet when you were first accosted?"

"Yes, I was."

"Did that person come up from behind you?"

"Yes, he did."

"Grabbed you from behind?"

"Yes, he did."

"You struggled at that point?"

"Yes, I did."

"Did that struggle take a long time?"

"Yes."

"About how long?"

"About ten or fifteen minutes."

"Now, there came a point when this individual took you from where you were first accosted into another area of the park. Is that right?"

"It wasn't another area. It was just further in."

"Further into the park?"

"Not further into the park but—on an outside the—we struggled outside the tunnel and then he took me inside the tunnel."

"Could you describe this tunnel for me?"

The questions were fast and furious. I had to breathe quickly to keep up. I couldn't see anything but Paquette's lips moving and the beads of sweat above them.

"Well, I keep calling it a tunnel because somebody told me that it was a tunnel leading up to the amphitheater. From what I see, and it doesn't have—you can't go farther into it than a distance of about ten feet. It is more like a cave and an arch. It has got stonework above it and a gate in front of it."

"How deep does it go in there, from the gate to the wall?"

"I would say about ten, fifteen feet at the most."

"At the most?" he said. It felt like a sudden, unexpected parry in a fencing match. "I ask you to take a look at exhibit number four, which has been received into evidence, and I ask you, do you recognize that?"

"Yes, I do."

"What is that?"

"That is the path by which he took me to the tunnel and that is the gate in front of the tunnel, the opening of the gate."

"So if we were looking at this picture, and would he have taken you farther down that path walking, and I would call it into the picture, or am I misstating—"

"The tunnel is behind the gate, or the cave is behind the gate."

Suddenly it dawned on me what he was doing. All the gate and tunnel questions, the rapid fire on where I was coming from, going to, how many feet it was or wasn't. He was trying to wear me out.

"Could you point out to me any other spotlight or streetlights that you see in the picture?"

I sat forward on my seat and studied exhibit four closely. I was attentive; I waited to form the answers that would equal him move for move.

"I don't see any streetlights, except right up here on that tip there is a light."

"Way in the back of the picture?"

"Yes."

"Are there any lights there that weren't depicted in this photograph?"

"Yes."

"There are?" he said, again the same disbelieving tone, meant to imply that I was really a bit insane, wasn't I? "They are missing from the picture?" he said. He smiled up at the judge, bemused.

"They are not in the picture, no," I said. "That is because the picture doesn't show the whole area."

All of what wasn't said in every move of his—his insinuations, what he implied—I tried to answer by being as clear and controlled as possible.

Quickly, he pushed forward another photo. "This is exhibit number five, do you recognize that?"

"Yes, I do."

"That is the area where you were assaulted; is that right?"

"Yes, it is."

"Is there any lighting in that picture, any artificial lights?"

"No. I do not see any lighting and you could see the place, and you—there must be some light."

"The question is," he said, pressing in, "do you see any artificial lighting? Of course there are police lights flashing into the picture."

"I see no artificial lights," I said, "and it is only a picture of the stone, and there can't be lights in the stone," I said, looking up at him and at the rest of the court.

"That probably would be true." His lips curled. "About how much time would you say that you spent in that area?"

"I would say about an hour."

"About an hour?"

"A little bit more."

"I am sorry?" He cocked his hand to his ear.

"I said an hour or a little bit more."

"An hour or a little bit more? How much time did you spend on the pathway that led up to the area we are talking about in exhibit number five?"

"On the pathway about two minutes. Right outside the cave about fifteen minutes." I wanted to get it right.

"All right. So you were on the pathway for about two minutes?"

"Right."

"The area outside of the cave, as depicted in exhibit five, for about fifteen minutes?"

"Yes."

"The area actually in the cave for about a little over an hour?"

"Right."

I was exhausted, felt as if I was being dragged here and there. The course of this man's logic was beyond me, and it was meant to be.

"Now, you saw this person on one other occasion, I think, and on that evening? I believe that you testified that that was as he was walking down the path?"

"Yes."

"And that was about how far from you?"

"That was about a hundred and fifty feet from me."

"About a hundred and fifty feet?"

Hearing my words back was maddening. He wanted me to falter.

"Yes."

"About fifty yards? Is that fair? About half a football field?"

"I would say," I said, "a hundred and fifty feet."

I sunk a nail in, but he pulled it out.

"Your glasses weren't on then, were they?"

"No, they were not."

"When did you lose those glasses?"

"During the time—" But he didn't like where I might be going, so he phrased my answer for me.

"During the fight on the path, right?"

"Yes."

"So within the first two minutes of this altercation you lost your glasses?"

I remembered my own time breakdown.

"During the fight which was off the side of the pathway."

So did he.

"So you were two minutes on the path and then fifteen minutes outside the gate, and it was during this fifteen-minute period that your glasses came off?"

"Yes, it was."

"Now, did you fight on the path, or did he sort of spirit you over to the area in front of the gate?"

His choice of words, "spirit you over," and his gesture, a hula-dancer-like push to the side with his hands, infuriated me. I looked down at his shoes to dissipate my rage. Gail's words came back to me: "If you ever get lost or upset, just tell, as best you can, what happened to you."

"He put his arms around both my arms, down at my side, and the other around the mouth, and so I couldn't really fight, and I agreed not to scream, and when he let go of my mouth, and I screamed, that is when we started fighting."

"Were you stationary at the first spot that you stopped at, at that point, or had you been moved?"

We were not in sync. I kept listening to what I knew to be the truth and I spoke from that place. He used language like *that you stopped at*, as if I had free will—a choice in the matter.

"I was walking, yes."

"He was standing behind you; isn't that right?"

"Yes, he was."

"You gave a—quite detailed description today, and I believe

that you testified that the person that was there was about five five to five seven, broad shoulders, small but very muscular, and you testified that he had a—I can't read my own writing—some kind of a line—"

"Boxer," I said.

"A pug nose?"

"Yes."

"Almond-shaped eyes?"

"Yes."

"Now, is it your testimony that you gave all of that information to the police on May eighth?"

"On May eighth, what I was to do was to put together a composite drawing from features."

"Did you give the police, who were going to go looking for the suspect, the information you gave us here today?"

"Could you repeat that?"

"Did you give the information that I just outlined, that you testified to today, did you give all that information to the police on May the eighth?"

"I don't recall if I gave them all of it. I gave most of it."

"Did you sign a statement on May eighth that set forth your version of the incident as it occurred?"

"Yes, I did."

"Would it refresh your memory if I were to show you the statement and give you an opportunity to review it?"

"Yes."

"I would ask this be marked as defendant's exhibit."

Paquette handed a copy to me and one to the judge. "I show you, to review the statement to yourself, and I guide your attention to the bottom paragraph, and I think that is where most of the description is, and review it to yourself and let me know when you are finished, and if your memory has been refreshed as to the description you gave to the police on May eighth, 1981."

He had succeeded in talking during the entire time I had to review the statement.

"Have you had an opportunity to review that?"

"Yes."

"Could you tell me what you told them on the eighth of May?"

"I said—'I wish to state the man I encountered in the park is a Negro, approximately sixteen to eighteen years of age, small and muscular build of one hundred and fifty pounds, wearing dark blue sweat shirt and dark jeans with short Afro-style haircut. I desire prosecution in the event this individual is caught.'"

"That doesn't say anything about the jaw or pug nose or any almond eyes, does it?"

"No," I said, "it does not." I was not thinking fast. How, if I had not mentioned them, could the composite have been made? Why didn't the police take those things down? When presented with the insufficiency of my statement, I was unable to reason that the lack in it had not been my fault. Paquette had won his point.

"Now, you saw this—individual on Marshall Street again, and this was in October; is that right?"

"Yes."

"I gather from your testimony that you made a—correct me if I am wrong—you made an effort to remember the features of that person so that you could go back and reconstruct it?"

"Yes, I did."

"Then what you did was, you went back to your dorm and reconstructed those features that you recall from that encounter on Marshall Street; is that true?"

"Also from the encounter on May eighth," I said. Anticipating his point, I rushed on, "And I could not have identified him as the man who raped me unless he was the man who raped me."

"Repeat that?"

I was glad to.

"In other words, I am saying that I would not have spotted him on the street as the man who raped me unless he was the man who raped me. So I knew those features. I had to know those features and what they looked like in order to identify him in the first place."

"You were on Marshall Street, and you saw this individual for the first time on that day? What was he doing?"

"I saw him for the first time on May eighth, and I saw him for the second time on October fifth."

I noticed Gail; she had been leaning forward listening to the cross. With that answer she sat back in her chair with a force of pride.

"That is what I said, for the first time on that day. I was try-ing—"

"I don't want to get tripped up," I said.

"Okay."

"Now," I started again, "the first time that I saw him, and I knew for sure that it was him—the man who had raped me—was when he was crossing the street and said, 'Hey, girl, don't I know you from somewhere,' and the first time I saw the same body was on the other side of the street, when he was talking to the man in the alley between Way Inn and Gino's and Joe's." I was being as exact as possible. "I had first spotted his body from the back—not becoming certain it was him until a few minutes later when he spoke to me and I saw his face."

"He was talking to someone in the alley there?"

"Yes."

"That is how far from where you were?"

"From where I was when?"

"Where you were standing when you saw him."

"I was walking, and when I saw him and it—it is just the street, he was on the sidewalk, and so it was just the street."

"You didn't say anything to him?"

"No. I said nothing."

"He didn't say anything to you?"

"He said, 'Hey, girl, don't I know you from somewhere?'"

Paquette was suddenly excited. "Did he say that? Are you say-ing that he said that then or after he came back down the street?"

"He wasn't in the alley," I said. I wanted to make certain of what I said now. I couldn't imagine the cause for Paquette's excitement. Wouldn't know for fifteen years that the defense had claimed Madison had been talking to Officer Clapper when he said, "Hey, don't I know you from somewhere?" I backtracked. There was something Paquette was after and I didn't know what. "He was talking to a man in the alley. He said that to me when I was on the other side of the street, the Huntington Hall side, and walking up and away from the Varsity. He said that as he was crossing the street and coming toward me."

"That would be the second time of that day that you saw him?"

"Yes. That was the first time that I knew for sure that that was the man who raped me."

"A lot of things happened," Paquette said. The tone he used was breezy, as if it had been a big and overwhelming day at the fair for me. As if I couldn't get my story straight because there was no straight story. "Did you contact the police and make a statement to the police on October fifth?"

"Yes, I did."

"That was the sworn statement that you signed?"

"Yes."

"You did ask the lieutenant to indicate that was full and accurate and complete?"

"Yes, I did."

"Did you tell the police on October fifth, 1981 that the man you saw on Marshall Street was the man who raped you, or did you say that you had a feeling that he might be the man?"

"I said that that was the man who raped me on May eighth."

"You are sure of that?"

He was setting something up. Even I could see that. The only thing I could do was stick to my story as he pinned me down.

"Yes, I am."

"So if the statement says something else, then the statement is wrong?"

I was in a minefield now; I kept walking.

"Yes, it is."

"But you signed the statement, didn't you?"

He was taking his time. I looked right at him.

196

"Yes, I did."

"Did you have a chance to read it over?"

"Yes, I did."

"Did they review it with you before you signed it?"

This was excruciating.

"They didn't review it. They gave it to me to read."

"Who are they?" he asked belligerently. He checked a note he'd made. He was grandstanding now. "You've had fourteen years of school," he said, "and you read it, and that was no problem, and you understood it all?"

"Yes, I did."

"Your testimony today is that you were sure that that is true. Even if the statement on October the fifth doesn't say that—"

Mastine objected. "Perhaps we could have a question and answer?"

"Sustained," said Gorman.

"Do you recall," Paquette began again, "saying in the statement to the police, 'I had a feeling that the black male—'"

Mastine stood. "I will object to the counsel reading from the statement or using the statement to impeach credibility; reading from the statement is improper, and in fact I object to it on that basis—"

"He could read from the statement," Gorman said to Mastine. "I believe, Mr. Paquette, you should form the question something like this, 'Do you recall giving the statement to the police, on such and such a date?' and read the statement. If you would, please."

"Sure," Paquette said. Some of his steam had been lost.

"Do you recall giving the statement to the police on October fifth?"

"Yes."

"Do you recall telling the police that 'I had a feeling that the black male might be the person that raped me last May in Thorden Park'?"

I had caught on to the game now. "I would like to see a copy of it just to be sure," I said.

197

"Sure, be happy to. I would ask that this be marked as defendant's C for identification, the statement made by Alice Sebold on October fifth.

"I ask you to review the statement and ask you if that refreshes your recollection as to the information you gave at the time?"

I scanned the contents of my affidavit. Immediately I saw the problem.

"Okay," I said.

"Did you advise the police in that statement that you were sure—"

I interrupted him. Suddenly I knew that the last few minutes were ones I could wrestle back from him.

"The reason why I said that I had a *feeling* at that point was because I had only seen his back and his mannerisms at that point. I was *sure* when I saw his face on the second time, when I was on the other side of the street. I had a *feeling*, because of his build and mannerisms on the first time, when I saw him from the back, but since I had then not seen his face at that time, I was not *sure*. When I saw his face I was sure that that was the man who raped me on May eighth."

"This statement was made after you had seen him both times on Marshall Street, wasn't it?"

"Yes, it was. They asked me to describe it and in chronological order, which I did."

"Does that statement in any way reflect a change in your stance from 'might be' to 'is'?"

"No, it does not."

"Thank you." He acted as if he had won something. He wanted out of that line of questioning and he took what he could get. He opted to muddy the water. Wasn't it clear from all this *feeling* to *sure, might be* to *is* that I was too confused to be believed?

"By the way," he said, reapproaching again, "on the day of the lineup in November, were there people from the Rape Crisis Center present in the building?"

"Yes, there were."

"Had you had counsel with them just prior to the lineup?"

"Counsel?"

"Did you talk to them and were they available?"

"Yes. She accompanied me to the Public Safety Building."

"As soon as you left the lineup, were they still available to you?"

"Yes, she was."

"*She* was?"

"Yes."

"You talked to her before and you talked to her after; is that right?"

"Yes."

"Are they here today? Is there anyone from the Rape Crisis Center here today?"

"No, they are not."

"They are neither in the courtroom or in the building?"

"No."

Paquette hadn't liked the point Mastine had made earlier, that Paquette, by not allowing Tricia in the room, could himself have had a hand in undermining the lineup as evidence.

"Now, there was a lineup procedure held, wasn't there?"

"Yes, there was."

"I believe that that was on November fourth?"

"Yes, it was."

"Do you remember an Investigator Lorenz being there?"

"Yes, I do."

"Had you recognized him from seeing him before?"

"Yes, I had."

"Where had you recognized him from?"

"He is the man who took my affidavit on May eighth."

"Did he ever tell you that he didn't believe the statement that you made on May eighth?"

I did not stop. Neither Gail nor Mastine had told me that Lorenz initially doubted me.

"No, he did not."

"Do you remember him advising you in any way when you first came into the lineup room?"

199

"He told me that my duty was to look at the five men and mark the box as to which one was the man in question."

"Do you recall who else was in the lineup room?"

I went through my head, reimagining the room and the bodies in it. "Mrs. Uebelhoer, the court stenographer, or the room stenographer—I don't know what you call them—and the other man was sitting there, and he did something, and me."

"Do you recall—"

"Yes, you."

His tone had switched suddenly. He was fatherly, shepherding. I didn't trust him.

"Do you remember an Investigator Lorenz advising you to take your time and look the people over and feel free to move around?"

"Yes. I do remember that."

"Do you recall me asking the investigator to explain to you how to—"

"Excuse me?"

"Do you recall me asking the investigator to explain to you how you should use the form?" His smile was almost benevolent.

"I don't recall you specifically," I said.

"You remember he did tell you that?"

"Somebody told me how to use it."

"In fact," he said, his smile gone now, "you did stand up and move around the room?"

"Yes."

"Didn't you even have the suspects make some sort of a motion; I think you had each of them turn to their left? Do you remember that?"

"Yes, I did."

"The investigator had each do that—'Number one, turn to your left'—and you remember that?"

He was dragging this out; it was his job to.

"Yes."

"At the end of that procedure, what did you do? What was the next thing that happened?"

200

"I counted down to four and five, and I chose five because he was looking at me."

"You chose number five?"

"Yes. I put the *X* in the box for five." I would say it a thousand times; I had done it.

"You signed that?"

"Yes, I did."

"Did you express in words, in that room, at that time, to anyone, any concern in your mind over it not being number five?"

"I didn't say a word in the room."

"You knew that by marking number five that what you were indicating was that he would be a suspect or might well be a suspect in a rape trial?"

"Yes." It seemed the wrongs I'd done were endless.

"So it wasn't until after you left the room that you discovered that number five wasn't the person that you should have picked?"

"No. I went to my rape crisis counselor and I said number four and five looked like identical twins. That is what I did."

"You didn't express that to anyone beforehand?"

"I did it in the room, and before that I hadn't seen them and I couldn't."

He didn't wish to linger long enough to clarify. I had meant the conference room this time, not the lineup room.

"You picked number five?"

"Yes, I did."

"I believe that your testimony is, then, that you were raped on May eighth?"

"Yes."

"That you didn't see your assailant again until Marshall Street?"

"October fifth, yes."

"Then you saw him on Marshall Street?"

"Yes."

"There was a police officer right there, wasn't there?"

"Yes."

"Did you approach that officer?"

"No. I did not approach the officer."

"Did you go to the nearest phone and call the police?"

"I went to the Hall of Languages, where I had a class, and called my mother."

"So you called your mother. . . ." He was snide. It brought me all the way back to the preliminary hearing, the way his colleague, Meggesto, had savored the words "Calvin Klein jeans." My mother, my Calvin Klein jeans. It was what they had on me.

"Yes."

"Then you talked to your professor?"

"I called my mother and then I called some friends, to try to get in contact with someone who could walk me back to my dormitory. I was very scared, and I knew I had to go to school. I couldn't get hold of anybody. I went upstairs to my teacher and told him why I wasn't attending class. I told him, and I walked to the library to find one of my friends to walk me the rest of the way home and go with me to the police and then I went back to my dorm and I had called the friend of mine who is an artist, so he could help me draw a picture, which he did not do. Then I called the police and they arrived with the Syracuse University security officers."

"Did you ever call security to give you a ride home?"

I began to cry. Was everything my fault?

"Excuse me," I said, apologizing for my tears. "They only do that after five or during night hours." I looked for Gail. I saw her staring intently at me. *It's almost over*, her look said. *Hang on.*

"How much time went by from the time that you saw him on Marshall Street?"

"Forty-five to fifty minutes."

"Forty-five to fifty minutes?"

"Yes."

"Now, you have not identified Mr. Madison from that moment until today; is that right?"

"Identified him, you know, in your presence?"

"Identified him here in the legal proceedings as the person that raped you."

"Not in legal proceedings, but I did today."

"Today you did. How many black people do you see in the room?"

Jumping the gun, knowing his insinuation. *How many other black people, besides the defendant, do you see in the room?* I answered, "None."

He laughed and smiled up at the judge, then swept his hand in the direction of Madison, who looked bored. "You see none?" Paquette said, emphasizing the last word. She really is quite *incredible*, he seemed to be saying.

"I see one black person other than—the rest of the people in the room."

He smiled in triumph. So did Madison. I wasn't feeling powerful anymore. I was guilty for the race of my rapist, guilty for the lack of representation of them in the legal profession in the City of Syracuse, guilty that he was the only black man in the room.

"Do you remember testifying about this lineup in a grand jury proceeding?"

"Yes, I do."

"Was it on November fourth, the same day as the lineup?"

"Yes, it was."

"Do you remember—looking at page sixteen of the grand jury minutes, line ten—'You picked him out of the lineup? Are you absolutely sure this is the one?'

" 'Number five; I am not absolutely sure. I was between four and five. But I picked five because he was looking at me.'

"So the juror says, 'What you are saying is you are not absolutely sure he was the one?'

" 'Right.'

" 'Number five is the one.'

" 'Right.'

"So you still weren't sure on November fourth?"

I didn't know what Paquette was doing. I felt lost. "That number five was the one? I was not sure five was the one, right."

"You surely weren't sure that number four was the one because you didn't pick him."

"He was not looking at me. I was very scared."

"He wasn't looking at you?" His syllables dripped with pitiless sarcasm.

"Yes."

"Did you notice anything unusual on May eighth, when you were accosted by this person, that you haven't told us about, about his features or scars or marks or anything, facial features, his teeth, fingernails, or his hands or anything?"

"Nothing unusual, no."

I wanted it to be over now.

"You said that you looked at your watch when you went in the park?"

"Yes."

"What time was it?"

"Twelve o'clock."

"You looked at your watch when you got to your dorm?"

"I didn't look at my watch. I—was very aware of what time it was because I was surrounded by police, and I may have also looked at my watch, and I knew that it was two-fifteen when I got back to the dorm."

"When you got back to the dorm? Were the police called when you got back to your dorm?"

"Yes."

"When you got back to the dorm, at two-fifteen, and there had been no police called yet?"

"Right."

"They came sometime after that?"

"Yes. Immediately after I got back to my dorm."

He had finally worn me down. It made awful sense that no matter how hard I tried, he would be left standing at the end.

"Now, you said, you testified that he kissed you; is that right?"

"Yes."

"Once or twice or a lot of times?"

I could see Paquette. Madison sat behind him, interested. I felt the two of them were coming in after me.

"Once or twice when we were standing and then, after he

had laid me down on the ground, a few times. He kissed me." The tears were just rolling down my cheeks now and my lips trembling. I didn't bother to wipe them. I had sweat through the Kleenex that I held.

Paquette knew he had broken me. That was enough. He didn't want this.

"May I have a moment, Your Honor?"

"Yes," Gorman said.

Paquette went to the defense table and conferred with Madison, then checked his yellow legal pad and files.

He looked up. "Nothing further," he said.

The relief in my body was immediate. But then Mastine stood.

"A couple of questions, if it please the court."

I was tired but knew now that Mastine would handle me gently if he could. His tone was firm but I trusted him.

Mastine was concerned with working Paquette's former territory, going back to strengthen weak lines. He made a quick five points. First he established how late it was and how tired I was when I gave my statement on the night of the rape. He had me detail all the things I had been through and on no sleep. Then he moved on to my statement on October 5, the one Paquette had gleefully put forth to me—the *feeling* versus *sure*. Mastine was able to establish that, as I had said, it was an affidavit in which I retold the encounter with Madison chronologically. I first saw him from the back and had a *feeling*. I then saw him face-on and was *sure*.

Then he asked me if anyone was with me. He wanted to point out that because my father was present, I had elected to decline the presence of a rape crisis representative.

"My father is waiting outside," I said. This fact didn't seem real to me. Far away, in the hall outside, he was reading. Latin. I hadn't thought of him since entering the courtroom. I couldn't.

Mastine asked me how long I had been under Madison in the tunnel and how far away from his face I was.

"One centimeter," I said.

Then he asked me a question I felt uncomfortable with, one I had known he might ask if Paquette's approach warranted it.

"Could you give the judge an idea of how many young black men you would see on a daily average in your travels, or class or dormitory or at all?"

Paquette objected. I knew why. It went straight to his case.

"Overruled," said Gorman.

I said, "A lot," and Mastine had me quantify. "More than fifty or less?" I said that it was more. The whole thing made me uncomfortable, separating the students I knew by their race, pooling them into columns, and tabulating their number. But this wouldn't be the first time, or the last, that I wished my rapist had been white.

Mastine had no further questions.

Paquette got up only to have me repeat one thing. He wanted me to repeat the distance of Madison's face from mine during the rape itself. I did: one centimeter. Later he would try and use my certainty against me. Quoting this distance in his final statement as to why I couldn't be trusted as a credible witness.

"No redirect," Mastine said.

"You are excused," Judge Gorman said, and I stood.

My legs were shaky underneath me and I had sweat through my skirt and stockings and slip. The male bailiff who had led me in came toward the center of the room and waited for me.

He took me out.

Down the hall, Murphy spotted me and helped my father gather his books. The bailiff looked at me.

"I've been in this business for thirty years," he said. "You are the best rape witness I've ever seen on the stand."

I would hold on to that moment for years.

The bailiff walked back toward court.

Murphy hustled me off. "We want to get away from the door," he said. "They'll be breaking for lunch."

"Are you okay?" my dad asked.

"I'm fine," I said. I did not recognize him as my father. He was just a person standing there, like all the rest. I was shaking and needed to sit down. The three of us, Murphy, my father, and I, returned to their bench.

They spoke to me. I don't remember what they said. It was over.

Gail breezed out of the courtroom and over to us. She looked at my father. "Your daughter's an excellent witness, Bud," she said.

"Thank you," my father said.

"Was I okay, Gail?" I asked. "I was worried. He was really mean."

"That's his job," she said. "But you held up under him. I was watching the judge."

"What did he look like?" I asked.

"The judge? He looked exhausted," she said, smiling. "Billy is really tired. I wanted to get up there so bad. We have a break until two and then it's the doctor. Another pregnant lady!"

It was like a relay race, I realized. The leg I'd run had been arduous and long, but there were still others—more questions and answers—more key witnesses, many more hours to Gail's day.

"If I learn anything I'll contact the detective," she said, turning to me. She extended her hand to my father. "Nice to meet you, Bud. You can be proud."

"I hope the next time we meet it's under more pleasant circumstances," he said. It had just hit him. We were leaving.

Gail hugged me. I had never hugged a pregnant woman before, found it awkward, almost genteel, the way both she and I had to lean only the upper halves of our bodies in. "You're incredible, kiddo," she said quietly to me.

Murphy drove us back to Hotel Syracuse, where we packed. I may have slept. My father called my mother. I don't remember those hours. My attention had been so focused that now I let go. I was aware that my case was still continuing as we folded clothes and waited for Murphy to pick us up later that afternoon. My father and I sat on the edges of the twin beds. Putting distance between us and the city of Syracuse was our unspoken goal. We knew the plane would do it. We waited.

Murphy came early to meet us. He brought news.

"Gail wanted to be the one to tell you," he said, "but she couldn't get away."

My father and I were in the carpeted lobby, our red American Tourister luggage waiting nearby.

"They got him," he said joyfully. "Guilty on six counts. He was remanded to jail!"

I went blank. My legs felt weak beneath me.

"Thank God," my father said. He said this quietly, acknowledging an answered prayer.

We were in the car. Murphy was chattering. He was high off it. I sat in the back of the car while my father and Murphy sat in the front. My hands were cold and limp. I remember feeling them distinctly resting on either side of me, useless.

At the airport, while my father and Murphy sat off at a distance in an airport lounge, I called my mother from a pay phone. Murphy offered to buy my father a drink.

I pushed in my home phone number and waited.

"Hello," my mother said.

"Mom, it's Alice. I have news."

I faced the wall and cupped the mouthpiece in both hands. "We did it, Mom," I said. "All six counts except the weapons one. He was remanded to jail."

I didn't know what *remanded* meant yet but I used the word.

My mother was ecstatic. She shouted up and down the house in Paoli, "She did it! She did it! She did it!" over and over again. She could not contain her joy.

I *had* done it.

Murphy and my father exited the bar. Our flight was boarding soon. I found out what *remanded* meant. It meant Madison would not be released between conviction and sentencing. They had handcuffed him inside the courtroom as the charges were read. This made Murphy gleeful.

"I wish I could have been there to see his face."

It had been a long, good day for John Murphy, and, as my father confided on the airplane, Murphy could really pack the drinks away. But who could blame him? He was heady, celebratory, off to see his Alice.

I was drained. Though it took me a while to realize it, I, too, had been remanded. I would be held over for a long time.

On June 2, I received a letter from the probation department of the County of Onondaga. They wrote to inform me that they were conducting "a pre-sentence investigation of a young man who was recently found guilty after trial of Rape First Degree, Sodomy First Degree and other related charges. These charges," the letter stated, "stem from an incident in which you were the victim." They wrote to inquire if I had any input on the sentencing recommendation.

I wrote back. I recommended the maximum sentence allowable under the law, and quoted Madison calling me "the worst bitch." I knew Syracuse had been voted the seventh-best city to live in that year, and I pointedly stated that having men like Madison on the streets wouldn't bolster this reputation. I knew my best hope to be heard was by making the point that a maximum sentence would make the men who sentenced him look good. That way they wouldn't be doing it for me, but for the people who elected them and paid their salaries. I knew this. Whatever skills I had, I used.

I closed my letter by signing it over my title: victim.

On July 13, 1982, in a court where Gorman presided, and Mastine, Paquette, and Madison were in attendance, Gregory Madison was sentenced. It was the maximum for rape and sodomy: eight and a third to twenty-five years. The larger sentences, along with lesser ones given for the four remaining charges, would run concurrently.

Mastine called to tell me. He also informed me that Gail had given birth. My mother and I went shopping for a gift. When I saw Gail fifteen years later, she brought the gift along to show me she remembered.

TWELVE

That summer I began my makeover. I had been raped but I had also been raised on *Seventeen* and *Glamour* and *Vogue*. The possibilities of the before-and-after that I had been presented with all my life took hold. Besides, those around me—namely my mother now, with my sister working in Washington before leaving for Syria, and my father off in Spain—encouraged me to move on with my life. "You don't want to become defined by the rape," she said, and I agreed.

I got a job in an ill-fated T-shirt shop where I was the only employee. I stamped badges in an unventilated attic and did sloppy silk-screening for local softball teams. My boss, who was twenty-three, was out hustling up business around town. Sometimes he was drunk and showed up with his buddies to watch TV. I was wearing huge clothes at the time, ones I made myself, what even my mother called tent dresses. And I wore a lot of them in the June and July heat of 1982. One day when my boss and his friends taunted me to show a little flesh, I turned around and walked out. I drove home in my father's car, covered in inks.

It was just me and my mother again, like the summer when I turned fifteen. I kept looking for another job—my journal is full of shoe-store interviews and office-supply-store applications—but like in any suburb during the summer, jobs were scarce once midsummer hit. Mom was trying to lose weight. I decided to join her. We watched *Richard Simmons* and bought an exercise bike. I have a memory of the Scarsdale diet, small, measured steak and chicken bits that we could barely get down. "This diet is costing a fortune," my mother said as we ate more meat that summer than I have since.

But I began to take off pounds. I would sit in front of the television in the morning and watch obese women cry with Simmons, setting off a sort of round-robin of tears among the guest, Simmons, and the studio audience. Sometimes I cried too. Not because I thought I was as fat as the women on the screen but because I thought I knew exactly how ugly they felt. I might have been able to get down the street without being called names and I could see my shoelaces over my belt, but I identified with Simmons's guests as I did with no one else. They were the walking, talking ostracized who had done nothing wrong.

So I cried. And I got on that bike. And I hated my body. I used that hate to shed fifteen pounds.

In late summer, after my father had returned from Spain, the three of us were out in the yard doing yard work. I was supposed to ride the ride-on mower. A typical Sebold fight erupted. I didn't want to, etc. Why did Mary get to go live in D.C. and then go to Syria? My father called me ungrateful. It escalated. Suddenly, just as it was traveling down the familiar path to all-out shouting, I burst into tears. I started crying but couldn't stop. I ran inside up to my room. Trying to sop up the tears was futile. I cried until I was spent, dehydrated, my eyes and the flesh around them a site map of broken capillaries.

Later, I didn't want to talk about it; I was putting the rape and the trial behind me.

Lila and I wrote back and forth to each other all summer. She was dieting too. Our letters to one another read like journal entries, long, pondering pieces written to have company during the writing as much as to really share any information bulletins about ourselves. We were hot and bored, nineteen and stuck at home with our parents. We told each other our life stories in those rambling letters. How we felt about everything from our individual family members to boys we knew at school. I don't remember writing her about the trial in detail. If I did, her letters don't reflect it. I got one postcard in the early summer congratulating me. That's it. It disappeared from our landscape after that.

As it did from almost everyone's. The trial seemed to have provided a very solid and heavy back door to the whole thing. Anyone who had actually entered that house with me, looked or walked into the rooms there, was very happy to finally leave the place. The door was shut. I remember agreeing with my mother that I had gone through a death-and-rebirth phenomenon in the span of one year. Rape to trial. Now the land was new and I could make of it anything I wished.

Lila, Sue, and I planned, via our letters, for the coming year. Lila was bringing a kitten down from a litter at home. I had made a pact with my mother: If I jumped up and down enough on a couch that she hated, we might convince my father when he returned from Spain that I should take it to school. I rented a truck with Sue, who lived nearby. My mother was cheery and sent me off with new clothes that fit my new figure. This was going to be the turnaround year. I was going to do what I called "live normal" now.

That fall, Mary Alice was in London in an exchange program. So were other friends. Tess was on leave. I missed them only vaguely. Lila was my living, breathing soul mate. We went everywhere together and cooked up crazy schemes. We both wanted boyfriends. I played the role of the experienced one to Lila's innocent. Over the summer I had made us matching skirts. We wore these and anything black whenever we went out.

Ken Childs was at a loss without Casey, who was also in London, and we began to pal around. I thought he was cute and, the most important fact, he already knew about me. The three of us went dancing together at on-campus clubs and art-student parties. I wanted to be a lawyer now. People liked hearing this ambition so I said it a lot. Because of Tess, I wanted to go to Ireland; I told people that too. I went to poetry and fiction readings and indulged in the wine and cheese. I took an independent study in poetry with Hayden Carruth and an independent with Raymond Carver, whom I've always thought Tess had assigned to baby-sit me.

One day I ran into Maria Flores on the street. I had written her a triumphant letter early in the summer about the trial. I told her that I had felt her there with me in the courtroom and that I hoped she could take some solace in this. Her letter back was, to be honest, too real for me. "I have a brace on my leg. My ankle is healed and I walk with a cane due to nerve damage. My suicidal tendencies have lessened though frankly, they aren't all gone." She worried about her cane inhibiting her from meeting new people and felt ashamed that she had not completed her job as a resident advisor. She ended the letter with a quote from Kahlil Gibran:

"We are all prisoners but some of us are in cells with windows and some without."

I couldn't see it for years but if one of us had a window, it was Maria who was looking out.

"I got off scot-free," I remember saying to Lila. "She'll wear the rape eternally."

I was dancing and falling in love. This time, a boy in Lila's math class: Steve Sherman. I told him about the rape after we had gone to see a movie and had a few drinks. I remember that he was wonderful with it, that he was shocked and horrified but comforting. He knew what to say. Told me I was beautiful, walked me home and kissed me on the cheek. I think he also liked taking care of me. By that Christmas, he became a fixture at our house.

At home my mother was on an upswing too. She was trying new drugs, Elavil and Xanax, and even biorhythm therapies, things she had never considered before. Group therapy was on the horizon. My mother trusting someone other than herself. "You inspire me, kiddo!" she wrote. "If you can go through what you did and go back out, I figure this old gal can too."

I had reached some positive ground zero; the world was new and open to me.

I worked on the literary magazine, *The Review*, and was chosen to be editor when I became a senior. The English department asked me to represent them in the Glascock Poetry Competition, which was held annually at Mount Holyoke College.

Years before, my mother had fled Mount Holyoke, leaving

behind a fellowship for graduate school. She recalls that it felt like a death sentence to her. All her friends were getting married and she, the egghead, was going off to a place full of "nuns and lesbians."

So I went back to reclaim something for my mother and to take the stage for rape. I didn't win. I came in second. I read "Conviction." Reading it aloud had made me shake with it, the truth of my hate. One of the judges, Diane Wakoski, took me aside and told me that subjects like rape had a place in poetry but that I would never win the prizes or cultivate an audience at large that way.

Lila and I thrilled at stupid movies and we saw one the day I got back from Massachusetts, Sylvester Stallone in *First Blood*. It played at the fifty-cent movie theater near our house. We laughed hysterically at the cartoonish action on the screen in front of us, guffawing so hard we were crying and could barely see or breathe. We would have been kicked out if anyone else had been in the theater to complain but we were alone in the old run-down movie house.

"Me Rambo, you Jane," Lila said, and beat her chest.

"Me good muscle, you girl muscle."

"Grrr."

"Tee-hee."

Near the end of the film someone cleared his throat quite audibly. Lila and I froze but kept staring at the screen. "I thought we were alone," she whispered.

"So did I," I said.

We kept it down and attempted a respectful silence during the final raging shoot-out scenes. We did this by digging our nails into each other's arms and biting our lips. We giggled but we did not erupt fully.

When it was over, and the lights went up, we were alone again. We started letting out what we had held back until we turned the corner and saw the manager of the theater standing there.

"You think Vietnam is funny?"

He was an imposing man; muscle gone to fat and with a pencil mustache that slid across his upper lip, like Madison's first attorney.

"No," we both said.

He blocked our way to the exit.

"Certainly sounded like you were laughing to me," he said.

"It's pretty exaggerated," I said, expecting him to see my point.

"I was in 'Nam," he said. "Were you?"

Lila was scared and holding on to my hand.

I said, "No, sir, and I respect the veterans that fought. We didn't mean to offend. We were laughing because we found the level of machismo exaggerated."

He stared at me as if I had blocked him with reason when what I had really blocked him with were words found inside me when under threat: a skill I now had.

He let us pass but warned us he did not want to see us again in his theater.

We didn't even try to get our giddy mood back. I was furious as we walked down the hill toward home. "It sucks being a woman," I said, stating the obvious. "You always get smashed!"

Lila wasn't ready to go there yet. She was busy trying to see his point. In my mind I was doing now what I did more and more of: fighting a man hand to hand and no matter how I played it, losing every time.

There were good men and bad, thinking men and muscle. I made that separation in my mind. I began to categorize them this way. Steve, who had a sort of ropy runner's body, was gentle in his movements and cared most about his studies. He would sit for hours until he had memorized—verbatim—the chapters of his textbooks. His Ukrainian-immigrant parents were paying cash for his education as they had for their cars and house. It was expected that he would study every day for hours.

I began a sort of unconscious lying to myself when engaged in sex. Steve's pleasure was all I focused on, the point of the journey, so if there were bumps and memories, painful flashes of the night in the tunnel, I rode over them, numbed. Happy when

Steve was happy, I was always ready to pop right out of bed and go on a walk or read my latest poem. If I could get back to the brain in time, like oxygen, the sex didn't hurt as much.

And there was the color of his skin. I could focus on a patch of white flesh and begin. As Steve was being gentle and ardent, inside I was talking myself down the path again. "This is not Thorden Park, he is your friend, Gregory Madison is in Attica, you are fine." It often worked to get me through it, like gritting your teeth on a frightening carnival ride that those around you appear to enjoy. If you can't do, mimic. Your brain is still alive.

By late in the year I had established myself as a sort of chubby New Age diva. The art students knew who I was and so did the poets. I threw a party with the confidence it would be packed and it was. Steve bought me white vinyl dance versions of my favorite songs and made dance tapes from them.

Mary Alice and Casey were back from London and showed up. The whole apartment house throbbed, but this time it was with *my* music and *my* friends. I had gotten *A*'s in Carruth's and Carver's independents and was now taking a class with a poet named Jack Gilbert. I couldn't believe my luck. Even Gilbert showed up! In the kitchen a trash can full of rotgut punch had more and more ingredients added as the party-goers got drunk. Lila's spices were being pitched in wholesale and small things, like forks and houseplants, joined the nutmeg and arrowroot.

Suddenly people we didn't know began to show up—boys. They were loud and strong and went for the pretty girls like magnets. This meant Mary Alice, who, by that time, was very drunk. The dancing on the dance floor got sexual. Steve almost had a fight with a stranger who was moving in on one of his female friends. The music got louder, a speaker blew, the booze ran out. All of this resulted in the sanest and soberest, who had not left already, peeling out. I stood like a barking Scottie by Mary Alice. When boys came toward her I steered them off. I threatened them with what they respected: a man. Mary Alice's boyfriend, I lied, was the captain of the basketball team and due soon with his teammates. If they doubted me I got up in their faces and did my straight-shooting act. I had listened to the detectives and how they talked, knew how to sound streetwise.

Mary Alice decided to leave and Steve and I found her a person we trusted to take her home. Near the door, as we were saying good-bye, she passed out. I and those around us stood and stared at her as she lay unconscious on the floor. I thought she was faking and at first said, "Come on, Mary Alice, get up." Her hair had been so beautiful as she fell, the long golden mane swinging up and out.

I got down on my hands and knees and tried to prod her. No luck. Steve came through the stragglers and strangers. As we stood over her in a circle, boys began to offer to take her home.

I can only think of dogs here. From barking Scottie to scrappy terrier to sudden superhuman strength. I wouldn't even let Steve carry her. I picked Mary Alice up in my arms—all 115 pounds of her—and carried her, with Lila and Steve clearing the way, back to Lila's room. We lay her out on the bed. She was a drunk coed but looked like a sleeping angel. The rest of my night was devoted to making sure she stayed that way. When cruisers showed up because of the complaints of neighbors, I watched the party break down and Steve and Lila escort the more intoxicated strangers out. Mary Alice spent the night. In the morning the place was sticky, and we discovered a friend of a friend of someone's who'd passed out and fell behind the couch.

The summer between my junior and senior years Steve and I lived in the apartment together and took summer school. Morally, my mother was able to adjust to the idea of me living with a man because, as she said, "it's nice to think you have a built-in security guard." Following summer school I got my first taste of teaching by assisting at an art camp for gifted students at Bucknell University. If I didn't become a lawyer, I decided, I would teach. I had no way of knowing then that teaching would end up being my lifeline, my way back.

* * *

By my senior year, I was a habitué of the poetry and fiction readings held on campus. I also worked as a waitress at Cosmos Pizza Shop, on Marshall Street, and my work schedule, combined with these evening readings, meant that I was out at night a lot. Lila seemed not to mind. She had the apartment to herself or shared it peaceably with our new roommate, Pat.

Lila found Pat via the anthropology department. He was younger than we were by two years and only a sophomore. Lila and I had discovered porn magazines in his room, fetish publications like *Jugs*, and one that featured only nude obese women. But he paid the rent and kept to himself. I was just happy that he didn't look the part of the regular bug eaters in anthropology. He was tall and slim with shoulder-length black hair. His Italian ancestry meant a lot to him, as did his love of shock. He showed Lila and me the speculum he had pilfered from a relative who was a gynecologist. He strung it to the light pull of his overhead.

The three of us had begun to adjust to one another by November of that year. After two months Lila and I were getting used to Pat's love of pranks. He liked to touch a spot on your collarbone and say, "What's that?" When you looked down, he chucked you under the chin. Or he would bring you a cup of coffee and, when you reached for it, pull it away. He teased us and when he went too far, Lila and I whined in response. Lila, who had a younger brother, told me that with Pat in the house, it was as if she had never left home.

In a course called Ecstatic Religion, I sat next to a boy named Marc. Like Jamie, he was tall and blond, and in small ways didn't fit in. He didn't go to Syracuse. He was getting a degree in landscape architecture from SUNY's forestry school, which, like a dependent little sister, shared buildings and grounds with Syracuse. He had also come of age in New York's Chelsea district. This made him wise beyond his twenty-one years, and sophisticated, or so it seemed to me. He had friends with lofts in Soho. Places, he promised, that he would show me someday.

After religion class we had chaste but passionate sessions

about that day's topics. The history of shamans and the occult garnered our intense intellectual scrutiny. He gave me tapes of Philip Glass and knew things about music and art that I didn't. He spoke wryly on subjects like Jacqueline Susann's adoration of Ethel Merman. He represented what my mother had always said was the best of New York—culture by birthright—even if the love trysts of "the Merm" and the author of *Valley of the Dolls* weren't what she meant.

Suddenly, Steve's earnestness, his caring attention to my pains and ills, didn't seem as attractive as Marc's "seen it all, done it all" world. When I told my jokes: "Why doesn't a rape trial rate a mention on ye ol' résumé?" Marc would laugh and join the riff whereas Steve would stop me, place a hand on my shoulder, and say, "You know that's not really funny, right?" Marc had a car, cable television, other girls thought he was cute. He wasn't afraid of drinking and he smoked cigarettes like a chimney. He cursed and because he was going to school for architecture, he drew.

He had also been honest and up front with me from the beginning. When we'd met, the year before at a party, we were clearly attracted to each other. He told me later that three boys had pulled him into the bathroom after they saw him talking to me.

"FYI, Marc. That girl's been raped."

Marc had said, "So?"

And they had looked at him dismayed. "Do we have to spell it out for you?"

But Marc was a natural feminist. His mother had been unceremoniously dumped for a much younger woman. One of his sisters was a lesbian and called her two male cats "the girls," the other was a lawyer with the Manhattan district attorney's office. He had read more Virginia Woolf than I had and he introduced me to the work of Mary Daly and Andrea Dworkin. He was a revelation to me.

I was to him as well. He knew names and theories I had never heard, but when he met me, I was the only woman he knew who had been raped. Or who he knew to have been.

I began having fun with Marc while I struggled with Steve.

"How many security guards does one girl need?" Lila asked one day after I'd been on the phone twice to each.

I didn't have an answer save to say I had never been popular with boys and suddenly I felt I was: Two boys both wanted me.

Our old roommate Sue had done a photo-essay for her senior project and she had left all sorts of makeup behind. One night, when Pat was at the library, I decided to play fashion photog and snap pictures of Lila. I dressed her up. I made her take off her glasses and we painted heavy kohl lines across her eyes. I really laid it on. Deep blues and blacks surrounded her eyes. Her lips were a horrible dark red. I posed her in the hallway of the apartment and began to point and shoot. We were having a wonderful time, just the two of us. I had her lie on the floor and glance up, or bring her shirt down over her shoulder for what we called "a skin shot." I mimicked what I thought real fashion photographers said to get models in the mood. "It's hot, you're in the Sahara, a beautiful man is bringing you a piña colada," or, "Somewhere, the only true love of your life is freezing to death in Antarctica. He has one precious photo of you to keep him alive and this is it. I want sex, sincerity, searing intelligence." When she wasn't distorting her features to achieve "the look," she was cracking up. I posed her in front of the full-length mirror on the outside of the bathroom door and took a long shot with me in it. I had her sit with her head in profile and her hands in black gloves.

My favorites back then were by far the more dramatic. In them, she is crawling on her hands and knees, blind eyes wide and lined with color, down the hall outside my bedroom. I think of them now as Lila's "before" shots.

THIRTEEN

A week before Thanksgiving 1983, the poet Robert Bly gave a reading in the auditorium of the Hall of Languages. I was anxious to see him, having greedily read his poems at the urging of both Tess and Hayden Carruth. Lila was at home studying for the kind of killer test that, as a poetry major, I no longer had to concern myself with. Pat had gone to study in Bird Library.

Tess and Hayden were both in attendance. So were the department heads. Bly was a big-name poet and the room was packed. I sat in the middle of the small auditorium. My friend Chris had graduated the year before and so now I attended readings solo. Twenty minutes into the reading, I felt sharp, stabbing pains in my abdomen. I looked at my digital watch. It was 8:56 P.M.

I considered toughing it out, but the pains were too intense. My stomach was cramping. At the end of a poem, I stood and noisily made my way between people's knees and the back of the row of seats in front of me.

Out in the hall, I called Marc. He had a car. I told him to meet me at Bird Library. I was too sick to take the bus home. I had used the same phone two years before to call my parents, but I had scrupulously avoided it since then. That night I failed to honor superstition.

Marc had to take a shower. "Twenty minutes at most," he said.

"I'll be the one cleaving to my abdomen," I tried to joke. "Try to hurry."

As I waited outside Bird, I began to tense up even more. Something was wrong but I had no idea what it was.

Finally, after forty minutes, Marc pulled up. We drove off

campus and up Euclid, where many students lived in run-down wooden houses.

We turned the corner onto my street. Up at the end of the block, where Lila and I lived, were five black-and-whites with their lights going. The policemen were out running around, talking to people.

I knew.

"Oh my God, oh my God," I started saying. "Let me out, let me out."

Marc was flustered. "Let me park, let me go with you."

"No, let me out, now."

He drove into a driveway and I got out. I didn't wait for him. All the lights were on in our building. Our front door was open. I walked right in.

Two uniformed policemen stopped me in the small foyer.

"This is a crime scene. You'll have to leave."

"I live here," I said. "Is it Lila? What happened? Please."

Involuntarily I started peeling off the layers of my clothing and letting them fall on the floor. My winter hat, my scarf, my gloves, jacket, and down vest. I was frantic.

In our living room, there were more cops. One of the uniforms made a gesture to someone there and began, "She says she lives—"

"Alice?" the plainclothes detective said.

I recognized him instantly.

"Sergeant Clapper?"

When I said his name, the uniforms ceased restraining me.

"It's Detective Clapper now," he said, smiling. "What are you doing here?"

"I live here," I said. "Where's Lila?"

His face fell. "I'm so sorry," he said.

I noticed the policemen looking at me differently than before. Marc entered the apartment. I told the uniforms he was my boyfriend.

"Alice Sebold?" one of them asked.

I turned back to Clapper. "Was she raped?"

"Yes," he said. "On the bed in the back bedroom."

"That's my room," I said. "Is she okay?"

"The female detective's in with her now. We need to have her examined at the hospital. You can drive with us in the car. She didn't struggle."

I asked to see her. Clapper said, "Of course," and went back to inform Lila I was there.

I stood there, feeling the eyes of the uniformed policemen on me. They knew my case because it had been one of the few convictions in a rape case in recent years. In their world, my case was famous. It had brought Clapper up in the ranks. Whoever worked on the case had benefited from it.

"I can't believe it. I can't. This can't be happening," I said over and over again to Marc. I don't remember what he said back to me. I was beginning to rally myself, to assume a control I didn't have.

"She doesn't want to see you," Clapper said, upon his return. "She's afraid she'll break down if she does. She'll be out in a few minutes and you can ride with them to the hospital."

I was hurt, but I understood.

I waited. I told Marc that I would be in for the long haul—the hospital, the police—and that he should go home and make his place nice. The three of us would sleep there, Lila and I in the bed, he in his living room.

The police made small talk. I started pacing. One of the uniforms gathered my clothes from the foyer and brought them over to the couch near me.

Then Lila was coming out of the room. She was shaken. Her hair was disheveled but I saw no marks on her face. A short, dark-haired woman in uniform trailed her.

She was wearing my robe, but it was belted with another tie. Her eyes were bottomless—lost. I couldn't have reached her then no matter how hard I tried.

"I'm so sorry," I said. "You'll be okay. You'll make it. I did," I said.

We stood there looking at each other, both of us crying.

"Now we really *are* clones," I said.

The female detective moved us along.

"Lila says you have another roommate."

"Oh my God, Pat," I said. I had forgotten him until that moment.

"Do you know where he is?"

"The library."

"Can someone get to him?"

"I want to go with Lila."

"Then leave him some kind of note; we don't want him touching things. And he should stay somewhere else tonight until we can secure that back window."

"At first, I thought it was Pat playing a prank on me," Lila said. "I came back from the bathroom and the door to my bedroom was farther out from the wall than usual, like someone was standing behind it. So I pushed it in and he pushed it out and back and forth until I got tired of it and said, 'Come on, Pat,' and walked into the room. He threw me on the bed."

"We've got an exact time," the female detective said. "She looked up at her digital clock. It was eight fifty-six P.M."

"When I felt sick," I said.

"What?" The female detective looked mystified.

I didn't know where to stand. I was not the victim. I was the victim's friend. The detective took Lila out to the car, and I hurriedly went into Pat's room.

I did something nasty. I used the speculum to weigh down the note. I left it on his pillow because the rest of the room was a mess. I could be certain he'd see it there: "Pat, Lila was raped. She is physically okay. Call Marc. You need to find somewhere else to stay tonight. I'm sorry to have to tell you this way."

I left the light on in his room and looked at it. I decided not to care about Pat—I couldn't. He would be okay, bounce back. It was Lila now.

We drove to the hospital in silence. I sat in the back with Lila and we held hands.

"It's horrible," she said at one point. "I feel filthy. All I want to do is shower."

I squeezed her hand.

"I know," I said.

We had to wait what seemed an interminable time in the emergency room. It was crowded and because, I've always assumed, she had not struggled and had no open wounds, could sit upright and talk coherently, she was made to wait. Repeatedly, I went up to the woman in admissions and asked her why we had to wait. I sat with Lila and helped her fill out the insurance form. There had been none of this for me. I had been wheeled directly in, from ambulance gurney to examination room.

Finally they called her. We walked down the hall and found the room. The examination was long and plodding, and several times we had to wait while the man examining her was called into various other rooms. I held her hand as Mary Alice had held mine. Tears rolled down my face. Toward the end Lila said, "I want you to leave." She asked for the female detective. I went and got her and sat in the waiting room, shaking.

My nightmares had never let Lila be raped. She and Mary Alice were safe. Lila was my clone, my friend, my sister. She had heard every part of my story and still loved me. She was the rest of the world—the pure half—but now she was with me. While I waited, I became convinced that I could have prevented Lila's rape. By coming home faster, by knowing instinctively that something was wrong, by never having asked her to be my friend in the first place. It didn't take me long before I thought, and then said, "It should have been me." I began to worry for Mary Alice.

I shook, and I wrapped my arms around my shoulders and rocked back and forth in my seat. I felt nauseous. My whole world was turning over; whatever else I'd had or known became eclipsed. There was no chance to escape, I realized; from now on this would be it. My life and the lives of those around me. Rape.

The female detective came out for me.

"Alice," she said, "Lila is going with Detective Clapper down to the police station. She asked me to go home with you and get some clothes for her."

I didn't know how to act. Even then I was beginning to realize that Lila didn't know what to do with me around. There was Alice her friend, and Alice the successful rape victim. She needed one without the other, but that was impossible.

The detective drove me home and I unlocked the door. Pat still had yet to come home. The light I had left on had been turned off by someone else. I plunged in. I remembered how Tree and Diane had brought me bad clothes—patched jeans and no underwear. I wanted Lila to have comfort. I pulled down a large duffel from her closet and opened her drawers. I packed all her underwear, all her flannel gowns, slippers, socks, sweatpants, and loose shirts. I threw in a book and from her bed a stuffed animal and a pillow.

I needed things too. I knew already that Lila and I would never sleep in that house again. I walked to the back, where my room was. The door was closed. I asked the detective if I could go in.

I said a little prayer to no one and turned the knob. The room was cold because of the open window through which he'd climbed. I switched on the light near the door.

My bed was stripped. I walked toward it. In the center was a small fresh bloodstain. Nearby were other, smaller ones, like tears.

She had come out of the shower, wrapped in a towel, gone to her bedroom, and played the door game, thinking it was Pat. Then the rapist had shoved her onto the bed on her stomach. She saw the clock. In the darkness, she saw him only for a few seconds. He blindfolded her with the tie from my robe, and then, turning her around on the bed, made her hold her hands in front of her chest in the prayer position while he tied her wrists with bungee cords and a cat leash we kept in the front closet. This meant he had gone through the house while she was in the shower. He knew no one else was home. He made her get to her feet and walk back to my bedroom, where he made her lie down on my bed.

That was where he'd raped her. He asked her where I was during the attack. Somehow knew my name. Somehow knew Pat would not be back until much later. At one point, he asked about the tip money I had on my dresser and took that. She did not struggle. She did as he said.

He had her put on my robe and left her there, blindfolded.

She started screaming, but the boys in the apartment above us were playing loud music. No one heard her or did anything if they had. She had to go through the front of the apartment, outside, and up the stairs, banging on their door until they answered. They held beers in their hands. They were smiling, expecting more friends. She asked them to untie her. They did. And to call the police.

Lila would tell me all of this in the coming weeks. Now I tried hard not to look at the blood, at my bed, at the possessions he had gone through. My clothes in the closet spilled onto the floor. Photos on my desk. My poems. I grabbed a flannel gown to match Lila's, and some clothes off the floor. I wanted to take my old Royal typewriter, but this would seem silly and selfish to everyone but me. I looked at it and looked at the bed.

As I was turning to leave, a gust of wind from the window slammed the door shut. All the hope I had had of living a normal life had gone out of me.

The detective and I drove to the Public Safety Building. We took the elevator up to the third floor and exited into the familiar hallway outside the bulletproof glass that looked onto the police dispatcher's station. The dispatcher pressed the button for the security door and we entered.

"Through there," a policeman said to the detective.

We walked toward the back.

The photographer was holding up his camera. Lila stood against a wall holding a number in front of her chest. Hers, like mine, was written in bold Magic Marker on the back of an SPD envelope.

"Alice," the photographer said upon seeing me.

I placed the duffel with our clothes in it on an empty desk.

"Remember me?" he asked. "I took evidence in your case in eighty-one."

"Hello," I said.

Lila remained against the wall. Two other policemen came forward.

"Wow," one said. "It's great to meet you. We don't get the opportunity to see many victims after a conviction. Do you feel good about your case?"

I wanted to give these men a response. They deserved it. They usually saw only the side of a rape case that Lila, forgotten against the wall, represented: fresh or weary victims.

"Yes," I said, aware that what was happening was all wrong, stunned by my sudden celebrity. "You guys were great. I couldn't have asked for better. But I'm here for Lila."

They realized the strangeness of it too. But what wasn't strange?

They posed her and while they did, they talked to me.

"She doesn't really have any marks. I remember you were real messed up. Madison worked you over good."

"What about the wrists?" I said. "He tied her up. I wasn't tied up."

"But he had a knife, right?" a policeman asked, anxious to review the details of my case.

The photographer went up to Lila. "Yeah," he said. "Hold up your wrist in front. There, like that."

Lila did as instructed. Turned to the side. Held her wrists up. Meanwhile the uniforms surrounded me and asked me questions, shook my hand, smiled.

Then it was time to make phone calls. They set Lila and me up at a desk in the opposite corner. I sat on the top of it, and Lila sat in front of me in a chair. She told me the number of her parents and I dialed.

It was late now, but her father was still up.

"Mr. Rinehart," I said, "this is Alice, Lila's roommate. I'm going to put Lila on now."

I handed her the phone.

"Daddy," she began. She was crying. She got it out and then handed the phone back to me.

"I can't believe this is happening," he said.

"She'll be okay, Mr. Rinehart," I said, trying to reassure him. "It happened to me and I'm okay."

Mr. Rinehart knew about my case. Lila had shared it with her family.

"But you're not my daughter," he said. "I'll kill the son of a bitch."

I should have been prepared for this kind of anger at her attacker, but instead I felt it to be directed at me. I gave him Marc's phone number. Told him we would be sleeping there that night, and that he should call with his flight arrival time. Marc had a car, I said; we'd meet him at the airport.

Lila went with the police to fill out an affidavit. It was late now, and I sat on the metal desktop and thought about my parents. My mother was just now back working again after having a two-year increase in panic attacks. Now I would ruin that. Logic was beginning to leave, draining away from me. With blame so heavy and nowhere to place it but the fleeing back of a rapist Lila could barely describe, I took it on.

I dialed.

My mother answered the phone. Late-night calls meant only one thing to her. She waited at home for the news of my death.

"Mom," I said, "this is Alice."

My father picked up.

"Hi, Dad," I said. "First, I need you to know that I'm okay."

"Oh, God," my mother said, anticipating me.

"There's no way to say it but flat out. Lila was raped."

"Oh, Jesus."

They asked a lot of questions. In answer I said, "I'm fine." "On my bed." "We don't know yet." "Inside the interrogation room." "No weapon." "Shut up, I don't want to hear that."

This last one was a response to what they would say over and over again. "Thank God it wasn't you."

I called Marc.

"We saw him," he said.

"What?"

"Pat called and I went over and we drove around looking for him."

"That's crazy!"

"We didn't know what else to do," Marc said. "We both want to kill the bastard. Pat can't see straight he's so mad."

"How is he?"

"Messed up. I dropped him off at a friend's house afterward. He wanted to stay with us."

I listened to Marc's story. They both had a few shots, then drove up and down the nearby streets in the dark. Marc kept a crowbar in the car. Pat would scan the lawns and houses as Marc slowed down and then sped up. Finally, they heard yelling, and then saw a man running out from between two houses. He ran onto the sidewalk and then, seeing Marc's car, turned quickly and headed back down the block, slowing his pace to a walk. Marc and Pat followed him. I can only imagine what they said and what they were planning.

"Pat was scared," Marc said.

"It might not have been him," I said. "Did you ever think of that?"

"But they say criminals sometimes stick around," Marc countered. "Besides the yelling and then the way he acted."

"You were following him," I said. "Marc, you can't do any-thing—that's the deal. Beating someone up doesn't help anyone."

"Well, he turned around and charged the car."

"What?"

"He just came at us, yelling and screaming. I almost shit my pants."

"Did you get a good look at him?"

"Yeah," he said. "I think so. It had to be him. He stood in the headlights yelling at us."

By the time Lila and I were driven to Marc's apartment on the other side of campus, I was too overwhelmed for further talk. I wanted to keep Lila safe from knowing about Marc and Pat's actions. I could understand it, but I didn't have much patience with it anymore. Violence only begat violence. Couldn't they see it left all the real work to the women? The comforting and the near impossible task of acceptance.

Inside Marc's bedroom Lila and I changed into our flannel gowns. I turned my back while she changed and I promised I would guard the door.

"Don't let Marc in."

"I won't," I said.

She got into bed.

"I'll be right back. I'll sleep on the outside edge, so you'll be safe."

"What about the windows?" she asked.

"Marc has bolts on them. He grew up in the city, remember?"

"Did you ever ask Craig to fix that back window?" Her back was to me when she asked this.

I felt the question, and its attendant accusation, like a knife at the base of my spine. Craig was our landlord. I had gone upstairs to his apartment two weeks before to ask him to fix the lock on my window.

"Yes," I said. "He never did."

I slipped out of the room and consulted with Marc. The only bathroom was through the bedroom. I wanted all details taken care of, down to this: If Marc had to urinate in the middle of the night, I told him to use the sink in his kitchen.

Back in the bedroom I slipped into bed.

"Can I rub your back?" I asked.

Lila was tucked into a ball with her back facing me. "I guess so."

I did.

"Stop," she said. "I just want to sleep. I want to wake up and have it be over."

"Can I hold you?" I asked.

"No," she said. "I know you want to take care of me, but you can't. I don't want to be touched. Not by you, not by anybody."

"I'll stay awake until you fall asleep."

"Do what you want, Alice," she said.

* * *

The next morning Marc knocked and then brought us tea. Mr. Rinehart had called with his flight number. I promised Lila I would get all of her stuff out of the apartment ASAP. She had a list of things she wanted her father and me to pack for the flight home. I called Steve Sherman. I needed a place to store my stuff. Lila had a friend who would take hers. Moving and packing: Her stuff was something I could take control of. I could serve her that way.

I stood at the same gate where Detective John Murphy had waited and watched for me. I had already met Lila's father once, on a visit to her house that summer. He was a huge, hulking man. As he approached me, I could see him begin to cry. His eyes were already red and swollen. He came up, put down his bags, and I held him as he wept.

But I felt like an alien in his presence. I knew the landscape, or so everyone imagined. I had been raped and through a trial and been in the papers. Everyone else was just an amateur. Pat, the Rineharts—their lives had not prepared them for this.

Mr. Rinehart was not kind to me. Eventually he said things to my mother and me about how they would handle their own. He told my mother that his daughter was nothing like me, and that they didn't need my advice or her counsel. Lila, he said, needed to be left alone.

But at first, on that day, he cried and I held him. I knew, more than he ever could, what his daughter had gone through and how impossible it was for him to do anything to fix it. In that moment, before the blame and separation set in, he was broken. My mistake was in not seeing how lost I had become. I behaved as I thought I should: like a pro.

At Marc's, Lila stood when she saw her father. They hugged and I shut the door to the bedroom. I went to stand as far away as I could to give them their privacy. In the tunnel that was Marc's attic kitchen, I smoked one of Marc's cigarettes. I counted, packing all our possessions in my head and distributing them to the homes of various friends. I thought a million different thoughts in every moment. When a spoon slipped in the sink, I jumped.

* * *

That night Mr. Rinehart took us out for dinner at the Red Lobster. Marc, myself, Pat, and Lila. It was all-you-could-eat shrimp night and he kept urging us on. Pat did his best and so did Marc, who preferred Szechwan noodles and snow peas. Neither Pat nor Marc were macho in the traditional sense; conversation stalled repeatedly. Mr. Rinehart's eyes were swollen and bloodshot. I don't remember what I said. I was uncomfortable. I could feel how much Lila wanted to leave. I didn't want to give her over to her parents. I thought of Mary Alice French-braiding my hair the morning of my own rape. I had sensed it almost from the start at the airport—there were going to be reasons put forth by people, by her parents, perhaps, that would prevent me from helping. I was to be banished. I had the disease, it was catching. I knew this, but I kept clinging. Clinging so hard, wanting to be with Lila in this shared thing so desperately, that my presence was bound to suffocate her.

We drove them to the airport. I don't remember saying good-bye to her. I was already thinking of the move out, of saving what was left to me.

I moved all our possessions, Lila's and mine, out of our apartment within twenty-four hours. I did it alone. Marc had classes. I called Robert Daly, a student who had a truck, and arranged for him to pick the stuff up after I had boxed it. I gave him my furniture—whatever he wanted he could take, I said. Pat was dragging his heels.

No one seemed to understand my urgency. In the midst of packing that day, I was in the kitchen and I knocked the table with my hip. A small, handmade bunny mug that my mother had given me after the trial fell on the floor and broke. I looked at it and cried, but then stopped. There was no time for that. I would not allow myself to be attached to things. It was too dangerous.

I had cleared my bedroom out first, in the early morning, and now, as Robert was due to arrive before dark, I turned the doorknob for one last scan of my room. I had been thorough. But on the floor near the dresser I found a photo of myself and Steve Sherman that had been taken on the porch of the house over the summer. We were happy in the photo. I looked normal. Then, in the closet, I found a valentine he had given me earlier that year. The photo, the valentine were ruined now—remains of a crime scene.

I had tried to be like everyone else. During my junior year, I had given it a go. But that wasn't the way it was going to be. I could see that now. It seemed I had been born to be haunted by rape, and I began to live that way.

I took the photo and valentine and shut the door of my bedroom for the final time. I drifted into the kitchen, holding them. I heard a noise in the other room. It echoed now that I had emptied the room out.

I jumped.

"Hello?" came a voice.

"Pat?" I walked into the other room. He had brought a green trash bag to get some of his clothes.

"Why are you crying?" he said.

I hadn't realized I had been, but as soon as he asked I became aware of the dampness on my cheeks.

"Aren't I allowed to cry?" I asked.

"Well, yeah, it's just that . . ."

"It's just that what?"

"I guess I expected you to be okay with it."

I yelled horrible things at him. We had never been best friends and now we would cease even to be acquaintances.

Robert Daly showed up. He was a rock. That is how I remember him. We shared a taste for honest criticism in our fiction workshop and a respect for Tobias Wolff and Raymond Carver. Robert and I weren't close either, but he helped me. I cried in front of him and he didn't like it when I apologized. He took my rocker and daybed and some other items. For a few years, until it became obvious I wouldn't come back for them, he dropped me cards to say my furniture was doing fine and wishing I were there.

* * *

I changed, but I didn't know it.

I went home for Thanksgiving. Steve Sherman came over from New Jersey to spend time with me. He had been Lila's friend first, before becoming my boyfriend, and the idea that both of us had been raped overwhelmed him. He told me that when he found out about Lila, he had been in the shower. His roommate had come in to tell him. He'd looked down at his penis and suddenly felt a self-hatred he couldn't describe, knowing that so much violence had come to his friends that way. He wanted to help. He stored the rest of my things and I slept in his spare bedroom. When Lila came back two weeks after her rape for the GRE's, she stayed in his house. He kept me company and volunteered as my security guard, walking me home from work or class.

The division that came was inevitable, I guess. People felt compelled to take sides. It began the night of the rape when the police had come up to me so openly. Lila's friends started avoiding me, looking away or to the side. During her overnight for the GRE's, the police came to Steve's house to do a photo lineup. I was in the bedroom with Lila and two policemen. They spread the small, wallet-size photos out on the desk. I looked over Lila's shoulder.

"I bet you recognize one of these," a uniformed policeman said to me.

They had put a photo of Madison and his lineup buddy, Leon Baxter, in the pack. I was so mad I couldn't speak.

"Is the one who raped her in here?" Lila asked. She was sitting at a desk in front of me. I couldn't see her face.

I left the room. I was sick. Steve reached his arms out and grabbed hold of me.

"What is it?"

"They put a photo of Madison in there," I said.

"But he's still in jail, isn't he?"

"Yes, I think so, yes." I hadn't even thought to ask.

"Attica," a uniform said in answer.

"To have to pick out her rapist and see *him* there, the focus is all wrong," I said to Steve. "It's not fair."

The door opened. Lila came out into the living room behind the officer who held the mug shots in an envelope.

"We're done here," a policeman said.

"Did you see him?" I asked Lila.

"She saw *something*," the policeman said. He wasn't happy.

"I'm stopping it now. I'm not going to pursue it," Lila said.

"What?"

"It was a pleasure getting to meet you, Alice," the officer said. He shook my hand. His partner did too.

They left and I looked at Lila. My question must have been obvious.

"It's too much," Lila said. "I want my life back. I watched what it did to you."

"But I won," I said, incredulous.

"I want it to be over," she said. "This way it is."

"You can't just will it away," I said.

But I felt her trying. She took her GRE's and returned home until after Christmas. Our plan was to live together in graduate student housing. Her family was going to loan her a car because it was the only way to get back and forth from campus. That, or the bus, which I would take.

I'll never know what the police said to Lila in that room or whether or not she saw her rapist among those men. At the time, I couldn't understand her decision not to pursue it, although I thought I did. The police had a theory that Lila might have been raped out of revenge. They based this on several things. Madison, though in Attica, had friends. He had been given a maximum sentence and would be inside a bare minimum of eight years. The rapist knew my name. Raped her on my bed. Asked after me while he did. He knew my schedule and that I was a waitress at Cosmos. All this could have been evidence of a connection to Madison, or it could just have been the thorough research of a criminal intent on finding his victim alone. I still choose to believe that part of the horror of the crime was in its cruel coincidence. Conspiracy seemed a stretch to me.

Lila didn't want to know. She wanted out of it.

The police interviewed my friends. They went to Cosmos and interviewed the owner and the man who flipped the pizzas inside the front window. But there were other rapes being done with a similar MO to Lila's. If Lila wouldn't prosecute, any link to me was now inconsequential. They had no witness and, with no witness, no case. The police dropped their investigation. Lila went home until January. She gave me a copy of her schedule. I told her teachers why she wouldn't be in attendance at finals. I called her friends.

My life became streamlined, and the fallout began.

I went home for Christmas.

My sister was depressed. She had graduated and won a Fulbright, but was now living at home and working in a garden shop. Her Arabic major was not translating into the job she had hoped for. I went to her room to cheer her up. At some point she said, "Alice, you just don't understand, everything comes so easily for you." I sputtered in my disbelief. A wall went up. I cut her out.

I had nightmares now even more vivid than before. My sporadic journal of those years is full of them. The recurring image is one I'd seen in a documentary of the Holocaust. There are fifty or sixty chalk-white and emaciated dead bodies. Their clothes have been stripped from them. The clip shows a bulldozer rolling them into a deep, open grave, the bodies plunging as a tangled whole. Faces, mouths, skulls with eyes set deep, the minds inside gone to unimaginable lengths in order to have survived. Then this. Darkness, death, filth, and the idea that one person could be struggling, trying to stay alive in there.

I woke up in cold sweats. Sometimes I screamed. I would turn over and lie facing the wall. Enter the next step: Awake now, I consciously played out the intricate plot of my almost death. The rapist was inside the house. He was climbing up the stairs. He knew, on instinct, which steps would betray him by a noise.

He was loping down the hall. A breeze came through the front window. No one would think to question it if they were awake in the other rooms. A light scent of another person, someone else in the house, would waft into them, but like one small noise, it would warn no one but me that something was going to happen. I would feel then my door opening, a sense of another presence in the room, the air changed to allow for a human weight. Far away, near my wall, something was breathing my air, stealing my oxygen. My breath would grow shallow and I would make a promise to myself: I would do anything the man wanted. He could rape me and cut me and take off my fingers. He could blind me or maim me. Anything. All I wanted to do was live.

Resolved, I would gather my strength. Why was he waiting like this? I would turn slowly around in the dark. Where the man stood so vividly in my imagination, there was no one, there was the door to my closet. That was all. Then I would turn on the light and check the house, going up to each door and trying the knob, sure it would give and there he would be, standing on the other side and laughing at me. Once or twice the noise I made woke my mother. "Alice?" she would call out.

"Yes, Mom," I said, "it's just me."

"Go back to sleep."

"I will," I said. "I'm just getting something to eat."

Upstairs in my bedroom, I would try to read. Not look at the closet, or, quickly, over to the door.

I never questioned what was happening to me. It all seemed normal. Threat was everywhere. No place or person was safe. My life was different from other people's; it was natural that I behaved differently.

After Christmas, Lila and I tried to make a go of it in Syracuse. I wanted to help her, but I also needed her. I believed in talking. To be with her after dark, I quit Cosmos. This was easy: They didn't want me back. When I had gone to ask about getting day shifts, the owner was distant and standoffish. The man who flipped the pizzas came up after the owner had left.

"Don't you get it?" he said. "The police have been in here asking questions. We don't want you here."

I left in tears and walked blindly into someone.

"Watch where you're going," the man said to me.

It was snowing. I quit the *Review*. The bus back to the place Lila and I were living broke down a lot. Tess was on leave. I stopped going to poetry readings. One night, I was a little later than usual getting home—it had grown dark—and Steve met me at the doorstep. "Where were you?" he asked. His tone was angry, accusatory.

"We needed food," I said.

"Lila called me because she was scared. She wanted someone to sit with her."

"Thanks for coming over," I said. I was holding a bag of groceries and it was cold.

"You should have been here."

I walked inside and hid my tears.

When Lila said it wasn't working out, that she didn't like the apartment, and she was going to go home for a few weeks and then move in with Mona, a friend she'd recently made, I entered a sort of shock. I thought we'd be in this together. Clones.

"It's just not working, Alice," she said. "I can't talk about it the way you want me to and I feel isolated here."

Steve and Marc were the only two people who had regularly visited the house. Both of them, though scrupulously avoiding each other, were more than willing to sit guard. But they were my friends—my boyfriends, to be exact—and Lila knew it. They were there primarily for me, and to help me out by helping her. She needed to separate. This is clear to me now. Then, I felt betrayed. We went through our record albums and other things that had been common property over our two years together. I cried, and if she wanted something, I gave it to her. I gave her things she didn't ask for. I left possessions behind me to mark my place. Could I ever get back to where I had been? Where was that? A virgin? A freshman in college? Eighteen?

I sometimes think nothing hurt me more than Lila's decision

to stop speaking to me. It was a total blackout. She did not return my phone calls when I was finally able to get her new number out of one of her friends. She passed by me on the street and did not speak. I called her name. No response. I blocked her path, she moved around me. If she was with a friend, they *indeed* looked at me—burning with a hatred I couldn't understand but nonetheless took in.

I moved in with Marc. In four months I would graduate. I stayed inside his apartment for everything but my classes. He drove me everywhere, a willing chauffeur, but mostly he stayed away from me. He was at the architecture studio late into the night; sometimes he slept there. When he was home I asked him to investigate noises, check the locks, to please just hold me.

The week before graduation, I saw Lila again. I was with Steve Sherman. We were in the student mall on Marshall Street. She saw me, I saw her, but she walked right by me.

"I can't believe it," I said to Steve. "We're graduating in a week and she still won't talk to me."

"Do you want to speak to her?"

"Yes, but I'm afraid. I don't know what to say."

We decided that Steve would stay where he was standing, and I would circle around again in the opposite direction.

I ran into her.

"Lila," I said.

She was not surprised. "I wondered if you'd try to speak to me."

"Why won't you talk to me?"

"We're different, Alice," she said. "I'm sorry if I've hurt you, but I need to move on with my life."

"But we were clones."

"That was just something we said."

"I've never been so close to anyone."

"You have Marc and Steve. Isn't that enough?"

We somehow got from that to wishing each other well at graduation. I told her Steve and I were going over to a nearby restaurant to have mimosas. She could come and join us if she wanted.

"Maybe you'll see me there," she said, then left.

I rushed into the bookshop we'd been standing in front of and bought her a book of Tess's poems, *Instructions to the Double*. Inside I wrote something that escapes me now. It was sappy and came straight from my heart. It said I would always be there for her, all she had to do was call.

We did run into her at the bar. She was tipsy and had a boy with her whom I knew she had a crush on. She didn't want to sit with us, but stood by our table while she talked about sex. She told me she had been fitted for a diaphragm and that I was right, sex was great. I was audience now, not friend or intimate. She was too busy doing what I was doing—proving to the world that she was fine. I forgot to give her the book. They left.

On our way home, Steve and I passed by another, posher student hangout. I saw Lila sitting inside with her crush and a bunch of people I didn't know. I told Steve to wait, and I rushed inside with the book. The people at the table looked up.

"This is for you," I said, offering it to Lila. "It's a book."

Her friends laughed because the fact that it was a book was obvious.

"Thank you," Lila said.

A waitress arrived to take drink orders. Lila's crush was watching me.

"I wrote something inside," I said.

As her friends ordered drinks, she looked up at me. I thought she pitied me then. "I'll read it later, but thank you. It looks like a good book."

I never saw Lila again.

On the day of graduation, I didn't attend. I couldn't imagine being there, trying to celebrate, seeing Lila and her friends. Marc had a project due. His school wasn't over yet. Steve was at graduation. Mary Alice was there too. I had told my parents I just wanted to get the hell out of Syracuse. They agreed. "The faster, the better," they said.

I packed my remaining possessions in a silver rental car. It was a Chrysler New Yorker; they'd run out of subcompacts. I drove this boat back to Paoli, knowing the car itself would get a laugh out of my parents.

Syracuse was over. Good riddance, I thought. I was going to the University of Houston in the fall. I was going to get an MA in poetry. I would spend the summer trying to reinvent myself. I had not seen Houston, never been south of Tennessee, but it was going to be different there. Rape would not follow me.

AFTERMATH

The night John got punched in the face was sometime in the fall of 1990. I was standing outside De Robertis on First Avenue, waiting for John to come back with the cheap heroin we both snorted. We had a routine. We always said that if he took too long I would come after him, shouting. It was a vague plan, but it kept from our minds the fact that something might happen that we couldn't control. That particular night it was cold out. But those days cloud together. By that time, this was the point of it all.

A year before, I had published a piece in *The New York Times Magazine*, a first-person account of my rape. In it, I beseeched people to talk about rape and to listen to articulate victims when they had a story to tell. I got a lot of mail. I celebrated with four dime bags and a Greek boyfriend who had once been my student. Then Oprah called, having read the article. I went on the show. I was the victim who fought back. There was another one who supposedly hadn't. Like Lila's, Michelle's resistance left no visible scars. But I doubt that Michelle flew back home to snort heroin.

I never made it through graduate school in Houston. I didn't like the city, yes, but to be honest, I wasn't cut out for it. I slept with a decathlete and a woman, I bought pot off a guy behind the 7-Eleven, and I drank with another student who also dropped out—a tall man from Wyoming—and sometimes, while the decathlete held me, or the man from Wyoming sat back and watched, I cried in hysterical trills that no one understood, least of all me. I thought it was Houston. I thought it was living in a hot climate where there were too many bugs and where the women wore too many ruffles and frills.

I moved to New York and lived in a minority low-income housing project on Tenth and C. My roommate, Zulma, was Puerto Rican and had raised her family in the apartment. Now she rented out her extra bedrooms. She liked to drink too.

I hostessed at a place in Midtown called La Fondue and then I landed (by meeting a drunk man in a bar called King Tut's Wawa Hut) a teaching job at Hunter College. I was an adjunct. I didn't have the requisite degrees and only a year of experience (I had been a teaching assistant in Houston), but the hiring committee was desperate, and they recognized some names: Tess Gallagher, Raymond Carver. During the interview, I took fifteen minutes to remember the word *thesis*, as in *thesis sentence*—the basis of all composition courses. When the chair called and Zulma handed me the phone, I had never been more surprised by what I took then to be the fortuitousness of drinking.

And my students there became the people who kept me alive. I could get lost in their lives. They were immigrants, ethnic minorities, city kids, returning women, full-time workers, former addicts, and single parents. Their stories filled my days, and their troubles in assimilating preoccupied my evening hours. I fit in with them in a way I had never fit in since before the rape. My own story paled when I compared it with theirs. Walking over the bodies of their countrymen to escape Cambodia. Watching a brother be stood against a wall and shot. Raising a handicapped child alone on waitressing tips. And then there were the rapes. The girl who had been adopted for the purpose by her father, who was a priest. The girl who was raped in the apartment of another student, and whom the police didn't believe. The girl who was a militant and tattooed dyke but who broke down in my office when she told me about her gang rape.

They told me their stories, I like to think, because I never questioned them, believed them utterly. They also thought I was a clean slate. I was obviously a middle-class white girl. A college teacher. Nothing had ever happened to me. I was too hungry for comfort to care that it was a one-way relationship. Like a bartender, I listened, and like a bartender, my position kept me at a safe remove. I was the ear, and the tragic stories of my students' lives medicated me. But I began to build up a resistance to them. By the time I wrote the article for *The New York Times*, I was ready to talk. Some students read it. They were shocked. Then came *Oprah*. Many more saw me there, holding forth, their English teacher, on her own rape. For the next few weeks I ran into former students on the street. "Wow," they would confide, "I never thought you, I mean, you know." And I did know. Because I was white. Because I grew up in the suburbs. Because without a name attached to my story, it remains fiction, not fact.

I loved heroin. Drinking had drawbacks—namely, the volume needed to reach oblivion—and I didn't like the taste or the history—my mother had done that. Cocaine made me sick. I went into paralytic cramps once on the floor of a club called the Pyramid. Rastas and white girls danced around my curled-up body. I did it a few more times just to double-check. Ecstasy and mushrooms and acid trips? Who wanted to enhance a mood? My goal was to destroy it.

I found myself in odd places. Vacant lots, alleyways, and Athens. One night I came to from a nod in a tiny cafe in Greece. In front of me, on a dish, were small silvery fish. Two men were sopping up the oil from my plate with bread. We went back to a house on a hill. I heard the name of my Greek student mentioned but he wasn't there. We smoked black tar and walked outside again. One of the men disappeared, the other wanted to sleep with me. I had been on American TV.

At the same house, with a new population shooting up in the back, I put on someone's jacket because I was cold. There was a used needle in the pocket. It stabbed me. I was startled for a moment, immediately I thought, AIDS, then I did what I had become good at: played the odds. It was Greece. How bad could the risk be?

After thirty days I went home. I wrote a travel article for *The*

New York Times, which appeared the following spring in time for people to plan their vacations. In the meantime, I flew back to Europe with another former student, John. He and a friend had scammed cheap tickets to Amsterdam through the friend's relative. We took the night train, high as kites, into Berlin. The wall was falling. It was after midnight by the time we reached the concrete separating West from East. John and Kippy pitched in. They borrowed a pickax from a group of raucous and euphoric German men and took their turns. I stayed at a remove. This wasn't my country and I was the only woman among men. A German man came over and offered me a cigarette, a bottle, said something to me, and grabbed my ass. Up along the wall, an East German border guard stared down.

It was sometime after that in New York that John was hit. I remember seeing him round the corner. He had been gone longer than usual. I could see his glasses were missing and his nose was bloodied. He was upset.

"Did you get it?" I asked.

He nodded his head. Didn't speak. We started walking.

"I got hit."

This, like the needle in Athens, startled me. The question was: How bad did it have to get? I didn't want John to cop alone anymore and made a point of that. He tried not to, but sometimes, when we were desperate, he went.

It got much worse, and then, in the spring of 1991, having just moved into an apartment on Seventh Street, something clicked. Something was wrong with me but I didn't know what. I lay in bed. I ate again, as I hadn't since college, and I wore my old flannel nightgowns. The boxes from the move remained unpacked. John was working grueling hours. He was uncomfortable around me now. When he came over I sent him out to buy me brownies. I gained weight. I stopped caring about what I looked like or how fast I could walk at a clip to a club. I wanted to be better but I didn't know how.

A friend of mine I'd known since we were teenagers called

to say I'd been quoted in a book. My friend was a doctor now, and he worked in Boston. My *New York Times* piece had been quoted in *Trauma and Recovery*, by Dr. Judith Lewis Herman. I laughed at this. I had wanted to write my own book but I couldn't seem to manage it. Now, almost ten years after Lila's rape, my name had appeared as a footnote in another person's. I thought about buying it but it was hardback—too pricey—and besides, I thought, I was done with all that.

In the next six months, John and I stopped seeing each other, I joined a gym, and I got a therapist. John kept using. Part of me wanted him back so desperately I did humiliating things. I begged. Part of me knew he was killing himself. First Avenue became a line I wouldn't cross. I felt the pull of my old neighborhood was too strong to resist and so, when an opportunity came to spend two months in California at a rural artists' colony, I took it.

Dorland Mountain Arts Colony, which sits in the mountains of rural, redneck California, is rustic by anyone's standards. The cabins are constructed of cinder blocks and plywood. There is no electricity. It is run on a shoestring budget.

When I arrived, I was met by a man named Robert Willis. Bob. He was in his early seventies. He wore a white felt Stetson, Wranglers, and a denim shirt. He had silver hair and blue eyes and was chivalrous but disinclined to talk.

He lit my propane lamp, came up the next day to check on me, drove me to town for food. He'd been there a long time and had seen a lot of people come and go. Odd as it was, we became friends. I told him about New York and he talked about France. He lived there half the year, in a similar caretaking capacity, on a horse farm. Eventually, in his cabin, after dark, by the light of the propane lamp, I told him about my rape and Lila's. He listened, saying only a few words. "That must have hurt." "You never get over certain things."

He told me about serving as an infantryman in World War II and losing all his buddies. Years later, in the winter of 1993, in France, he had stared out a window down at a tree.

"I don't know what it was," he said. "I had seen that tree from that window hundreds of times, but I started sobbing like a baby. On my knees sobbing, like you'd never seen. I felt ridiculous but I couldn't stop myself. While I was doing it, I realized it was my buddies, that I had never cried for them. They were all buried in a graveyard in Italy near a tree like that, so far away. I just lost it. Who would have thought something that happened that long ago could have such power?"

Before I left, we had dinner one last time. He made what he called army vegetables—canned corn and canned tomatoes heated up on the stove—and bacon. We drank cheap wine, jug cheap.

Dorland could be a spooky place in the daylight. At night it was pitch black, only a few kerosene or propane lights dotting the hill. After dinner, as we sat on the porch of his cabin, we saw what Bob took to be a truck's lights on the dirt road that led up from the highway.

"Looks like we've got a visitor," Bob said.

But then the truck's lights went off. We didn't hear it move.

"You wait here," he told me. "I'm going to investigate."

He went into the back and got his rifle from where he kept it hidden from the fragile liberal arts colonists and Dorland's board of directors.

"I'm going to circle back through the brush and come up on the road," he whispered.

"I'll shut off the light."

I stood absolutely still on the porch. I strained to hear anything, gravel under a tire, a twig snapping, anything. In my mind the men in the truck had hurt or killed Bob, and now they were advancing toward the cabin. But I had made a promise to Bob. I would not move.

Moments later I heard a rustle in the leaves on the far side of the cabin. I started.

"It's me," Bob's whisper came through the dark. "Stay still."

We watched the road. We never saw the lights on the truck go on. Eventually, Bob stepped through the chaparral with Shady, his faithful wolf-malamute, and we lit the propane light again. Both of us were amped up, went through the course of events a dozen times, shared our perception of it, talked about threat and how you could sense it. How we were lucky for war and rape because it gave us something no one else had: a sixth sense that turned on when we felt danger near us or those we loved.

I went back to New York, but not the East Village. Too many memories. I moved with a boyfriend to 106th Street between Manhattan and Columbus.

My parents had visited me twice in ten years on my home turf. My mother had stood in an apartment of mine and said, "You can't tell me you want to spend the rest of your life this way." She was talking real estate and apartment size but they were words, as I came to repeat them, that took on a different meaning for me.

That fall I quit dabbling in heroin. It had as much to do with losing easy access to it as it did with anything. I drank again and smoked cigarettes but so did everyone. Then I bought Dr. Herman's book. It was out in paper. I reasoned I should have a record of anyplace my name appeared in print.

Herman chose to use one sentence from my article at the beginning of her chapter called "Disconnection." The sentence, as it appeared, is this: "When I was raped I lost my virginity and almost lost my life. I also discarded certain assumptions I had held about how the world worked and about how safe I was." It appeared on page fifty-one of a three-hundred-page book. I read the sentence and my name again in the bookstore before purchasing it. It was not obvious to me until I was riding home on the subway. In a book called *Trauma and Recovery*, I was cited in the first half. I decided not just to keep the book as a memento, but to actually read it.

They do not have a normal "baseline" level of alert but relaxed attention. Instead, they have an elevated baseline of arousal: their bodies are always on the alert for danger. They also have an extreme startle response to unexpected stimuli . . . People with post-traumatic stress disorder take longer to fall asleep, are more sensitive to noise, and awaken more frequently during the night than ordinary people. Thus traumatic events appear to recondition the human nervous system.

Paragraphs like this began the most gripping read I had ever had: I was reading about myself. I was also reading about war veterans. Unfortunately, my brain went into overdrive again. I spent a week in the main reading room of the New York Public Library plotting a novel that would use PTSD as the great equalizer, bringing together women and men who suffered from the same disorder. But then, in the midst of the narratives I read, I lost the will to intellectualize it.

There was a collection of first-person accounts of Vietnam that I read over and over again and kept on reserve. Somehow, reading these men's stories allowed me to begin to feel. One particularly affected me, the story of a hero. He had seen heavy action, and watched as his friends were cut down. He bore it all stoically. I couldn't help but think of Bob.

This vet got home, received decoration, held down a job. Years later, he fell apart. Something gave. The hero could not hold. He became a man by crumbling. The account left off in process. He was out there somewhere, working on it. I'm not part of any religion but I prayed for that vet and for Bob.

I read Herman's entire book. It wasn't a magical cure but it was a start. I also had a good therapist. She had actually used the words *post-traumatic stress* a year before but I had dismissed them as so much psychobabble. True to form, I did everything the hard way: wrote a column, got it quoted, bought the book, and recognized myself in the case histories of the sick. I had post-traumatic stress disorder, but the only way I would believe it was to discover it on my own.

While I was living on 106th, my boyfriend worked late bartending, and I spent the evenings alone. I watched a lot of television. It was an old tenement house in a bad neighborhood. It was what

I could afford in New York City on an adjunct's salary. I lived behind gated windows, and the nights were regularly peppered with automatic fire. Tech-9's were the gun of choice in the neighborhood then.

One night I'd turned the toaster on while coffee was brewing. I blew a fuse. The fuse box was down in the basement. I had to go outside and down a dark stairwell to get there. I called my boyfriend at work. He was brusque. A large crowd had just entered the bar. "What do you want me to do about it? Take a flashlight and do it or sit in the dark. Those are your choices."

I decided I was being stupid, helpless. I used something I had learned in therapy, "inner talking," to psyche myself up for the chore. It was around 11:00 P.M. I reasoned this was not as bad as 2:00 A.M. To say the least, my inner talking was faulty.

Down two flights and out into the street, around the corner, over a wrought-iron gate whose lock had rusted shut, down the outdoor stairs, turn on the flashlight. I found the keyhole, inserted the key, got inside. I turned the latch on the inside and stood for a moment against the wall. My heart was racing. It was pitch black and windowless in the basement. My flashlight trailed across a far wall with rooms tunneling into the back. I made out the possessions of a Dominican man who had been evicted a month or two before. I heard rats squeaking in annoyance as my light discovered them. Focus, I said to myself, the glass fuse cold in my hand, and then I heard a noise. I shut off my light.

It was outside. Against the door. People. Soon, by listening through the door to their Spanglish, I understood I would have to wait awhile. I stood two feet from them as he slammed her against the door. "Fuck me, bitch," he yelled. I stepped back as far as I could, but staying near the fuse box, what I had come to do, seemed better than going farther into the dark rooms of a sealed-off basement. Once the landlord's nephew had lived down here, my boyfriend told me. He had been a crackhead and someone had come in one night and shot him to death.

"That's why she won't rent to Dominicans anymore," he told me.

"But she's Dominican."

"Nothing makes sense up here."

Outside, the man grunted and the woman didn't make a sound. Then the two of them finished. They left. He called her some name in Spanish and laughed at her.

For the first time, I allowed myself to feel really scared. I changed the fuse and worked myself up to get back inside. My only goal was safety now, and inside the building upstairs was safer than down here, buried in the dust with the rats, the ghost of a murdered crackhead, and a door against which a girl had just been fucked.

I made it.

That night I decided to leave New York. I remembered reading that many of the men, upon returning from Vietnam, were drawn to places like rural Hawaii or the Florida Everglades. They were recreating the environment they knew best, where their responses to things seemed more natural than they did inside suburban homes scattered across the less lush and green United States. This made sense to me.

I'd always lived in bad neighborhoods except once, when I lived over a wife beater, in Park Slope, Brooklyn. New York meant violence to me. In the lives of my students, in the lives of those on the street, it was commonplace. All this violence had reassured me. I fit in with it. The way I acted and thought, my hypervigilance and nightmares, made sense. What I appreciated about New York was that it didn't pretend to safety. On the best of days it was like living in a glorious brawl. Surviving this year by year was an honor mark that people wore proudly. After five years you earned bragging rights. At seven you began to fit in. I had made it to ten, almost dyed-in-the-wool by the projected East Village shelf life, then, all of a sudden and to the surprise of those who knew me, I left.

I went back to California. I took Bob's job at Dorland while he was away. I lived in his cabin and took care of his dog. I met the colonists and showed them around, taught them how to light a fire in their woodstoves and taunted them with the specter of kangaroo rats, mountain lions, and the supposed ghosts that roamed the place. I didn't talk about myself much. No one knew where I was from.

On the Fourth of July, 1995, I was working on a story inside my cabin. It was dark out. The place was deserted. The colonists had gotten together and gone into town. I was alone except for Shady. I hadn't written much in the past two years, since the two months I'd been at Dorland as a colonist. It seemed unfathomable to me that it had taken so many years to come to terms with my rape and Lila's, but I had begun to accept that it had. It left me with a feeling I couldn't describe. Hell was over. I had all the time in the world ahead.

Shady ran into the cabin and rested her chin on my lap. She was scared.

"What is it, girl?" I said, patting her head. Then I heard it too; it sounded like thunder, a summer rain coming on.

"Let's go see what it is, okay?" I said. I grabbed my heavy black flashlight and shut off my lamp.

Outside I could see into the distance. The cabin had a porch and one chair. Very far away and partially obscured by the side of a dark mountain, I could see fireworks going off. I reassured Shady then and sat down on the chair.

The fireworks lasted a long time. Shady kept her head on my lap. I would have raised a glass if I'd had one but I didn't.

"We made it, girl," I said to Shady, rubbing her side. "Happy Independence Day."

Eventually it was time to move on. The night before I left Dorland I slept with a male friend of mine. I hadn't had sex in over a year. A self-imposed celibacy.

The sex that night was short, fumbling. We had gone out to dinner and had one glass of wine. In the kerosene light I focused on his face, on how my friend differed from a violent man. We both agreed later, when we talked on the phone from opposite coasts, that it had had a special quality about it. "It was almost virginal," he said. "Like you were having sex for the first time."

In some sense I was, in another this was impossible. But it is later now, and I live in a world where the two truths coexist; where both hell and hope lie in the palm of my hand.

AFTERWORD

It has been thirty-six years since I was raped, eighteen years since *Lucky* was first published, and only two months since a multiple molester and proud pussy-grabber was elected the forty-fifth president of these United States.

For me, as for many women who have survived sexual assault, I was horrified, though perhaps not shocked, by the outcome of the 2016 election. In the life of most victims of rape, unfathomable injustice is par for the course. My own story remains, thirty-six years later, more just in how it ended than most. My story had the beginning, middle, and end that the majority of rape cases don't. The rapist was arrested, brought to trial, convicted, and served nearly two decades in jail. Compare this to the two- or three-month slap-on-the-wrist sentences we've seen recently and you begin to understand that I chose the title *Lucky* both because I had indeed been truly lucky, but also because the ironies of how we define luck never seem to stop.

In the immediate aftermath of my rape in 1981, I made a promise to myself that if I survived I would write about it. I was an eighteen-year-old freshman and I read and wrote poetry obsessively. I devoured obscure journals and dug deep in old bookshops for back issues of *Poetry* or *American Poetry Review* (*APR*). Poetry was my oxygen. Even to me that sentence now sounds a bit off-putting, but when I was eighteen I believed wholeheartedly in, to put it broadly and in the terms I thought of it then, "the power of art." Though my fervent belief in poetry might have seemed naive, perhaps the most shocking proof of innocence was that at eighteen I still believed in a just world. Also, unlike many of the women and men I began hearing from

255

after *Lucky* was published, I knew instinctively that what had been done to me in that tunnel was wrong. Also, here's luck: I'd been beaten up enough that there was no way to hide it.

In the end, it took another eighteen years to write a book about my rape and a switch from poetry to prose along the way, and even though no little girl dreams of growing up, getting raped, and then writing a book about it, I was not unhappy with its publication. I say not unhappy because what I wanted to write was a novel, not a memoir, and though that novel would come two years later and do well enough in the world to allow *Lucky* to reach more readers, I now feel I was destined to write *Lucky*. Many of us have a purpose we do not choose but that instead finds us in the dogged way such things do—I used the thing that I loved the most, which was language, to translate into prose the worst violence I had ever known. Dodging that, I eventually realized, for the sake of myself and for the sake of those victims who remain silenced by shame or family or cultural imperative, was not an option.

After *Lucky* came out and my story was known, and especially after *The Lovely Bones* was published, I began meeting men and women, young girls and boys, who had been raped and molested, and this, along with the amount of mail I received that contained detailed accounts of rape and incest, overwhelmed me. I had unwittingly created a space where people who had experienced sexual violence could tell their story. And for many, I was the first person with whom they had ever shared these stories. The rushed disclosures in book-signing lines or the long single-spaced letters and, most poignantly perhaps, the still-childlike handwriting on ruled paper would frequently include this phrase: "What happened to me isn't as bad as what happened to you." But the accounts of sexual violations that followed often seemed far worse than my own.

I received a shocking number of letters from girls or boys who had been raped by family members who believed that what had happened to me was worse, because I'd been raped by a stranger.

Evidence, if any were needed, of how a perpetrator can rape not just the body but also the brain. I now understand that "what happened to me isn't as bad as what happened to you" is part of a pattern that begins in the seconds after an attack. If you have been shoved deep underwater, you do anything to reach the surface and to pull in as much life-giving air as you can to survive. This includes dismissing or diminishing the gravity of experience in order to distance oneself from horror and, given the circumstances, what may well have been death. The police said I was lucky because I wasn't murdered; my father said he was glad it happened to me and not my sister because in his mind I was tougher. And then there was this: "I'm glad it happened because I wouldn't be who I am now if it hadn't." This last one is said by people who have survived war, cancer, been orphaned by natural disaster, become paralyzed in a road accident. It was, for a very long time, said by me.

The harder truth is this: if I could take a magic eraser to that night in 1981, I'd do so in a heartbeat, and if I could have told every young person who had been raped by a relative that in comparison to them I was *indeed* lucky, I would have done that too. But all I could do was write one book and tell one story. Unfortunately, there are no do-overs, and the greatest challenge, after gaining safety, remains living with the knowledge of the life that was taken from you.

This is how I was introduced at the first public reading I gave for *Lucky* in 1999:

> Alice Sebold is here today to read to us from her memoir concerning the horrible thing she experienced from which she has now thankfully recovered.

Though it would be easy to make fun of the ladies luncheon at which I was a guest speaker that day, I can't help but defend them. Compared to countless other venues, they took me on despite the apparently sordid, unmentionable topic I'd had the temerity to write about. Still, as I made my way to the podium, I began to feel an old familiar fury grow inside me.

I now find anything that tries to obfuscate the truth of rape and its aftermath infuriating because it represents a further deceit of the world at large and the victim herself. It's like slapping a smiley face on a corpse. In our desire to protect people from the truth we do them a disservice by attempting to hide it. This only creates a new level of distraction from what is most important, which is coming to terms with the cards you were dealt.

Eighteen years after I'd been raped, and despite the stamp of an esteemed publisher on my story, the woman introducing me didn't feel able to use a simple four-letter word. In avoiding it, she perpetuated the idea that rape was still taboo. Her omission made me do something that goes against my basic character, as I've never been a fan of audience participation. But what inspired me that day was a sort of rage against shame. I would not permit what I saw as censorship, even if enacted by a blameless woman who more than anything probably wanted to be polite. I took a moment at the mic to make eye contact with members of the audience, making sure to include those in the front and back and to my left and right. When I did speak, I was so calm in my delivery that it would seem as if I did this every day.

"Rape, that's the horrible thing that happened to me. We at least have to learn to say the word. Let's all do it together, okay?"

I felt as if I had turned the clock back and was reliving the day nearly two decades earlier, where I had insisted on saying the word aloud in my parents' living room in front of my favorite church lady, Myra Narbonne. (I want to pause here to note that Myra, a spitfire to the end, lived well into her nineties, and when *Lucky* came out, there was no bigger fan.)

Encouraging an audience to say "rape" was never going to be easy, but after a few rounds of me going it alone and adding encouragement, more and more people went from mortified silence to whispering the word to finally joining me in saying it aloud over and over. Doing this together, in such an unexpected way, resulted in a quality of exchange with my audience that

I went on to feel was my responsibility to bring to any public event I did. I didn't always succeed, but I was smart enough to know that just as inside any courtroom, the success of my presentation may have been based not only on the power of my words but also on my appearance and behavior.

Sometimes readers would say they were surprised at how funny I was during the Q&A, which of course meant that I didn't seem to be who they expected a rape victim might be. Many men felt compelled to apologize for what had happened to me. I thanked them for their kindness but would also smile and say, "You didn't rape me, so we're cool." At this point in history the male gender cannot bear all the blame. Just ask men who were raped by their mothers.

But I also see now that I had a tendency to joke in the face of readers' sincerity, because for years I'd remained uncomfortable with the feeling of being "other than."

In the end, we tell each other our deepest secrets because we want these stories to be acknowledged; we also dream that when acknowledged by a few, we might then be understood. If the full narrative of one's life is embraced by others, this opens up the possibility of intimacy or community; if instead it is met with awkward silence or a change of subject on the part of the listener, then the doors of the heart begin to shut down. The message has been received: no one wants to hear your story; no one actually cares. Locked alone in a room with a secret deemed so unspeakable it can't be shared, the imprisoned person will go to any lengths to escape. One need search no further for the origins of addiction and other self-harming behaviors. Anything is preferable to being sentenced to suffer such pain all by yourself.

It makes sense then that I've never felt more engaged than when I spoke to readers, or even nonreaders, about their lives. Because of *Lucky*, I have met many more rape victims than I ever thought possible. The youngest one was eight. She was an incest victim and haunted by night terrors. She had not read *Lucky* but her mother had, and she brought her daughter to a reading so the little girl could shake my hand. The oldest was a woman in Australia, who, when she reached the table at which I was signing books, told me the story of being gang-raped in the 1940s. When this elderly woman, through tears, told me that she had never told anyone this, I felt nearly as lost at sea as I had when I shook the hand of the eight-year-old. Often, after a reading, a few men and women will thank me for coming, and though they may say nothing more than this, a flash of eye contact will let me know that a version of what happened to me, happened to them. Some will actually use those words as I sign a book or shake a hand. For a moment, any sense of what I'd felt was my essential otherness evaporates. Given the opportunity an afterword affords, I want to thank them.

Perhaps because I had decided to prosecute my rapist and had never denied the fact that I'd been raped, my well-meaning mother and the friends who knew about my past would send me clippings and later links to news stories or court decisions they thought might be of interest to me. I never had the heart to tell them that I rarely read or clicked on them. It's the black humor version of the good humor story my father would tell—namely that having worked in an ice cream parlor and been allowed to eat all the ice cream he wanted for free, he had gone off the stuff. I never once called to find out when or if my rapist had been granted parole, and I did not keep up to date on the tics of progress or the avalanches of setbacks in the justice system as far as various sex crimes were concerned. I share this trait with many former soldiers I've met. In some way you are never *not* aware of the topic people may most closely associate you with because you are living its aftermath every day. Even for me, who put her name to a book about rape, there remains a continual push and pull between my sense of responsibility to other victims and what, barring that experience, I would have been doing had I never been raped. I am a writer so I wrote about rape.

In light of a presidential election where the experience of women was deemed irrelevant, if even truthful, by millions of American men and women, it was hard to come to the writing of this afterword in a cheery frame of mind. It may be the very fact that we're hearing more stories of rape and sexual assault that marks our greatest progress. Yet it goes without saying that this is not enough progress, that it has not come soon enough, and that there are still too many cases where privileged young men have gotten what equates to a slap on the wrist after being proved in court to be unapologetic rapists. But given that collective action can only happen if there are enough voices to form a collective in the first place, it's a start. As I write this, the state of California has voted to rescind the statute of limitations in rape cases: clear proof of the power of victims telling their stories.

Another striking example of the progress to be had by creating a collective can be seen in the 2015 documentary *The Hunting Ground*. The film centers around two young rape victims—Annie E. Clark and Andrea Pino—who, while enrolled at the University of North Carolina, Chapel Hill, were raped by fellow students. After finding themselves further abused by the lack of support from UNC, Clark and Pino reached out and essentially created their own grassroots network of sexual assault victims from colleges across the country. Ultimately they and many other student rape victims would go on to sue these schools for discrimination under Title IX, which provides that a school must ensure that all students have equal access to education, regardless of gender, sexual orientation, or gender identity. This means that a school can be found legally at fault if they do not actively respond to a student's claim of sexual harassment or sexual assault and take steps to ensure the victim's safety and well-being. As a drama alone, *The Hunting Ground* is riveting to watch, and it also serves as a mini education on why silencing reports of rape is currently the choice for those in power. (The filmmakers have said that it was the response on college campuses to their previous documentary, *The Invisible War*, concerning rape in the military, that inspired them to make *The Hunting Ground*.)

The film unmasks the lengths to which a college will often go to protect a potential perpetrator over his victims, for the sake of the all-mighty dollar. The financial incentives to dump the student victim and defend the student perpetrator are too great to ignore because so often the perpetrator is either a star athlete, which directly translates to revenue for the institution he attends, or a member of a highly funded campus fraternity. Rip away any romantic notions of colleges as ivory towers and know that in order to survive they have become businesses first and foremost. Rape charges made public threaten alumni support and healthy enrollments, and while we assume—perhaps at our children's peril—that a college's mandate is to both nurture and protect all of its students, institutions that have vigorous athletic departments and many with nationally ranked teams that serve to increase the schools' status in a commercial world end up being guilty of further abuse against their very own students. Just as many countries downplay the incidence of violence against women so as not to harm tourism, many colleges would prefer that parents and students remain in the dark about a very real threat.

If, even in the atmosphere of what is deemed "higher learning," those who report being assaulted by fellow students are frequently accused of lying by both the administration and their peers, why wonder that almost a carbon copy of this form of injustice played out repeatedly in the run-up to our presidential election? Donald Trump stated and/or implied that all of the women who came forward to say he had made unwanted advances toward them or, worse, had actually fondled them, were liars. He also stated that many were not good looking—as if to imply that being molested by him was an honor and he did not deem these women hot enough for such greatness to be bestowed. As a result of Trump's denials and their tone, many versions of his slanderous comments were repeated and then further hideously embroidered by certain supporters of his campaign. These women, who had been brave enough to tell stories they had never intended to share but who were motivated to do so for the sake of their country, in the end added up to zero in a large block of our voting public's consciousness.

The day after the election I saw a young woman in my local dog park. We don't know each other's names. I am distinguished only by the fact that I have a dog that her dog likes to chase. Even though the question "How are you?" would end up being double loaded that day, I asked it reflexively. When she answered me, her eyes were rimmed with tears but her words seethed with ill-concealed rage.

"Can you imagine coming forward about being raped by your boss in Trump's America?"

Though she couldn't know it, I'd seen the look in her eyes countless times before. I still don't know her name, but I believe I do know something more about her than I had before that day. I also worry her experience may now become something she will fear to confide the details of, to anyone.

I would spend years trying to find someone who had been through what I had and was also interested in talking about it. The attempts I made at this, over many years, were blind and almost always fruitless. The lack of finding others became a permanent ache, and so I eventually ended up on the safe but deadly shores of self-isolation. In case you missed it, and I can understand why you might, the progress that I saw reflected in *The Hunting Ground* is the fact that more sexual assault victims are telling their stories, which frees others to do the same. United, voices turn into action. Though I can't change the facts of my past, I found myself wishing for something equally futile—that, if raped, it would have happened in a time where it was a bit less difficult to make contact with others and by doing so perhaps have access to a certain solace bred of commonality.

At the few public events I did upon *Lucky*'s publication and then at the many more I did after the unexpected success of my novel *The Lovely Bones*, I would tell readers that when it came to violent sexual assaults, mine was actually comparable to an introductory course if judged alongside sex crimes committed around the world every day. I even called it Rape 101.

Women are a degraded class across the globe. In many places they are treated worse than animals, whose value is deemed higher. The female body is a physical commodity easily traded for profit or status. If violated against her will, the woman herself is frequently blamed and then disposed of by family and community as one might a soiled rag. I remember being horrified the first time I heard about the virgin cure in South Africa. In the belief that by raping a virgin one could be cured of AIDS, the incidence of rapes and gang rapes, many of them fatal, escalated wildly in the populations of girls under five.

When I called my own experience Rape 101, I was indulging my penchant for dark humor, but in all honesty my deepest hope was that if a reader saw what had happened to me as unjust, then *Lucky* might stand as a doorway from which rape could be seen more clearly as the entrenched cultural imperative it has been for centuries—the surest form of living genocide committed almost exclusively by one gender against another.

I was thirty-seven when *Lucky* was first published; I am fifty-four now. I still believe, as I did at eighteen, that the key to effecting true change is to attach individual faces and names to crimes of sexual assault. One of the most striking magazine covers of recent years came from *New York* in July 2015. It was a portrait of thirty-five of the women who had publically accused Bill Cosby of assault. They were pictured in four rows running across the white page, and all were seated in identical chairs. One empty chair remained, begging the question of those who were still too afraid to speak.

It was a little more than a year from the time of my rape to the final trial. During those twelve months there was an arrest followed by a lineup, various pretrial motions and hearings, the grand jury trial, and many phone calls concerning details that needed to be followed up. The nights I could sleep were often full of nightmares. On other nights, I would lie awake and imagine spearheading a movement to get famous women who had been raped to reveal their past. Not that I wished ill on anyone, but I couldn't help thinking how powerful it would have been if Queen Noor of Jordan or Jackie Joyner-Kersee or the then newly appointed Supreme Court Justice Sandra Day O'Connor had been through what I had and come forward. I do remember my mother or father telling me about an actress they knew who had been raped and that hearing this was a godsend. There she was, accomplished in her field and famous by then for decades. On top of this she was also long married and an iconic beauty.

On September 19, 2014, I read a column by Charles M. Blow in the *New York Times*. A political and cultural journalist, he was coming forward to tell the story of being molested by an older cousin of his when he was a boy. It made me raise my fist and weep. The tears came in simple solidarity, the fist because I knew how powerful his story would be for men who had been sexually assaulted and stayed silent for years.

For centuries now, the shame and resulting silence surrounding crimes that have at their center a sexualized act has damned any hope of building strength through numbers. And though obviously no one wants to qualify to be a member of this group, the only other alternative is isolation, from the self first and, as a result, from those around you. Both of these make true intimacy between people impossible. Rape is not about sex but uses a sex act to convey brutality; true intimacy is not about sex, but sex is one of the surest ways to express our love.

If rape victims in 2016 are still too often disbelieved, disowned, or degraded, there has also been undeniable positive change. Because of the increase in sexual assaults now reported, and the rise of the internet, citizens themselves have begun to vocalize in revolt against cases of obvious injustice. In *People vs. Turner*, a Stanford student was found guilty of having raped an unconscious woman with a foreign object. Sentenced to only six months in jail, the rapist was out in three. An outraged public called for the removal of the judge while the victim's fiercely articulate impact statement was read aloud on CNN, and after being posted online, has been read by well over ten million people.

The more citizens who show up at rallies such as those that followed in the wake of the Turner case, the more likely it is that women and men who have experienced sexual assault will understand that what happened to them has nothing to do with who they are, but everything to do with the fact that those who attacked them are criminal deviants even if they hide behind the guise of a loving father, a college athlete, coach, or a billionaire businessman.

As a culture, America favors stories of triumph. It complements our whitewashed origin myth. Complication, nuance, or the reality of the constantly shifting weights and balances of real life—on those we are not so keen.

In writing *Lucky* I was aware that the bones of my story could easily be made to fit the always appealing tragedy-to-triumph rubric. If I began as a virgin rape victim, I then went on to see my rapist found guilty of six of the seven felonies with which he was charged. But triumph, like happiness, is an elusive state. It flickers briefly before diminishing. Even within the first few years after the events described in *Lucky*, life began to hand me more challenges. My roommate was raped on my bed. I experienced physical abuse from a partner (though I did not stick around long enough to be apologized to a second time), and I encountered, over and over, the truth about why some of us are judged to have triumphed over adversity while others are not. Luck—there's that word again—has so very much to do with it. My rapist was poor, black, and uneducated, and came from a family with an entrenched criminal record. I was a middle-class white girl attending an expensive university and I was raped not on property owned by the college, but in a public park on the edge of it. The fact that I was proven to have been a virgin by the medical examination, and had been visibly beaten, was gravy when it came to making it an obvious case of rape in the eyes of the legal system. And, like the victim in the Stanford case, I knew that my words mattered. Take the exact same case but Mad Lib the roles and specifics. Example: The rapist is a middle- or upper-class white professional from a well-respected family. He rapes a transgender Filipina prostitute in a hotel room. The crime itself is exactly the same, but the chances of conviction? Not even in the same ballpark. A male student at an elite university is held down by members of an elite fraternity and anally raped with a bottle of Jack Daniel's. Chances of a conviction if the victim is brave enough to come forward? You tell me.

There are few windows where large groups united can affect a culture for the good. If not taken advantage of, these windows close swiftly, and opportunity is lost. So here I am hoping that if we can resist the urge to subdivide our nation post-election, we might continue to grow a powerbase and, in doing so, find light enough to progress. In the weeks following the election, I thought of one of my favorite books from childhood: *The Sneetches* by Dr. Seuss. In a land populated by upright Seussian beasts I turned the pages to watch them descend into lives of ludicrous waste based purely on the fact that some Sneetches had stars on their bellies while other Sneetches lacked "stars upon thars." I know I'm not alone in having thrilled at the one-for-all, all-for-one mentality that, after much righteous recrimination and posturing, these Sneetches end up adopting. Sadly, having been taught this philosophy as children, it is not how most of us try to live our lives.

When I was raped, no one used the term *survivor*; such subtle semantic changes had not yet taken hold. And because the idea that the word *victim* was not just a word but could be an identity was also something I hadn't heard prior to being raped, I never saw the term *rape victim* as anything but a descriptor. I was a rape victim in the same way I was a brunette, or a United States citizen, or the child of an alcoholic. All were fixed truths. But in the years following my experience, this simple descriptor was parsed to such an extent that by inflating its meaning it became robbed of simple context. I began to be scolded when I failed to use the word *survivor* in place of *victim*. In print interviews I gave after becoming an author, the journalist, or perhaps it was his or her editor, hit "replace all" and without my consent changed *victim* to *survivor*. Pigheadedly, I continued to use the word *victim* in public, where particularly concerned people might inform me that what they liked about me was that I had so clearly never been a victim, that I was a survivor through and through. My response to the victim vs. survivor debate (talk about Sneetches!) is to agree to split the difference. I'll agree that I'm both, but first and foremost I'm a writer. What matters more to me than anything is to maintain my right of word choice.

Before coming to this afterword, I reread *Lucky* for the first time since recording the audio book back in 2002. Looking again at these pages I find that I now have more empathy for those who tried to help me without any instruction manual or cultural common knowledge. But perversely I also now have greater empathy for those who couldn't or didn't know how to help me or, worse still, those who may have inadvertently hurt me. With the clarity that comes with time, one's luck is laid bare, and although I will never forgive my rapist, I do possess compassion for what circumstances in his life and mind might have led him to devastate mine. I also may wish that I had never been raped and therefore left unwritten both *Lucky* and *The Lovely Bones*—but I was and I did. In the end I think my greatest luck has been in finding the words to tell my story and in the fact that they were heard.

Alice Sebold, January 2017

ABOUT THE AUTHOR

A lice Sebold is the author of three #1 bestselling books, including the novels *The Lovely Bones* and *The Almost Moon*. Her books have been translated into more than fifty languages. Sebold's work has appeared in the *New York Times*, the *Chicago Tribune*, and the *Guardian* among other publications, and she has contributed to numerous anthologies and edited *The Best American Short Stories 2009*. Born in Madison, Wisconsin, Sebold earned her BA from Syracuse University and her MFA from the University of California at Irvine. She is a member of the National Leadership Council for RAINN.org (Rape, Abuse & Incest National Network). She lives in California.

A SCRIBNER READING GROUP GUIDE

LUCKY

Alice Sebold

Introduction

In a memoir hailed for its searing candor as well as its wit, Alice Sebold reveals how her life was transformed when, as an eighteen-year-old college freshman, she was brutally raped and beaten in a park near campus. What propels this chronicle is Sebold's indomitable spirit—as she struggles for understanding; as her family and friends sometimes bungle their efforts to provide comfort and support; and as she ultimately triumphs, managing through grit and coincidence to help secure her attacker's arrest and conviction. In a narrative by turns thrilling and inspiring, Sebold illuminates the experience of trauma victims and imparts a wisdom profoundly hard-won: "You save yourself or you remain unsaved."

Questions for Discussion

1. *Lucky* opens with an incredibly brutal scene. Immediately after the rape, Alice tells her attacker she forgives him. Why?
2. "I was learning that no one—females included—knew what to do with a rape victim" (page 78). How did Alice's friends and classmates react to her story?

3. Alice writes that she was "raised in a house where my mother's problems provided the glue of family" (page 167). Discuss the Sebold family dynamic. In what ways did Alice's family provide the support she needed in the aftermath of the rape? In what ways did they fail? How did her role in the family evolve?

4. What effect did Alice's rape have on her relationship with her sister? Do you think Alice and Mary were closer before the rape or after? Why?

5. Discuss the role of race in this story. Sebold mentions what she calls "the cosmetics of any rape case." What does she mean by this?

6. Picture that October afternoon when Alice found herself face-to-face with her attacker. Would your reaction have been different from Alice's?

7. "Remember everything," Alice's professor and notable memoirist Tobias Wolff tells her as she heads to the police station. How was this advice helpful to her?

8. Reflecting on a poem for her workshop with Tess Gallagher, Alice wrote, "You could not be filled with hate and be beautiful" (page 103). Discuss her poem "Conviction" and the reactions it elicited.

9. Alice fails to identify Gregory Madison in the police lineup. In what ways does Alice's lawyer's comment that "rights are weighted on the side of the defendant" (page 145) ring true?

10. What seems to drive Alice forward as the prosecution of Gregory Madison continues? What did you learn about a rape trial by reading *Lucky*?

11. If Alice had been sexually active before the rape, how might her recovery have been different? At the trial, was Alice's virginity a factor in securing Gregory Madison's conviction?

12. Discuss Alice's response to Lila's rape. How does that impact the relationship between the friends?

13. "It is not just forcible intercourse; rape means to inhabit and destroy everything" (page 127). Discuss how this applies to Alice's experience.